First World War
and Army of Occupation
War Diary
France, Belgium and Germany

62 DIVISION
186 Infantry Brigade
Duke of Wellington's (West Riding Regiment)
1/5th Battalion
5 August 1917 - 2 May 1919

WO95/3086/3

The Naval & Military Press Ltd
www.nmarchive.com
Published in association with The National Archives

Published by

The Naval & Military Press Ltd

Unit 10 Ridgewood Industrial Park,
Uckfield, East Sussex,
TN22 5QE England
Tel: +44 (0) 1825 749494

www.naval-military-press.com

www.nmarchive.com

This diary has been reprinted in facsimile from the original. Any imperfections are inevitably reproduced and the quality may fall short of modern type and cartographic standards.

© **Crown Copyright**
Images reproduced by permission of The National Archives, London, England, 2015.

Contents

Document type	Place/Title	Date From	Date To
Heading	WO95/3086-3		
Heading	62nd Division 186th Infy Bde. 2-5th Bn Duke Of Wellington's Regt 1918 Feb-1919 Apl		
Heading	War Diary Of 5th Duke Of Wellington's (W.R.) Regt. 1st To 28th Feby. 1918 (Volume.)		
War Diary	Ref Maps Lens 11 1/100000 Sheet 57 1/20,000	01/02/1918	28/02/1918
War Diary		00/02/1918	00/02/1918
Miscellaneous	5th West Riding Regt Operation Order	08/02/1918	08/02/1918
Operation(al) Order(s)	5th Duke Of Wellington's Regt Operation Order No. 2	10/02/1915	10/02/1915
Operation(al) Order(s)	5th Duke Of Wellington's Regt Operation Order No 3		
Miscellaneous	Appendix "A" to be attached to Operation Order No.3.	18/02/1918	18/02/1918
Miscellaneous	All Recipients Of 0. 0.3.	18/02/1918	18/02/1918
Miscellaneous	Appendix "B" to be attached to Operation Order No.3.	18/02/1918	18/02/1918
Miscellaneous	All Recipients Of O.O. 3.	18/02/1918	18/02/1918
Miscellaneous	Appendix "A" to be attached to Operation Order No.3.		
Miscellaneous	Appendix "B"		
Miscellaneous	Appendices		
Heading	186th Infantry Brigade 62nd Division 5th Battalion The Duke Of Vellington's Regiment March 1918		
War Diary	Ref Maps Lens 11 1/ 100,000 Sheet 51.b. N. W1/20,000	01/03/1918	08/03/1918
War Diary	Ref Map Maroeuil Combined Sheet	09/03/1918	09/03/1918
War Diary	Ref Map Maroeuil Combined Sheet1/20 ,000	09/03/1918	30/03/1918
War Diary	Ref Map 57d NE 1/20000	31/03/1918	31/03/1918
Miscellaneous	Narrative Of Operations In Which The 5th Bn Duke Of Wellington's Regt	25/03/1918	25/03/1918
Operation(al) Order(s)	5th Duke Of Wellington's Regt Operation Order No 5	08/03/1918	08/03/1918
Operation(al) Order(s)	5th Duke Of Wellington's Regt Operation Order No 6	08/03/1918	08/03/1918
Operation(al) Order(s)	5th Duke Of Wellington's Regt Operation Order No 7	04/03/1918	04/03/1918
Operation(al) Order(s)	5th Duke Of Wellington's Regt T.F. Operation Order No 8		
Operation(al) Order(s)	5th Duke Of Wellington's Regt Operation Order No 9	24/03/1918	24/03/1918
Miscellaneous	5th Duke Of Wellington's Regt Operation Order No 9 by Lt Col J. Walter	01/04/1918	01/04/1918
Heading	62nd Division 186th Infantry Brigade 5th Battalion The Duke Of Wellington's Regiment April 1918		
War Diary	Ref. Map. 57d. NE.1/20000	01/04/1918	30/04/1918
Operation(al) Order(s)	5th Duke Of Wellington's Regt Operation Order No 10	07/04/1918	07/04/1918
Miscellaneous	Operation Order by Lt Col J. Walker Command 5 Duke of Wellingtons Regt	17/04/1918	17/04/1918
Miscellaneous	Operation Order 5th Bn Duke of Wellingtons Regt	23/04/1918	23/04/1918
Heading	War Diary Of 5th Bn Duke Of Wellington's Regiment (W.R.)		
War Diary	Ref. Map. 57. D. 1/4 0000	01/05/1918	14/05/1918
War Diary	57 D. N. E.1/20000	14/05/1918	19/05/1918
War Diary	Ref. Maps. 57. D. 1/40000	20/05/1918	20/05/1918
War Diary	57 D. N. E.1/20000	20/05/1918	23/05/1918
War Diary	Ref. Maps. 57. D. 1/4000	23/05/1918	23/05/1918
War Diary	57 D. N. E.1/20000	24/05/1918	30/05/1918
War Diary	Ref. Maps 57. D.1/4000	30/05/1918	30/05/1918

War Diary	57 D.N.E. 1/20000	31/05/1918	31/05/1918
Miscellaneous	Appendices		
Operation(al) Order(s)	5th Duke Of Wellington's Regt Operation Order No. 14	15/05/1918	15/05/1918
Miscellaneous	Appendix "A" to be attached to Operation Order No.14.	16/05/1918	16/05/1918
Operation(al) Order(s)	5th Duke Of Wellington's Regt Operation Order No. 1 5	19/05/1918	19/05/1918
Operation(al) Order(s)	5th Duke Of Wellington's Regt Operation Order No 16		
Heading	War Diary Of 5th Duke Of Wellington's (W.R.) Regt. (T.F) 1st To 30th June 1918 (Volume 5		
War Diary	War Diary Of 5th Duke Of Wellington's (W R) Regt (T.F.) 1st To 30th June 1918 Volume 5		
War Diary	Ref Map 57.d. N. E. 1/20000	01/06/1918	30/06/1918
Miscellaneous	Honours Awards		
Miscellaneous	Appendices		
Operation(al) Order(s)	5th Duke Of Wellington's Regt Operation Order No 17	01/06/1918	01/06/1918
Operation(al) Order(s)	5th Duke Of Wellington's Regt Operation Order No 18	09/06/1918	09/06/1918
Operation(al) Order(s)	5th Duke Of Wellington's (W.R.) Regt Operation Order No 19		
Miscellaneous	Ref O.O 19 Para 2	16/06/1918	16/06/1918
Operation(al) Order(s)	5 Duke Of Wellington Regt Order No. 20	16/06/1918	16/06/1918
Heading	War Diary Of 5th Duke Of Wellingtons Regiment 1st To 31st July 1918 Volume 5		
Heading	186 Brigade 62nd Division 5th Bn. Duke Of Wellington's (W R) Regt July 1918		
War Diary	Ref Map Sheet 57. d.1/40000	01/07/1918	15/07/1918
War Diary	Ref Map French Map 50 Chalons & Arcis No 67	16/07/1918	19/07/1918
War Diary	Ref Map Reims S O 1/50000 French	19/07/1918	30/07/1918
War Diary	Ref Map Chalons 1/100,000	31/07/1918	31/07/1918
Miscellaneous	Appendices		
Operation(al) Order(s)	Order General No. 63		
War Diary	Special Order By Lieutenant-General Sir A.J. Godley K.C.B. K.C.M.G. Commanding XXII Corps	31/07/1918	31/07/1918
Operation(al) Order(s)	5th Duke Of Wellington's Regt Operation Order No 126		
Operation(al) Order(s)	Order Of The Day No 63	30/07/1918	30/07/1918
Miscellaneous	Headquarters XII Corps	30/07/1918	30/07/1918
Miscellaneous	Special Order Of The Day By Major General W.P. Braithwaite C.B. Commanding 62nd (West Riding) Division	31/07/1918	31/07/1918
Map	Map		
Map	Arcis		
Map	Chalons		
Heading	War Diary Of 5th Duke Of Wellington's Regiment 1st To 31st Augt 1918 Volume 6		
War Diary	Ref Map Chalons (French) 1/8000	01/08/1918	04/08/1918
War Diary	Ref Map 57.d. 1/40000	05/08/1917	31/08/1917
Miscellaneous	Appendices		
Miscellaneous	5th Duke Of Wellington's Regt	24/09/1918	24/09/1918
Miscellaneous	H. Qs. 62nd (W.R.) Division	27/08/1918	27/08/1918
Map	German Trenches In Blue		
Map	France		
Heading	War Diary Of 5th Duke Of Wellington's (W.R.) Regt. 1st To 30th. Septr.1918. (Volume 7).		
War Diary	Ref. Map 57.c. N.W. 1/20000	01/09/1918	09/09/1918
War Diary	Ref. Map 57.c. 1/40000. 57.c.N.E.57.c.S.E. 1/20000	10/09/1918	15/09/1918
War Diary	Ref. Map. 57.c. 1/40000	16/09/1918	26/09/1918
War Diary	Ref. Map. 57.c.N.E. 57.b.N.W. 1/20000.	26/09/1918	30/09/1918
Miscellaneous	Appendices		

Type	Description	Date From	Date To
Operation(al) Order(s)	5th Duke Of Wellington's Regt Operation Order No 134	08/09/1918	08/09/1918
Miscellaneous	All Recipients Of O.O. 134.	09/09/1918	09/09/1918
Operation(al) Order(s)	5th Duke Of Wellington's Regt Operation Order No. 135.	09/09/1918	09/09/1918
Miscellaneous	March Table		
Map	U.T.S. Map No. 415		
Miscellaneous	Message Form		
Miscellaneous	62nd. (W.R.) Division.	09/09/1918	09/09/1918
Miscellaneous	185th. Infantry Brigade.	14/09/1918	14/09/1918
Miscellaneous	62nd. (W.R.) Division	12/09/1918	12/09/1918
Operation(al) Order(s)	5th Duke Of Wellington's Regt Operation Order No. 137		
Operation(al) Order(s)	5th Duke Of Wellington's Regt Operation Order No. 138	15/09/1918	15/09/1918
Miscellaneous	62nd. (W.R.) Division.	16/09/1918	16/09/1918
Miscellaneous	5 Duke Of Wellingtons Regt. Operation Order		
Operation(al) Order(s)	5th Duke Of Wellington's Regt Operation Order No. 140.		
Operation(al) Order(s)	5th Duke Of Wellington's Regt Operation Order No. 140.	26/09/1918	26/09/1918
Miscellaneous	Addendum To Operation Order No. 140.		
Miscellaneous	Extract From British Official Communique	28/09/1918	28/09/1918
Miscellaneous	H.Q. 62nd (post Riding) Division	01/10/1918	01/10/1918
Heading	War Diary Of 5th Duke Of Wellington's (W.R.) Regiment 1st To 31st October 1918 (Volume 22)		
War Diary	Ref. Maps. 57c 1/40,000 Valenciennes 1/100,000.	01/10/1918	08/10/1918
War Diary	57b 1/40,000	09/10/1918	16/10/1918
War Diary	Ref Map 57 B N.E. 251a SE 1/20000	17/10/1918	31/10/1918
Miscellaneous	Appendices		
Map	France		
Map	Map		
Miscellaneous	Message Form		
Map	Map		
Map	France		
Miscellaneous	Battalion Operation Order By Lieutenant Colonel J. Walker, D.S.O. Commanding 5th West Riding Regt. No. 142. G/17. 10. 18.	17/10/1918	17/10/1918
Miscellaneous	5 Duke of Wellington Regt. Operation Order No Ref Map. 51a S.E. & 5 of B.G.E. 1/20000.	19/10/1918	19/10/1918
Miscellaneous	62nd (W.R.) Divn. H.Q	20/10/1918	20/10/1918
Miscellaneous	5 Duke Of Wellington Rgt Operation Order	22/10/1918	22/10/1918
Miscellaneous	Copy for War Diary		
Operation(al) Order(s)	5th Duke Of Wellington's Regt Operation Order No 143	30/10/1918	30/10/1918
Map	Map		
Map	France		
Miscellaneous	51 A S E "B"coy		
Heading	War Diary Of 5th Duke Of Wellington's (W.R.) Regiment 1st To 30th November, 1918 (Volume-9)		
War Diary	Ref. Sheets 57.c.57.a.51. 1/40,000	01/11/1918	03/11/1918
War Diary	Reference Sheet 51a 1/40,000	04/11/1918	17/11/1918
War Diary	Ref. Map. Namur.B. 1/100,000.	18/11/1918	30/11/1918
Miscellaneous	5th Battn. Duke Of Wellington's Regt.		
Miscellaneous	5th Battn. Duke Of Wellington's Regt.	02/11/1918	02/11/1918
Miscellaneous	5th Battn. Duke Of Wellington's Regt.	03/11/1918	03/11/1918
Miscellaneous	Instruction No 4	03/11/1918	03/11/1918
Miscellaneous	Amendment To Instruction No. 1		

Miscellaneous	Special Order Of The Day	06/11/1918	06/11/1918
Miscellaneous	62nd Division	06/11/1918	06/11/1918
Miscellaneous	62nd (West Riding) Division. Special Order of The Day by Major General Sir R.D. Whigham K.C.B. D.S.O.	10/11/1918	10/11/1918
Miscellaneous	5th Duke Of Wellington's Regt.		
Miscellaneous	62nd (West Riding) Division	11/11/1918	11/11/1918
Operation(al) Order(s)	5th Duke Of Wellington's Regiment Operation Order No. 144	16/11/1918	16/11/1918
Heading	War Diary Of 5th Duke Of Wellington's (W.R.) Regiment 1st To 31st December, 1918. Volume 10.		
War Diary	Ref Map Marche 1/100,000	01/12/1918	14/12/1918
War Diary	Ref Map Germany I M 1/100,000	15/12/1918	31/12/1918
Miscellaneous	Appendices		
Miscellaneous	Special Order Of The Day To all ranks of The 62nd (West Riding) Division		
Operation(al) Order(s)	5th Battn Duke Of Wellington's Regt Operation Order No. 146	15/12/1918	15/12/1918
Miscellaneous	Reference Maps		
Miscellaneous	62nd (West Riding) Division.	03/12/1918	03/12/1918
Miscellaneous	Commanding Officer 5th Battn. West Riding Regiment	30/11/1918	30/11/1918
Heading	War Diary Of 5th Duke Of Wellington's (W.R) Regt 1st To 31st January 1919 Volume 11		
War Diary	Ref. Map Germany I.L. 1/100,000	01/01/1919	31/01/1919
Miscellaneous	Appendices		
Miscellaneous	Special Order By Major General Sir R.D. Whigham K.C.B. D.S.O. Commanding 62nd (West Riding) Division	31/12/1918	31/12/1918
Heading	War Diary Of 5th Duke Of Wellington's (W.R.) Regt. 1st To 28th February 1919. Volume 12		
War Diary	Ref Map Germany I L 1/100,000	01/02/1919	28/02/1919
Miscellaneous	Appendices		
Heading	War Diary Of 5th Duke Of Wellington's Regt. 1st To 31st March 1919 (Volume-13)		
War Diary	Ref Map Germany I L 1/100,000	01/03/1919	31/03/1919
Miscellaneous	Appendices		
Operation(al) Order(s)	5th Duke Of Wellington's Regt Order No 148	07/03/1919	07/03/1919
Miscellaneous	All Recipients Of Order 148	07/03/1919	07/03/1919
Operation(al) Order(s)	5th Duke Of Wellington's Regt Order No 149	07/03/1919	07/03/1919
Operation(al) Order(s)	5th Duke Of Wellington's Regt. Order No. 150	30/03/1919	30/03/1919
Heading	War Diary Of 5th Duke Of Wellington's Regt.1st To 30th April 1919 (Volume 24.)		
War Diary	Ref. Map. Germany. I.L 1/100000. Namur. 1/100000.	01/04/1919	02/05/1919
Operation(al) Order(s)	5th Duke of Wellington's Regt Order No 151		
Map	Map		
Map	France		
Map	Namur		
Diagram etc	Belgium		
Map	Belgium		
Map	Germany		
Diagram etc	Belgium		
Map	Germany		

moss/rose (3)

moss/rose (3)

62ND DIVISION
186TH INFY BDE.

2/7TH BN DUKE OF WELLINGTON'S REGT

~~JAN 1917 — DEC 1918~~
1918 FEB — 1919 APL

FROM 49 DIV 147 BDE

SECRET.

CONFIDENTIAL

WAR DIARY

- of -

5TH. DUKE OF WELLINGTON'S (W.R.) REGT.

1st. to 28th. Feby. 1918.

(Volume /.).

ORIGINAL
9/2/14

[signature]...Lieut.Col.
Commdg. 5TH. DUKE OF WELLINGTON'S REGT.

Army Form C. 2118.

5th BATTALION, WEST RIDING REGIMENT.

No. 25/2/18

ORIGINAL WAR DIARY or INTELLIGENCE SUMMARY.

(Erase heading not required.)

Instructions regarding War Diaries and Intelligence Summaries are contained in F. S. Regs., Part II. and the Staff Manual respectively. Title pages will be prepared in manuscript.

Place	Date	Hour	Summary of Events and Information	Remarks and references to Appendices
REF. MAPS. LENS 11. 1/100000. SHEET 57¢5L⁶⁰⁶ 1/20,000.	1918. Feb.1.		The new amalgamated Battalion continued its reorganisation during the day and became 5th. Duke of Wellington's (West Riding) Regiment on the merging of the 1/5th. and 2/5th. Battalions. Lieut.Col. J. Walker (Commanding Officer of 1/5th. West Riding Regiment) was appointed Commanding Officer, Lieut.Col. F. Brook (Commanding Officer of 2/5th. Duke of Wellington's) was appointed Second in Command, Capt. K. Sykes M.C. (Adjutant of 1/5th. West Riding Regiment) remained as Adjutant of the new battalion. Company Commanders were "A" - Capt. G.L. Tinker (of 2/5th.) "B" Capt. G.V.Ransome M.A (of 2/5th.), "C" - Capt. C.G.H. Ellis (of 1/5th.) "D" - Capt. H.O. Browning M.C. (of 1/5th.) "A" and "B" Companies consisted of the old 2/5th. Battalion men and "C" and "D" Companies were made up by the nucleus of 1/5th. Battalion and drafts from the disbanded 2/6th. Duke of Wellington's Regiment. In the evening the battalion left billets at ST. AUBIN and relieved the 2/5th. York and Lancaster Regiment and the 2/5th. King's Own Yorkshire Light Infantry in the left sub-section of the GAVRELLE SECTOR. The battalion entrained on light railway at ST.AUBIN at 5.pm. and detrained at CHANTECLER SIDING (G6.d.7.4.) From there the troops marched into the line. The battalion held the line from the GAVRELLE ROAD (C.25.a.6.6.) to B.18.d.70.00. Companies were disposed as follows :- "C" Company the right of MILL POST (C.19.c.65.15) to C.19.c.80.70, "B" Company left of MILL POST (C.19.c.80.70) to C.19.c.45.35), "A" Company - BRADFORD POST (C.19.a.20.50 to B.24.b.85.75) "D" Company were in support with three platoons in MARINE TRENCH (B.30.a. central to B.24.d.25.80) and the fourth platoon in support to "A" Company. Relief went smoothly and was completed by 11.30pm.	
	2nd.		Dull day. Slightly misty in the morning. Quiet during the day. A little trench mortaring on the left of MILL POST in evening, one man wounded.	
	3rd.		Dull, cold and wet in early morning, but cleared into a bright day afterwards. A little scattered shelling during the day round "C" Company's Headquarters. Considerable hostile trench mortar activity on the left Company in MILL POST as a result of which No. 2 Post and a wiring party from 186th. Pioneer Company suffered 10 casualties (4 killed 6 wounded) It appeared as if it was a prelude to a raid but nothing transpired.	

Army Form C. 2118.

ORIGINAL

WAR DIARY
of
INTELLIGENCE SUMMARY.

(Erase heading not required.)

Instructions regarding War Diaries and Intelligence Summaries are contained in F. S. Regs., Part II. and the Staff Manual respectively. Title pages will be prepared in manuscript.

5th BATTALION,
W............

Place	Date	Hour	Summary of Events and Information	Remarks and references to Appendices
REF. MAPS. LENS II. 1/100000. SHEET 57d.b.N.W. 1/20,000.	1918. Feb.4.		Bright clear day. Considerable aerial activity. Widely scattered hostile artillery activity.	
	5th.		The battalion was relieved by 2/7th. Duke of Wellington's Regt. at night. On relief the battalion moved into Brigade Support. Battalion H.Q. and A and B Companies were accommodated in dugouts at CHANTECLER (H.1.c.50.55) C Company went back to WAKEFIELD CAMP and D Company took over BAILLEUL POST (B.28 central) in the REDLINE	
	6th.		Bright clear day. The Battalion found working parties during the day and night. Parties of officers reconnoitred the GREEN LINE.	
	7th.		Dull day with slight showers. Battalion all out on working parties.	
	8th.		The battalion was relieved by 1/2nd. London Regiment. Troops entrained at CHANTECLER SIDING on light railway (G.6.d.7.4.) at 5.30pm and went into billets for the night at MAROEUIL.	
	9th.		Battalion entrained at MAROEUIL at 12.10pm and went to TINCQUES. From there the battalion marched via CHELERS and MONCHY BRETON to LA THIEULOYE. Billets quite good. Men marched well. The battalion became (with Division) Corps and G.H.Q. Reserve.	
	10th.		Men cleaned up and reorganised at LA THIEULOYE.	
	11th.		The battalion moved from LA THIEULOYE and marched via ROCOURT, MAGENCOURT and FREVILLERS to VILLERS BRULIN and GUESTREVILLE. Billets were moderately good. "A" Company was billeted at GUESTREVILLE, "B" "C" "D" and H.Q. at VILLERS BRULIN and Transport at BETHONSART.	
	12th.		Men cleaned up and had baths at Divisional Baths TINCQUES.	
	13th.		Very wet day. Divisional Commander (Maj.Genl. Braithwaite C.B.) visited the battalion during morning but on account of the wet saw no training.	

Army Form C. 2118.

5th BATTALION,
WEST RIDING
REGIMENT.

No. ....
Date ....

ORIGINAL
WAR DIARY
or
INTELLIGENCE SUMMARY

(Erase heading not required.)

Instructions regarding War Diaries and Intelligence Summaries are contained in F. S. Regs., Part II. and the Staff Manual respectively. Title pages will be prepared in manuscript.

Place	Date	Hour	Summary of Events and Information	Remarks and references to Appendices
REF.MAPS. LENS 11. 1/100,000. SHEET 57.b.NW. 1/20,000.	1918. Feb. 14th.		Fine day. Battalion did Training in the morning and Recreational Training in afternoon.	
	15th.		- Ditto -	
	16th.		- Ditto -	
	17th.		- Ditto -	
	18th.		The battalion had baths at the Divisional Baths TINCQUES morning and afternoon. Through the generosity of the people of Huddersfield the battalion had Christmas Dinners at the various billets.	
REF.MAPS. LENS 11. 1/100,000. 51.b.NW. 1/20,000.	19th.		The battalion left VILLERS BRULIN Area and entrained at TINCQUES at 2.pm. Detrainment was made at ECURIE STATION. The battalion then marched to STEWARTS CAMP A.29.b.3.7. and relieved 2/4th. Duke of Wellington's Regiment. The camp was a good one consisting of Nissen Huts. There was plenty of good accommodation. The Regimental Transport moved by road from BETHONSART to standings at BRAY near EGOIVRES.	
	20th.		All four Companies were employed on wiring the Corps Line under 461st.(W.R.) Field Company R.E. and 457th.(W.R.) Field Company R.E. Hours of work were from 9.am to 3.30pm. A and D Companies were working about G.6.c. and C and B Companies about A.22.d. H.Q. Company were employed on making revetments round the huts against bombing and also making new latrines.	
	21st.		All available men were out wiring on Corps System under the direction of 457 Coy.R.E. and 461st Coy. R.E.	
	22nd.		- Ditto -	
	23rd.		- Ditto -	

Army Form C. 2118.

5th BATTALION,
WEST RIDING
REGIMENT.

No. ....
Date ....

ORIGINAL
WAR DIARY
or
INTELLIGENCE SUMMARY.
(Erase heading not required)

Instructions regarding War Diaries and Intelligence Summaries are contained in F. S. Regs., Part II. and the Staff Manual respectively. Title pages will be prepared in manuscript.

Place	Date	Hour	Summary of Events and Information	Remarks and references to Appendices
REF.MAPS LENS 11. 1/100,000. 51.b.NW. 1/20,000.	1918. Feb.24th.		All available men were out wiring on Corps System under the direction of 457th. Company R.E. and 461st Coy. R.E.	
	25th.		- Ditto -	
	26th.		- Ditto -	
	27th.		- Ditto.	
	28th.		All available men on Corps wiring parties as usual. Weather wet.	

Commdg. 5TH. [signature] Lieut.Col.
DUKE OF WELLINGTON'S REGT.

Army Form C. 2118.

5th BATTALION,
WEST RIDING
REGIMENT.

No..........
Date..........

ORIGINAL
WAR DIARY
INTELLIGENCE SUMMARY
(Erase heading not required)

Place	Date	Hour	Summary of Events and Information	Remarks and references to Appendices
	1918 February		APPENDICES.	
		J.S.	CASUALTIES etc.	
			Killed. 3 other ranks.	
			Wounded. 11 other ranks.	
			Lieut. E. Bond - To Hospital - 19.12.17. To England to Machine Gun Corps 18.2.18.	
			2/Lieut. A. Walker - To Hospital 14.2.18. Returned 22.2.18.	
			" D.A.S.Haigh - To Hospital 19.2.18.	
			" H.J. Weighill - To Hospital 22.2.18.	
		J.S.	TRANSFERS etc.	
			2/Lieut. C.S. Floyd - To England - six months light duty 14.2.18.	
		J.S.	" H. Dean - To M.G. Corps. 18.2.18.	
			DRAFTS.	
			3.2.18. 6 other ranks.	
			5.2.18. 2 " "	
			16.2.18. 4 " "	
			19.2.18. 3 " "	
			21.2.18. 1 " "	
			25.2.18. 4 " "	
			26.2.18. 1 " "	
			27.2.18. 2 " "	
			HONOURS & AWARDS.	
		J.S.	LIEUT.COL. J. WALKER awarded the BELGIAN CROIX DE GUERRE d/ . ;	
			No.240358 C.S.M. FISHER W. awarded the BELGIAN CROIX DE GUERRE d/ . ;	
			No.240135 Corpl. J.H.HAIGH awarded the MILITARY MEDAL for bravery in the Field d/11.2.'18.	

Secret.   5th West Riding Regt
          Operation Order.   7/8/18

1. **Move**
   The Battalion will move to LA THIEULOYE
tomorrow. Entrain at MARŒUIL 12.10pm.
Detrain at TINCQUES. March from there to
billets at THIEULOYE.

2. **Entrainment**
   Coys will march independently to
MARŒUIL to be there by 11.45am. Silence to be
maintained during entrainment. Each Coy
will send a complete marching out state
to the Adjutant by 10 am tomorrow shewing
details to be entrained (a) Officers (b) other
ranks.

   OC 'A' Coy will detail a picquet
of 1 Officer and 10 other ranks who will
prevent men leaving the train without
permission during the journey.

3. **March Discipline**
   Particular attention is to be paid to
march discipline. Intervals of 200 yards
will be maintained between Companies.

4. **Transport**
   The Regimental Transport will move

independently so as to arrive in new area
by 4.0pm.

Blankets (rolled in bundles of 10)
Officers Valises etc. to be collected into one
dump per Company by 9.15am. The QM
will detail 3 lorries to collect these dumps
at 9.30am.

Cookers to be ready for removal by
8.45am

Officers Mess Cart and Maltese Cart
will report at BHQ at 8.30am.

5. Food arrangements etc.

Breakfasts will be had at 7.30am.
Men will take haversack rations with
them. Dinners to be cooked on field
kitchens 'en route' and ready on arrival
in new area.

Sick parade at Battn HQ 7am.

7. Reports

Capt B Mollett MC will report to RTO
MARCEUIL at 11.45am with complete
marching out state of Battalion which
he will obtain from the Adjutant.

OC B Company will detail an
Officer to obtain certificate of cleanliness
of Billets from Town Major MARCEUIL

Companies will report settled in

Billets on arrival in new area

K S[?] Capt Adjt
5th West Riding Regt

Copies to:-
A B C D & HQ Coys
Office
War Diary (2)
TO & QM

SECRET.   Copy No. #9

5TH. DUKE OF WELLINGTON'S REGT.

Operation Order No.2

Ref. Map.   LENS. SHEET 11.   1/100,000.   Feby 10th

1. **MOVE.** The Battalion will move by march route from LA THIEULOYE to VILLERS BRULIN and BETHONSART tomorrow. March via ROCOURT, MAGNICOURT, FREVILLERS.

2. **ORDER OF MARCH.** Companies and Transport will pass LA THIEULOYE CHURCH in the following order at times stated -

"D" Coy.	11.15am.
"C" Coy.	11.17am.
H.Q. Coy.	11.19am.
"A" Coy.	11.21am.
"B" Coy.	11.23am.
Transport.	11.25am.

   Distances of 200 yards will be maintained between Companies and between "B" Company and the Transport.
   Each Company will send an Officer to synchronise watches with the Adjutant at 9.am.
   Usual halts (10 minutes to the hour) will be made on the march.

3. **ADVANCE AND REAR PARTIES.**
   (a). Billeting party under Major T. Goodall D.S.O., M.C. has proceeded in advance and will meet the Battalion at the entrance to the village of BETHONSART.
   (b). Lieut. Yates is detailed to remain behind with 1 N.C.O. and 3 men per company to hand over billets clean. A certificate to this effect will be obtained from the Area Commandant's Representative and forwarded to Orderly Room.
   (c). The Orderly Officer and Orderly N.C.O's will march in rear of the Battalion to pick up any stragglers on the march.

4. **TRANSPORT.** Mens' Blankets (rolled in bundles of 10) will be sent to Q.M. Stores by 9am.
   Officers' Valises will be stacked in one dump per Company by 9.30am. and collected under arrangements to be made by the Quartermaster.
   T.O. will arrange for Mess Cart and Medical Cart to be at H.Q. at 10.15am.
   Horses for Company Commanders will be at respective billets at 11.am.
   Horses for C.O., Adjutant, M.O. and Capt. Jackson D.S.O. to be at Battalion H.Q. at 11.am.
   Orderly Room Boxes to be collected at 10.am.

5. **REPORTS.** Companies will report 'Settled in Billets' on arrival in new area and will notify Orderly Room of Location of their Coy. H.Q.

                                               ....Capt. & Adjt.
                                               5th. Duke of Wellington's Regiment.

Copies to -   A, B, C, D & H.Q. Coys.
              T.O. & Q.M.
              War Diary (2)
              Office.

SECRET.   Copy No...7...

5TH. DUKE OF WELLINGTON'S REGT.
OPERATION ORDER NO. 3.

Ref. Map. LENS. SHEET 11. 1/100,000.

1. **RELIEF.** The battalion will relieve the 2/4th. Duke of Wellington's Regiment at STEWARTS CAMP in forward area on the 19th inst.

2. **TRAIN ARRANGEMENTS.** Train arrangements will be notified later as appendix "A".

3. **ADVANCE PARTIES.** Advance Parties as follows will move to the new area tomorrow 18th inst. travelling by rail between SAVY and MAROEUIL.

Strength.	Depart.	Billeting Area.	Area Commandant.
Lt Mollett, M.C Capt.H.S.Jackson D.S.O. 1 N.C.O. per Coy. & H.Q., 1 representative from Transport, 1 runner and 1 servant.	SAVY. 1.30pm.	STEWARTS CAMP.	A.C. Nine Elms. A.28.b.7.2.

Transport Lines at BRAY near ECOIVRES.
Report to Area Commandant ECOIVRES.
This party will take 2 days rations with them.
Parade at Orderly Room 12.30pm.

4. **TRANSPORT.** Transport arrangements will be notified later as Appendix "B".

5. **WORKING PARTIES.** There will be no interruption of working parties. O.C. 2/4th. Duke of Wellington's will provide the working parties in the forward area on the 19th inst.

6. **BILLETS.** All billets will be left clean. Lieut. Mollett M.C. is detailed to obtain usual certificate of satisfaction and cleanliness from representative of 2/4th. Duke of Wellington's on the morning of 19th inst.

7. Acknowledge.

.....K Syhes......Capt. & Adjt.
5th.Duke of Wellington's Regiment.

Copies to - A,B,C,D & H.Q. Coys.
            Office.
            Bde.
            War Diary (2).
            Adjutant.
            Capt.H.S.Jackson D.S.O.
            QM
            T.O.

APPENDIX "A"
to be attached to Operation Order No.3.

(a). The battalion will parade at zero minus 60 minutes outside Chateau Gate VILLERS BRULIN in following order - D, B, C, A, H.Q.
March to SAVY STATION by Companies. 200 yards distance between each Company. March down Chateau Avenue to SAVY.

(b). Entrainment and Detrainment will be done in silence.
O.C. C Company will detail Train Picquet of 1 Officer and 10 other ranks to prevent men getting out of the train without permission.

(c). Entraining strengths to reach the Adjutant by 10am tomorrow shewing (a) No. of Officers (b) No. of other ranks.

(d). Zero will be notified later. It will probably by 1.pm.

18.2.18.

TO - All recipients of O.O. 3.

   Previous appendices "A" and "B" are cancelled and the attached appendices are substituted.

   The covering memo. still holds good.

<u>CLAIMS Certificates of ~~cleanliness~~ will be obtained for each billet or stable by all concerned.</u>

         ...K. Sykes... Capt. & Adjt.
         5th. Duke of Wellington's Regiment.

18.2.18.

APPENDIX "B"
to be attached to Operation Order No. 3
- -

(a). Mens' blankets rolled in bundles of 10, Officers Valises (lightly packed), Orderly Room Boxes will be stacked in one dump per Company by 9.am tomorrow. 2 Dumps for H.Q. will be at Orderly Room and at Chateau Guard Room. All other Companies will have one dump only.
Q.M. will arrange to collect these dumps with the lorries at his disposal and take to STEWARTS CAMP.

(b). 4 Cookers, Mess Cart, Medical Cart, 4 Lewis Gun Limbers and 1 Water Cart will leave VILLERS BRULIN at 12 noon and proceed to STEWARTS CAMP. Horses will be left there for Mess Cart, Medical Cart and Water Cart. Horses for L.G. Limbers wand Cookers will return to Transport Lines at BRAY.

(c). Remainder of Regimental Transport will proceed direct to BRAY under Transport Officer's arrangements.

(d) T.O. will arrange for Riding Horses for C.O., 2nd in Command, Adjutant and M.O. and 1 spare to be at MAROEUIL STATION at zero plus 60 minutes.

(1).

(e).   T.O. will arrange for Mess Cart to be at H.Q. Mess at 11.am
and Medical Cart at Regimental Aid Post at same time.

18.2.18.

TO - All Recipients of O.O. 3.

Herewith Appendices A and B to be attached to O.O. 3.

Breakfasts will be as usual tomorrow. Companies must arrange for men to have TEA at 11.am and for dinners to be served on arrival at STEWARTS CAMP. R.S.M. will arrange for H.Q. Coys Tea and Dinner to be cooked proportionately on B, C and D Coys' Kitchens.

1 N.C.O. and 3 men (Signallers) will be attached to Battalion H.Q. from Brigade for rations and accommodation from tomorrow.

................K. Sykes......Capt. & Adjt.
5th Duke of Wellington's Regiment.

18.2.18.

APPENDIX "A"
to be attached to Operation Order No.3
- -

(a). The battalion will entrain at TINCQUES at 1.pm tomorrow and will arrive at the Station at 12.30pm.   Detrainment will be at ECURIE.   Companies will pass GUESTREVILLE - VILLERS BRULIN - BETHENCOURT - VILLERS BRULIN Roads fork roads in the following order at times stated -

        D Company.   11.45am.
        B Company.   11.47am.
        C Company.   11.49am.
        A Company.   11.51am.
        H.Q.   11.53am.

200 yards distance between each Company.

(b). Entrainment and detrainment will be done in silence.
O.C. C Company will detail train picquet of 1 Officer and 10 other ranks to prevent men getting out of the train without permission

(c). Entraining strength to reach the Adjutant by 10am tomorrow shewing (a) No. of Officers (b) No. of other ranks.

APPENDIX "B".

(a). Mens blankets rolled in bundles of 10, Officers Valises (tightly packed) Orderly Room Boxes, will be stacked in dumps by 8.30am.
Two dumps for H.Q. will be at Orderly Room and at Chateau Guard Room.

All other companies will have one dump only.

(b). Two motor lorries only will report to the Battalion at 8.30am tomorrow. These lorries will first be loaded up with blankets which will be conveyed to TINCQUES STATION and dumped under a guard of 1 N.C.O. and 3 men to be provided by O.C. B Company, -
Pending loading on troop train under orders of R.T.O.
A loading party of 1 N.C.O. and 12 men from D Company will report at TINCQUES STATION by 12 noon.
After dumping blankets lorries will return to VILLERS BRULIN and convey remainder of stores to STEWARTS CAMP.

(c). 4 cookers, Mess Cart, Medical Cart, 4 Lewis Gun Limbers and one water cart will leave VILLERS BRULIN at 11.30am and proceed to STEWARTS CAMP.
Horses will be left there for Mess Cart, Medical Cart and water

cart.
Horses for Lewis Gun Limbers and cookers will return to Transport Lines at BRAY.

(d). Remainder of Regimental Transport will proceed direct to BRAY under T.O's arrangements.

(e). H.Q. Riding Horses will be sent to STEWARTS CAMP with Transport mentioned in para. c.

(f). T.O. will arrange for Mess Cart and Medical Cart to be at H.Q. Mess and Regimental Aid Post respectively at 10.30am.

Army Form C. 2118.

5th BATTALION,
WEST RIDING
REGIMENT.

No...........
Date...........

ORIGINAL
WAR DIARY
or
INTELLIGENCE SUMMARY.
(Erase heading not required.)

Instructions regarding War Diaries and Intelligence Summaries are contained in F. S. Regs., Part II. and the Staff Manual respectively. Title pages will be prepared in manuscript.

Place	Date	Hour	Summary of Events and Information	Remarks and references to Appendices
			A P P E N D I C E S (continued)	
			THE BATTALION on amalgamation was made up as follows :-	
			1/5TH. WEST RIDING REGIMENT. 11 officers 199 other ranks.	
			2/5TH. DUKE OF WELLINGTON'S REGT. 35 officers 677 other ranks.	
			2/6TH. DUKE OF WELLINGTON'S REGT. 4 officers 101 other ranks.	

186th Infantry Brigade.
62nd Division.

WAR DIARY

5th BATTALION

THE DUKE OF WELLINGTON'S REGIMENT

MARCH 1918

Appendices attached:-

    Report on Operations 25th-30th March
    Congratulatory Messages.
    Operation Orders.

ORIGINAL

5TH. Bn. DUKE OF WELLINGTON'S (W.R.) REGT. T.F.

Army Form C. 2118.

WAR DIARY
or
INTELLIGENCE SUMMARY.

(Erase heading not required.)

Instructions regarding War Diaries and Intelligence Summaries are contained in F.S. Regs., Part II. and the Staff Manual respectively. Title pages will be prepared in manuscript.

Place	Date	Hour	Summary of Events and Information	Remarks and references to Appendices
REF. MAPS. LENS 11. 1/100,000. SHEET 51.b. N.W. 1/20,000.	1918. Mch. 1st.	K.S.	The battalion was relieved in STEWARTS CAMP, ROCLINCOURT by 2nd. Battalion Irish Guards On relief the battalion marched to LANCASTER CAMP, ECOIVRES via ECURIE and ANZIN. The new battalion band appeared on parade for the first time and played quite creditably. Weather was very variable with intervals of rain and sleet.	
	2nd.	K.S.	Cold, raw, snowy day. The Battalion did Training (Close Order Drill under Regtl. Sergt. Major and Company Training) in the morning. The afternoon was devoted to Recreational Training.	
	3rd.	K.S.	Very cold day with falling sleet most of the time. The battalion marched from LANCASTER CAMP, ECOIVRES to SPRINGVALE CAMP near ECURIE and relieved 10th Battn. East Yorks Regt., 31st Division in Divisional Reserve. The camp was a comfortable one.	
	4th.	K.S.	A very wild wet day. Very cold. A little training was done by companies during the morning. "C" Company went forward area making a cable trench to Brigade Battle H.Q. West of the BOIS DE LA VILLE at B.7.b.7.7.	
	5th.	K.S.	A very bright day. Windy but sunny. "B" Company were employed on making Cable Trench at B.7.b.7.7. "A" Company made 100 concertina wire entanglements in camp for use in the line "B" and "C" Companies were training in the morning on the Range and Assault Course in Camp.	
	6th.	K.S.	Usual working party for 186th Brigade Signals.- Making buried cable trench. Remainder of the Battalion training.	
	7th.	K.S.	——— Ditto ———	
	8th.	K.S.	——— Ditto ———	
Ref.Map. MARCEUIL Combined Sheet.	9th.	K.S.	A very brilliant day. The battalion relieved the 2/4th. Duke of Wellington's Regt. as battalion in Brigade Support to ACHEVILLE Sector L.2. The relief was carried out during the morning and was completed by 12.15pm. without incident. The route taken to the trenches	

Army Form C. 2118.

WAR DIARY
or
INTELLIGENCE SUMMARY.
(Erase heading not required.)

Place	Date	Hour	Summary of Events and Information	Remarks and references to Appendices
Ref.Map. MAROEUIL Combined Sheet 1/20,000.	1918. Mch. 9th.		was ARRAS - LENS Road, past THELUS Cross Roads, MERSEY, C.P.R. and HUDSON Communication Trenches. Dispositions on relief were as follows:- Battalion H.Q. in VANCOUVER ROAD T.28.a.5.2. "B" Company in CANADA TRENCH from Right Brigade Boundary (T.28.d.3.5. to T.28.b.6.7. with Company H.Q. at T.28.b.8.1. "D" Company in CANADA TRENCH from T.28.b.6.7. to Left Divisional Boundary T.22.c.3.4. with Company H.Q. at T.28.b.5.7. "A" Company were accommodated in dugout in Railway Embankment at B.2.a.9.3. "C" Company were accommodated at CUBITT CAMP A.9.a. central.	
	10th.		A very fine day. The battalion found many working parties from A,B, and D Coys. for work under the direction of 457th Coy. R.E. and for wiring in front of CANADA TRENCH.	
	11th.		A brilliant day. Many working and wiring parties found by the battalion. Two of our aeroplanes were brought down in aerial combat during the afternoon. One crashed within the enemy's lines and the other came down on the ARRAS - LENS Road. In the evening a heavy trench mortar bombardment was put down on the front line battalion from 10.15pm to 10.30pm. A certain amount of enemy gas shelling (mustard) was evident during the evening but none came very near the battalion.	
	12th.		A very bright fine day. Usual working parties on the Support Line Defences and Communication Trenches. Instructions were received during the afternoon that indications pointed to an attack by the enemy in the neighbourhood of ARRAS involving the front of this Corps. This attack being expected possibly tomorrow. The Division was ordered to maintain a state of instant readiness. "A" Company manned Strong Points BEEHIVE T.27.d.3.7. WAKEFIELD T.27.d.7.7. BARNSLEY T.27.d.8.3. SHEFFIELD T.28.a.1.7. one platoon of "C" Company manned FOVANT S.P. Remaining 3 platoons and Company H.Q. of "C" Company moved from CUBITT CAMP A.9. to dugout on Railway Embankment B.2.a.9.3. vacated by "A" Company Our artillery considerably harassed the enemy all night who appeared to be very apprehensive by the unusual number of Very Lights he sent up.	

ORIGINAL.

Instructions regarding War Diaries and Intelligence Summaries are contained in F. S. Regs., Part II. and the Staff Manual respectively. Title pages will be prepared in manuscript.

5TH. Bn. DUKE OF WELLINGTON'S (W.R.) Regt. T.F.

WAR DIARY
or
INTELLIGENCE SUMMARY.
(Erase heading not required.)

Army Form C. 2118.

Place	Date	Hour	Summary of Events and Information	Remarks and references to Appendices
Ref. Map. MAROEUIL Combined Sheet 1/20,000.	1918. Mch. 13th.		The battalion stood to arms from 5.am until 8.am. Nothing unusual transpired except for increased harassing fire by our artillery and an energetic reply by the enemy on forward Battalion H.Q. in WINNIPEG ROAD.	
	14th.		After a very quiet night the Battalion "Stood to" from 5.am to 8.am again but nothing unusual occurred. A much cooler day with very little sun.	
	15th.		The battalion was relieved by 2/7th. Bn. Duke of Wellington's Regt. in Support Trenches. On relief the battalion relieved 2/4th. Bn. Duke of Wellington's Regiment in the front line system of ACHEVILLE SECTION. The section consists of one post named HUDSON POST. The post extends from T.30.b.05.80 to T.24.a.30.45. Dispositions of companies on relief was as follows - "A" and "C" Companies in front and close support in North and South TRIUMPH and NOVIA SCOTIA Trenches. Right front company (C) holding posts 1 to 8 with its Company Support in South TRIUMPH. Left front company (A) holding posts 9 to 16. "D" Company in Battalion Support in BRANDON TRENCH and "B" Company in Battalion Reserve in NEW BRUNSWICK TRENCH. Battalion H.Q. was established in NEW BRUNSWICK TRENCH (T.22.d.9.2.) The relief was carried through very quietly and was completed by 2.pm. Remainder of the day was very quiet. The trenches were on the whole very good ones. Weather very fine and bright.	
	16th.		A brilliant day again. Very quiet day. There was some Gas Shelling of back areas in direction of WILLERVAL which did not affect the Battalion Area very much, although the mustard and sneezing gas were felt. The Division on our right (56th) carried out a raid at 10.pm but it did not affect our front	
	17th		A very clear bright day. There was much aerial activity on both sides during the day. A raid on the enemy trenches was successfully carried out by 2/7th. Duke of Wellington's Regiment at 11.pm. The raiding party consisted of 2 officers 10 N.C.Os and 66 men from 2/7th. Bn. Duke of Wellington's Regt and 6 sappers detailed by G.R.E. 62nd. Division. The objectives were enemy front line T.24.d.52.20 to T.24.d.42.35, Support Trench T.24.d.64.00 to	

ORIGINAL.

Army Form C. 2118.

Instructions regarding War Diaries and Intelligence
Summaries are contained in F. S. Regs., Part II.
and the Staff Manual respectively. Title pages
will be prepared in manuscript.

5TH. Bn. DUKE OF WELLINGTON'S (W.R.) REGT T.F.

WAR DIARY

or

INTELLIGENCE SUMMARY.

(Erase heading not required.)

Place	Date	Hour	Summary of Events and Information	Remarks and references to Appendices
Ref. Map. MARŒUIL Combined Sheet. 1/20,000.	1918 Mch. 17th		T.24.d.63.15 TULIP Communication Trench T.24.d.63.15 to T.24.d.34.24. the Raiding Party went out through our No.1 Post. Wire had previously been cut by 6" Trench Mortars. At zero - 10 at dummy barrage was put down on the enemy trenches S.E. of ARLEUX, which was successful in deviating the enemy's attention from the front to be raided. The gaps in the enemy's wire were completed by the explosion of Bangalore Torpedoes and the raiding party entered the enemy's Trench immediately after the barrage lifted. The raiders having completed their task, withdrew at Zero plus 15 minutes. Five prisoners of the 469th I.R. (240th Division) were captured and 2 more killed in the trench. At Zero plus 10 minutes, the enemy opened a light barrage and between plus 15 minutes and 30 minutes a fairly heavy barrage of Light Shells and Trench Mortar's were put down on No Man's Land. Then barrage then increased in intensity, particularly on ARLEUX, also on BRANDON and WINNEPEG Support Trenches. Our line was considerably thinned out during the Raid and men put under shelter with the result that only two casualties occured. Remainder of night was very quiet.	
	18th		A day of very good visibility and in consequence many balloons were up on both sides. Damage to trenches caused by enemy counter barrage during the Raid was repaired. The Corp Commander, Divisional Commander and Brigade Commander visited Battalion Headquarters during the morning. A quiet day.	
	19th		A very wet day. Enemy did a little Light Trench Mortaring on No.5 Post in Right Company front line about 7 a.m. causing 3 Casualties, otherwise quiet.	
	20th		Enemy artillery was more active than usual on our Trench system. During the night 20th/21st there was a change in enemy attitude. An unusual amount of Movement and talking in the enemy trench was heard. Two enemy patrols were seen and dispersed during the night.	
	21st		At 5 a.m. a heavy counter Battery fire was opened by the enemy. At first, the fire on our front was at a much slower rate than on front of Corps on our right, but increased in	

ORIGINAL

Army Form C. 2118.

5TH. BN. DUKE OF WELLINGTON'S (W.R) REGT. T.F.

WAR DIARY
or
INTELLIGENCE SUMMARY.
(Erase heading not required.)

Instructions regarding War Diaries and Intelligence Summaries are contained in F.S. Regs., Part II. and the Staff Manual respectively. Title pages will be prepared in manuscript.

Place	Date	Hour	Summary of Events and Information	Remarks and references to Appendices
Ref.Map. MAROEUIL Combined Sheet. 1/20,000	1918. Mch. 21st.		intensity about 5-30 a.m. About 10 a.m. the situation quietened down. The Battalion was relieved by the 2/7th Duke of Wellington's Regt during the day in the ACHEVILLE SECTION, on relief B & D. Coys and Battalion Headquarters moved to SPRINGVALE CAMP, Nr. ECURIE. A & C. Companies went into dug-outs on Railway Embankment near FARBUS STATION.	
	22nd.		The Battalion received hurried orders to move to LANCASTER CAMP, MONT.ST.ELOI. This was done during the afternoon after relief by two companies of Canadian Corps.	
	23rd.		The Battalion received Warning Orders to be prepared for active-operations at very short notice. All detached Officers and men began to rejoin the Battalion.	
	24th.		Battalion marched from MONT.ST.ELOI to ETRUN AREA and the Brigade concentrated into one hutment camp. Orders were received that the Brigade was likely to have to man the Green Line south of ARRAS (FICHEUX-TELEGRAPH HILL Line) on the following day.	
	25th 26th 27th 28th 29th 30th		See Special Narrative attached.	
Ref.Map. 57.d.N.E. 1/20,000	31st.		Battalion remained in Support in trenches in E.30.b.	

Lieut-Colonel.
COMMDG. 5TH. BN. DUKE OF WELLINGTON'S (W.R) RGT

Original.

5th Duke of Wellington (W.R.) Regiment J.F.

Army Form C. 2118.

WAR DIARY
or
INTELLIGENCE SUMMARY.
(Erase heading not required.)

Place	Date	Hour	Summary of Events and Information	Remarks and references to Appendices

APPENDICES.

CASUALTIES etc.
Lieut.Col. J. Walker, wounded at duty 26.3.18. 1st Lt.J.W.Sherrick (U.S.M.C.) wounded 28.3.18.
Major F. Brook, wounded at duty 28.3.18. Capt.G.L. Tinker, wounded 29.3.18.
2/Lieut. F. Chapman, wounded at duty 29.3.18. Capt. T. Goodall, D.S.O., M.C. wounded 29.3.18.
2/Lieut. J. Sugden, killed 29.3.18. 2/Lieut. M.H. Weighill, wounded 28.3.18.
2/Lieut. P. Mosley, killed 28.3.18. Lieut. B. Mollett M.C. wounded 28.3.18.
2/Lieut. A. Cawthra, missing 29.3.18. Capt.H.O. Browning M.C., wounded 27.3.18.

          OTHER RANKS
    Missing.   56.
    Killed.   31.
    Wounded. 115. /2/ Died of wounds /

Lieut. H.S. Jackson D.S.O. - 6 month's light duty in England 15.3.18.
Lieut. G. Dyson - Medical Board whilst on leave to England 27.2.18.
2/Lieut. R. Denham - Transferred to Machine Gun Corps 18.3.18

DRAFTS
  27.2.18. 56 other ranks.
   4.3.18. 29   do. 10.3.18. 1 other rank.
   7.3.18.   4   do. 24.3.18. 13 do.
                              27.3.18. 26 do.

PROMOTIONS, RELINQUISHMENTS, etc.
Lieut. (Acting Lieut.Col.) F. Brook relinquishes the acting rank of Lieut. Col. on ceasing to command battalion 14.2.18, when he reverts to acting rank of Major whilst employed as Major on Headquarters.
2/Lieut. W. Yates to be Lieut. 5.2.18.
2/Lieut. (A/Capt.) C.G.H. Ellis to be Lieut. 29.1.18.
2/Lieut. C.S. Floyd to be Lieut. 18.1.18.
Capt. T. Goodall DSO,MC, relinquishes the acting rank of Major on ceasing to be employed as second in command dated 13.2.18.
Lieut. H.S. Jackson to be acting captain (additional) dated 16.2.18.

ORIGINAL.

5th. Bn. DUKE OF WELLINGTON'S (W.R.) REGT. T.F.

Army Form C. 2118.

WAR DIARY
or
INTELLIGENCE SUMMARY.

(Erase heading not required.)

Instructions regarding War Diaries and Intelligence Summaries are contained in F. S. Regs., Part II. and the Staff Manual respectively. Title pages will be prepared in manuscript.

Place	Date	Hour	Summary of Events and Information	Remarks and references to Appendices
			A P P E N D I C E S (continued)	
			Lieut. A.R. Haigh)	
			Lieut. W. Yates.) Relinquish the acting rank of captain on ceasing to command companies,	
			Lieut. F.H. Waite.) dated 1.2.18.	
			Lieut. G. Dyson.)	
			2/Lieut. B. Mollett M.C. relinquishes the acting rank of Captain (additional) dated 1.2.18.	
		Ditto	Authority A.G. List No. 176 dated 24.2.18.	
		Ditto	2/Lieut. B. Mollett M.C. to be lieutenant dated 5.2.18.	
			Authority London Gazette dated 22.2.18.	

NARRATIVE
of

Operations in which the 5th. Bn. Duke of Wellington's (W.R.) Regt. T.F. was engaged.

25th. March to 30th March
1918.

Ref. Map. 57.D. N.E. 1/20,000.

25TH. MARCH

1.30am. Battalion received orders to move with Brigade from ETRUN AREA at 3.5am to AYETTE. Accompanied by Transport the Battalion marched via WARLUS, BEAUMETZ, RANSART to AYETTE. Roads were all very congested with moving troops and guns and the march was a slow and tedious one. Before reaching AYETTE at 7.50am. orders were passed down the column that the division had to go on to BUCQUOY to concentrate there. On arrival at BUCQUOY about 2.pm. the battalion marched up the ACHIET LE PETIT Road and had dinners on the common in front of BUCQUOY. The area was one mass of moving artillery and guns moving in a rearward direction. Ammunition, bombs etc. were issued to the men from Regimental Reserve and Packs were dumped. Orders were received for the brigade to advance at about 4.30pm. and take up a position in front of ACHIET LE PETIT to guard the railway in a S.E. direction. The 2/7th. West Riding Regt. was on the left and 5th. Bn. West Riding Regiment on the right with 2/4th. West Riding Regiment in Reserve.

Battalion advanced in artillery formation of platoons and encountered no opposition.

Dispositions of the battalion were - "A" Company took up defensive position across the Railway S.E. of ACHIET LE PETIT with 2/7th. West Riding Regiment on their left. "B" Company were on the right of "A" Company. "C" Company in Support of "A" Company and "D" Company in Support of "B" Company. "D" Company provided one platoon to watch the MIRAUMONT VALLEY. No organized troops were on our right flank. Large numbers of men of 41st, 19th, 25th, 42nd, and 51st Divisions straggled back through our lines retiring from the direction of LOUPARD WOOD and GREVILLERS followed by the enemy.

Before dusk parties of the enemy were clearly seen on skyline in front N. of IRLES. The only artillery which remained to cover the battalion was a battery of 3 guns who drew out about 11.pm. After darkness the enemy approached our positions both from the front and from the MIRAUMONT VALLEY. In encounters three prisoners were captured by us and several killed. During the night orders were received to alter our dispositions and take up a position on the high ground overlooking the Railway and the MIRAUMONT VALLEY on the crest S. of ACHIET LE PETIT. These positions were taken up accordingly and a line of posts dug.

MARCH 25TH.

At 3.30am orders were received for the Brigade to retire before dawn, and take up a position on the high ground between BUCQUOY and PUISSEUX. The 2/7th. West Riding Regiment to be on the left with its left flank on BUCQUOY and the 5th. West Riding Regiment on the right with its right flank on PUSSIEUX. The dividing line between battalions to be a point midway between PUSSIEUX and BUCQUOY. The 2/4th. West Riding Regiment remained in Support.

The retirement from ACHIET LE PETIT was a hurried one as orders were received so late and actually some of the Companies left in broad daylight. The battalion was very closely followed by the enemy in large numbers, especially in the MIRAUMONT - PUISSEUX Road where B Company encountered e-v an enemy cyclist patrol 40 strong with light machine guns, but which was dispersed by our Lewis Gun Fire. Covered by our retirement a large amount of ammunition was removed from ammunition dump on the road leading from BUCQUOY to the ACHIET LE PETIT - PUISSEUX Road. Remainder of this ammunition was blown up as we retired. The enemy clearly saw our retirement and subjected us to Machine Gun Fire from Ridge S. of ACHIET LE PETIT as soon as we moved. A few casualties were caused. During the retirement a Lewis Gun Team of B Company and a few men got cut off and were probably taken prisoner by troops of the enemy moving up the MIRAUMONT VALLEY.

The battalion formed a defensive line 200 yards E. of the BUCQUOY - PUISSEUX Road with Lewis Guns pushed forward. Three Companies were put in the line (A,B,C, right to left) with D Company in Support along the road. Each Company had three platoons in the line with 1 platoon in company reserve. Patrols were sent into PUSSIEUX. At this stage (about 8.30am) a section of 4 Machine Guns reported and were placed - 2 immediately N. of PUISSEUX to cover the MIRAUMONT - PUISSEUX VALLEY and 2 to cover the approaches from direction of ACHIET LE PETIT, where they at once came into action, the enemy being close up. Shortly afterwards the enemy were reported to be in PUSIEUX and on the high ground S. of PUSIEUX. "A" Company was then withdrawn and placed on the right flank facing southwards towards PUSIEUX to protect this flank. The enemy pressed vigorously but were held back. The 9th. Durham Light Infantry were in support in trenches about 200 yards W. of PUSIEUX - BUCQUOY Road and liaison was established.

At about 10.am the enemy were seen in large numbers attempting to encircle our right flank. In conjunction with the 9th. Durham Light Infantry the right flank was then extended company by company along the high ground N. of the PUSIEUX - GOMMECOURT Road and the enemy's attempt to outflank us was frustrated. "D" Company had been brought up from Reserve and were attached to the Durhams on the right flank. Having secured the right flank the left companies were withdrawn to the line of trenches W. of BUCQUOY - PUSIEUX Road lately occupied by the Durhams. During this withdrawal the enemy pressed very hotly and the movement was carried out with considerable difficulty. The H.Q. Company being used to provide covering fire for alternate withdrawals

The 2/4th. Duke of Wellington's were in position in rear of this Battalion. It was then reported that enemy cavalry was operating on the right flank and it therefore become necessary to withdraw still farther to the right flank which necessitated a frontal withdrawal. This brought the battalion on to the line occupied by the 2/4th. Duke of Wellington's Regt. and the withdrawal was carried out by both units. Up to this time the left flank of the battalion had also been exposed as we were not in touch with 2/7th. Duke of Wellington's Regt.

This withdrawal was carried out orderly, the companies

giving mutual support and the line was established running from the S.E. corner of ROSSIGNOL WOOD toward the S.E. corner of BUCQUOY. The 2/4th. Duke of Wellington's Regt. being on our left. Efforts were made to gain touch with 2/7th. West Riding Regiment on our left but without success. Our right flank was completely exposed ~~and was in fact the right flank of the Third Army at the time.~~ It was not until next day that touch was obtained with 2/7th. Duke of Wellington's Regt.

The following line was then occupied and consolidated - "D" Company K.12.d.70.95 along trench to L.7.c.S.1. where block was established, then down communication trench from L.7.c.1.7. to L.7.a.5.0. "B" Company was in support to "D" Company and held trench from K.12.b.9.5. to L.7.a.5.0. "A" Company from this point along trench to L.7.c.95.80 Then 1 company of 9th. Durham Light Infantry continued along this trench to L.7.d.3.8. "C" Company held a line of shell hole positions from this point running N.E. to about L.7.b.7.1. where it joined up to the 2/4th. Duke of Wellington's Regt. Battalion H.Q. was established at L.7.b.2.7. in an old gun pit.

Eleven tanks were in support about L.7.b.3.7. and came under orders of O.C. Battalion.

During the afternoon numbers of the enemy were seen on ridges extending from FORK WOOD and L.7.c. and d. They were also seen to be occupying ROSSIGNOL WOOD. They endeavoured to advance toward our positions in small bodies but were easily driven off by Lewis Gun and Rifle Fire, considerable casualties being inflicted. During this time the battalion was subjected to much sniping both from machine gun and rifle fire but the position of our line did not change. About 7.pm the enemy made a demonstration and owing to some misunderstanding a general withdrawal of this battalion, the 9th. Durham Light Infantry and 2/4th. Duke of Wellington's Regt. took place. The Tanks were sent forward and the men rallied and advanced to their original positions and the enemy fled.

During the night patrol encounters took place and prisoners were taken while endeavouring to reach our position.

MARCH 27TH.

During the morning enemy aerial activity was very marked and large numbers of the enemy were observed filling trenches S.W. of FORK WOOD and in L.7.d. At 12.30pm. our right company was attacked both across the open and along the trenches. The attack in the open was easily driven off by Lewis Gun Fire and Rifle Fire. The bombing attack up the trenches was very persistent and was difficult to hold back owing to our shortage of bombs. A bombing block was established at L.7.c. 2.5. and the left platoon of the right company withdrawn. Bombing Fighting continued at this point and also on the flank adjoining ROSSIGNOL WOOD from which position the enemy kept up continued sniping fire. During the afternoon and evening several enemy demonstrations were made in L.7.c. and d but by means of Lewis Gun Fire and Artillery Fire no further attack developed.

About 7.pm. the battalion on our right was seen to be bombed out of their position by the enemy and our right flank again became completely exposed. B Company and a platoon of 9th. D.L.I. were then turned into a defensive flank and the battalions position made secure. During the night patrols were sent out over the whole battalion front. Enemy patrols were encountered and driven off and 2 prisoners taken. Supplies of ammunition were got up to the companies and further consolidation carried out.

MARCH 28TH.

Battalion H.Q. was moved to L.1.c.8.2. in an old dugout shaft. At 9.25am the enemy put down a very heavy barrage on our front line system and the trenches and ridges in rear. The enemy was then seen to be massing between ROSSIGNOL WOOD and the Ridge S.W. of the Wood. At 10.20am a message was received that the enemy was attacking along the whole battalion front, the barrage continuing to fall on the trenches around battalion H.Q. Our artillery put down a counter barrage in L.7.c. and d and a stiff fight ensued and in no case did the enemy succeed in getting to our line. Time after time the enemy massed to make fresh attacks but was decimated by our accurate rifle and Lewis Gun Fire at each attempt. During the rest of the day the enemy were seen crawling back towards ROSSIGNOL WOOD. During these attacks several prisoners were taken, the attacking troops proving to be 2nd. Reserve Guards. In conjunction with the attack in the open a very strong enemy bombing attack took place east of ROSSIGNOL WOOD and No. 13 platoon of D Company became isolated at about K.12.d.95.60. At 1.5pm. this platoon was reported to be still holding out. Several attempts were made to bomb to their rescue but when they were finally reached it was found that the platoon under 2/Lieut. A. Cawthra had been overwhelmed and none were left alive. At 3.15. pm. the enemy were reported to be again massing in L.7.d. and L.8.c. Artillery action with very satisfactory results was at once taken and no attack developed. It was then reported from the 2/4th. York and Lancaster Regt. that ROSSIGNOL WOOD was in enemy occupation so "D" Company was withdrawn into line with "B" and "A" Companies a block being established at L.7.c.40.95. Bomb fighting continued during the afternoon on the right of "B" Company and the riflemen were concentrated against enemy snipers in ROSSIGNOL WOOD with satisfactory results. During the night instructions were received for the right company to be prepared to attack along the east side of ROSSIGNOL WOOD in conjunction with an attack of the 8th. West Yorks Regiment but as this Battalion did not proceed beyond our line no attack was made by "B" Company.

MARCH 29th.

Enemy got up a considerable amount of artillery and trench mortars were established in ROSSIGNOL WOOD and our line was subjected to a heavy bombardment some casualties being sustained. During the day enemy rifle, Machine Gun and Sniping was particularly active. This was replied to by our rifle and Lewis Gun Fire and Stokes Mortars.

At 7.30pm. in the evening a further demonstration was made in L.7.c. and d but by means of Lewis Gun and Rifle Fire and good artillery work the enemy concentration was broken up.
Patrols were sent out as usual during the night and the enemy was quiet.

MARCH 30th.

The day passed quietly except for increased shelling and sniping. Enemy field guns appeared to enfilade our positions from direction N. of ROSSIGNOL WOOD causing us serious casualties.

At night the battalion was relieved by 8th. West Yorks Regt. and 2/8th. West Yorks Regt. and went into support in trenches in K.30.b.

During operations 24th. March to 30th March the battalion sustained the following casualties -

	Officers.	Other ranks.
Killed.	2.	30.
Wounded.	6	126.
Missing.	1.	50.

Sd. J. WALKER................Lieut.Col.
Commdg. 5th. Duke of Wellington's (W.R.) Regt. T.F.

3.4.18.

TO - 5th. Duke of Wellington's (W.R.) Regt.

Divisional Commander wires aaa Men are doing splendidly aaa Congratulations aaa I know how tired they are but we have got to stick it aaa ANZAC Division are now joined up to 5th. Australian Bde Fort COLINCAMP to S. of HEBUTERNE aaa.

(sd).............Capt.
186th. Infantry Brigade.

27.3.18.

C O P Y.

TO - 5th. Duke of Wellington's (W.R.) Regt.

Following message from GENL. BRAITHWAITE aaa begins aaa congratulate 5th. West Riding Regiment on their fine fighting and congratulate Colonel WALKER on his leadership aaa The fight put up by the isolated platoon is worthy of proudest traditions of the Regt. to which it belongs aaa ends aaa Brig. Genl. Commdg 186th. Inf. Bde adds his congratulations.

(sd)..........Capt.
186th. Infantry Brigade.

28.3.18.

TO 5th. Duke of Wellington's (W.R.) Regt.

Following from lV Corps timed 10.30am. begins aaa The Corps Commander congratulates 42nd, 62nd, and N.Z. Divisions and the 4th. Australian Bde on their magnificent behaviour during the last few days fighting aaa. Numerous heavy attacks by the enemy have been completely repulsed with heavy loss and the capture of prisoners and machine guns aaa. He heartily thanks the troops for their courage and endurance and is confident that they will continue to hold the line against all attacks aaa ends.

(sd)............Capt.
186th. Infantry Brigade.

29.3.18.

SECRET.   Copy No......
                    5TH. DUKE OF WELLINGTON'S REGT.

                         OPERATION ORDER NO.5

Ref. Map. 51.b.N.W.   8.3.18.

1.   The 186th. Inf. Bde will relieve the 92nd. Inf. Bde in the
        line on 8.3.18.

2.   The 5th. Duke of Wellington's Regt. will relieve the 11th.
        East Lancs. Regt. in Reserve at SPRING VALE CAMP (A.22.c.6.4.)
        Relief to be complete by 11.30am.

3.   The battalion will move by march route. The first Company
        to pass point on road opposite H.Q. Mess at 8.30am.

4.   Order of march will be H.Q., D, C, B, A. 100 yards distance to
        be kept between Companies.

5.   ROUTE. If weather fine - by overland track direct to SPRING VALE
        CAMP.   If wet - by road via ANSIN, BOURIE, SPRING VALE CAMP.

6.   The band will march 20 minutes with each Company commencing
        with H.Q. Company.

7.   All defence schemes, aeroplane photographs, maps etc. will
        be taken over and list of same will be forwarded to Battalion
        O.R. by 1.pm.

8.   The C.Q.M.S. of each company, 1 representative from Transport
        and Q.M. Stores, will report to Lieut. Armitage at Headquarters
        Mess at 6.pm to-night and will proceed to SPRING VALE CAMP as

advance party, travelling by train leaving BOUVARES at 6.45pm. and detrain at ECURIE.

9. TRANSPORT. T.O. will arrange for Mess Cart, MALTESE Cart, Cov. Officers Horses, and horses for Lewis Gun Limbers etc. to be at LANCASTER CAMP by 7.30am.
Baggage wagons will report to Q.M. at 7.30am.
Lorries will be notified later.
Transport will join Battalion at a entry bex. *as arranged with TO*
Blankets (rolled in bundles of 10) and valises will be dumped at Junction of Road and trench from Company lines and opposite H.Q. Mess respectively at 7.30am.
Officers Mess Boxes and Orderly Room Boxes will be dumped opposite H.Q. Mess by 8.am.
Packs of band will be dumped with blankets at 7.30am.

10. REAR PARTY. 1 Representative per Company will report to Lieut. B. Mollett H.Q. at H.Q. Mess by 8.15am. Clearing certificates will be obtained from Town Major before the party leaves.

11. Acknowledge.

.... Capt. & Adjt.
5th. Bn. of Wellington's Regiment.

Copies to - A,B, C,D and H.Q. Companies.
T.O.
Q.M.
Adjutant.
186th. I.B. (for infm.)
Office.

SECRET.   Copy No.........

                        5TH. DUKE OF WELLINGTON'S REGT.

                        Operation Order No. 6   8th.March.1918.

            Reference - MARCHEUIL 1/20,000.   Secret 186th. Inf. Bde Map 1/20,000.

1. RELIEF.   The battalion will relieve 2/4th. Duke of Wellington's
                    Regiment in Support to the ACHEVILLE SECTION tomorrow. Relief
                    to be complete by 12 noon.

2. DISPOSITIONS   Companies will be disposed as under -
                    "D" Coy. 5th.Duke of Wellington's will relieve "A" Coy. 2/4th
                    Duke of Wellington's in the RED LINE.
                    "B" Coy. 5th.Duke of Wellington's will relieve "B" Coy. 2/4th.
                    Duke of Wellington's in the RED LINE.
                    "A" Coy. 5th.Duke of Wellington's will relieve "D" Coy. 2/4th.
                    Duke of Wellington's in Railway Embankment B.2.a.9.5.
                    "C" Coy. 5th. Duke of Wellington's will relieve "C" Coy.2/4th.
                    Duke of Wellington's at CUBITT CAMP, NEUVILLE ST. VAAST.

3. ORDER OF   "D" "B" "A" Coys. will leave camp in this order by platoons at
   RELIEF,   100 yards interval.   First platoon to leave camp at 8.30am.
   ROUTES etc.   Route - ARRAS - LENS ROAD, DUCKBOARD TRACK from ARRAS - LENS
                    ROAD, MERCEY, C.F.R. and HUDSON Communication Trenches.
                    Guides for D and B Coys will be at Battalion H.Q. VANCOUVER
                    ROAD at 11.am.
                    Lewis Guns and stretchers will be carried so as not to show
                    above the parapet.
                    C Company will move independantly to CUBITT CAMP to be
                    there before 10am.

4. DRESS etc.   Dress for all troops, except C Company - Fighting Order -
                    Haversack on back - waterbottles (full at side, Steel helmets
                    with covers - Box Respirator in alert position - Greatcoats
                    to be worn - Rifle Covers and Rifles.
                    Battle kit will be taken by each Company as follows - 8 prs.
                    wirecutters - 4 prs. hedging gloves - 4 very pistols - 16
                    vigilant periscopes - 4 compasses - 24 cup attachments.
                    All other Battle Kit will be returned to Q.M. by O.C.M.B.

5. LEWIS GUNS.   Lewis Guns will be taken with 20 magazines per gun (except
                    A.A. Lewis Guns which take 4)
                    B and D Coys. will take their anti-aircraft guns with them.
                    B company will man anti-aircraft position in RED LINE and D
                    Company will man similar position at Battalion H.Q.
                    C Company will attach 4 Lewis Guns and teams to A Company
                    whilst the battalion is in Support.   Anti-aircraft Guns of
                    A and C Coys will be utilised by Brigade School.

6. TRANSPORT.   The T.O. will provide 1 limber for A,B,D Coys. at 8.15am
                    tomorrow to take Lewis Guns to Duckboard Track on ARRAS -
                    LENS Road.   2 Representatives from each Company to accompany
                    these limbers.

                                        (1).

One limber will be provided for Battalion H.Q. at 8.15am to take Signalling Equipment etc. to the Duckboard Track. The Transport Officer will arrange for C Company's Cooker, Valises and blankets to be removed to CUBITT CAMP during the day.

Officers' Mess Boxes, Orderly Room Boxes, etc. required to go up to the line at night will be stacked outside Orderly Room by 8.am tomorrow.

Mens' blankets, Officers' Valises, Orderly Room Boxes, Mess Boxes etc. not required in the line will be dumped on Camp Road opposite Company Officers' Quarters by 8.am and removed to Q.M. Stores under T.O's arrangements.

7. RATIONS & WATER Meat for A, B, D and H.Q. Companies is being cooked to-day. Rations for tomorrow for these companies will be taken on the man. Dixies for these companies will be sent up with Rations tomorrow night by the Q.M.

The T.O. will send 2 water carts up to Battalion H.Q. nightly to fill two tanks there. 20 tins of water will be sent up to A Company nightly.

8. MAPS etc. Secret maps, Defence Schemes, Aerial Photographs and Trench Stores will be taken over. Work in progress and contemplated and anti-aircraft positions for Lewis Guns will be taken over.

9. REPORTS. 'Relief complete' will be reported by wiring the words '1000 Mills Grenades'
Trench Stores List, Company Dispositions, copy of Company Defence Scheme will be sent to Battalion H.Q. as soon as possible after relief.

10. Acknowledge.

..........K. Sykes.......Capt. & Adjt.
5th. Duke of Wellington's Regiment.

Copies to - 1 to 5. A, B, C, D & H.Q. Coys.
6. Q.M.
7. T.O.
8. Adjutant.
9. 2/4th. Duke of Wellington's Regt. (for infm.)
10. 186th. Inf. Bde (for infm.)
11 & 12. War Diary.
13. Office.

Copy No 13

5th Duke of Wellington's Regt.
Operation Order No 7

Ref. MARCEUIL 1/20,000
Sheet 186 G.B. 1/20,000   11th March 1918

1. Relief. The Battn. will be relieved by 2/4th D. of Ws Regt. tomorrow. On relief the Battalion will relieve 2/4th D. of Ws Regt in the ACHEVILLE SECTION.

2. Company Relief. A Coy 5th D of Ws will be relieved by 'D' Coy 2/4th D. of Ws by 10.30am. On relief A Coy will relieve D Coy of 2/4th D. of Ws in left front line.
B Coy 5th D. of Ws will be relieved by C Coy 2/4th D. of Ws by 10.30am. On relief B Coy will relieve A Coy 2/4th D. of Ws in NEW BRUNSWICK TRENCH
C Coy 5th D of Ws Platoon in FOVENT S.P will be relieved by a platoon of 2/4 D. of Ws before dawn. On relief this platoon will join remaining 3 platoons at Railway Embankment. C Coy will leave the Railway Embankment at 10.30 am and relieve B Coy 2/4th D of Ws in right front line.

"A" Coy 3rd D. of W. will be relieved by "B" Coy 4th D. of W. On relief "B" Coy will return to Coy H.Q. "D" of W. in BURDON TRENCH
"B" Coy 3rd D. of W. on relief by H.Q. Coy 3/4th D. of W. will relieve H.Q. 3/4th D. of W. in WINNIPEG ROAD
Advance parties as already detailed will proceed to the front line to-day and stay the night.

3. **Movement** etc. — Platoons will move at not less than 50 yds intervals. Lewis guns will be carried so as not to show above the parapet.
C.P.R & HUDSON C.Ts will be used.

4. **Rations** etc. — Rations & water for A.C.D & H.Q. will be brought up by Light Railway at night.
Rations and 30 petrol tins of water for B Coy will be brought up by limber.

5. **Maps** etc. — Secret maps, Defence schemes, aerial photographs, Patrol Form and Trench Stores will be taken and handed over. Work in progress and contemplated and any anti-aircraft positions for Lewis guns

report the same over.

6. Relief complete will be reported by wiring the words "100 Screw Pickets".
Trench stores list (in duplicate) Company Dispositions and copy of Company Defence Scheme will be sent to Battalion H.Q. as soon as possible after relief tomorrow.

7. Acknowledge by wire.

K Sykes.
CAPT. & ADJUTANT
5th BN. DUKE OF WELLINGTONS REGT.

Copies to -
1-5. A B C D & H.Q. Coys
6.   Q.M. & T.O.
7.   Adjutant
8.   2/4th Duke of Wellingtons Regt (for infm)
9.   2/4th
10.   186th I.B. (for infm)
11.   Office
12 & 13. War Diary.

SECRET.   Copy No. ...17.

5TH. DUKE OF WELLINGTON'S REGT.

Operation Order No. 8.

Ref. Map. HAISNES. 1/20,000.

1. **RELIEF.** The battalion will be relieved by 2/7th. Duke of Wellington's
   Regiment tomorrow 21st inst.
   Companies will be relieved as follows –
   "A" Coy.5th.D.of W's.Regt. by "B" Coy.2/7th. D. of W's. Regt.
   "B"   "   "   "   "   "   "   "A"   "   "   "   "   "   "
   "C"   "   "   "   "   "   "   "D"   "   "   "   "   "   "
   "D"   "   "   "   "   "   "   "C"   "   "   "   "   "   "

   On relief companies will move independently.
   B and D Companies and H.Q. to SPRINGVALE CAMP (H.28.c.5.2.)
   3 platoons of A Coy. to No. 1 dugout at FARBUS STATION, 1
   platoon of "A" Coy to SPRINGVALE CAMP, 2 platoons of C Coy.
   to No. 1 dugout at FARBUS STATION, 1 platoon of C Coy. to
   No. 2 dugout at FARBUS STATION, 1 platoon of C Coy.
   SPRINGVALE CAMP.
   Platoons of A and C Companies to SPRINGVALE CAMP will be
   attached to C and B Companies respectively for rations and
   administration.

2. **Movement.** Platoons will move at not less than 50 yards interval.
   Lewis Guns and stretchers will be carried so as not to show
   above the parapet.

3. **ROUTE.** HUDSON C.T., C.P.R., MERSEY, DUCKBOARD TRACK to LENS – ARRAS
   ROAD to SPRINGVALE CAMP.

4. **GUIDES.** 1 guide per platoon from each company will report to
   Intelligence Officer at Battalion H.Q. at 10.45am. tomorrow
   and will then report at H.Q. 2/7th. Duke of Wellington's Regt.

5. **ADVANCE PARTY.** 2/Lieut. Lord and C.S.M.S. of B, D and H.Q. Coys. will take
   over camp vacated by 2/4th. Duke of Wellington's Regt. A and
   C Companies will send Advance Party of 1 officer and 1 N.C.O.
   per platoon to take over accommodation in RAILWAY EMBANKMENT
   from 2/4th. Duke of Wellington's Regt.   These parties
   to report at respective destinations at 9.am.

6. **TRENCH STORES.** All trench stores, petrol tins, defence schemes, aeroplane
   photographs, maps, details of work in hand and contemplated
   will be carefully handed over. Lists (in duplicate) to be
   forwarded to Orderly Room as soon as possible after relief.

7. **TRANSPORT.** The T.O. will arrange for 3 limbers to be at junction of
   HUDSON TRACT with LENS – ARRAS Road at 2.pm to convey
   Lewis Guns, signalling equipment etc. to SPRINGVALE CAMP.
   All Companies will send any surplus baggage requiring to be
   moved to Transport Lines or to SPRINGVALE CAMP to Battalion
   H.Q. by 10.am tomorrow.
   O.C. A Company will detail a guard of 1 N.C.O. and 3 men
   for this camp. It will be collected at dusk by the T.O. and
   delivered to proper quarter.

8. **REPORTS.** Completion of Relief will be reported to Battalion H.Q. by
   wiring the words "No iron rations required".

9. **RESERVE.** Whilst in Brigade Reserve the battalion will be in readiness
   to move at 1½ hours notice between 7.pm and 7.am.

10. Acknowledge.

                                        K. Sykes ....Capt.& Adjt.
                                        5th. Duke of Wellington's Regiment.

SECRET.   Copy No.

5TH. DUKE OF WELLINGTON'S REGT.

Operation Order No.9

1. The Brigade moves to Y Huts near DUISANS L.2.c. (Sheet 51.c.) on Transfer to XVll Corps to-day.
   All transport including baggage waggons will accompany the battali
   Following intervals to be maintained on march - Between Battalions 500 yards. Between companies and between last company and transport 100 yards.

2. Head of Battalion will pass starting point (Cross Roads F.8.d.4.1.) at 2.5pm. following Bde H.Q. Route - Road junction E.29.b.8.3.

3. Nucleus personnel will accompany the battalion into XVll Corps area. Orders for disposal will be issued later.

4. It is expected that the division will be employed at first on work on the FICHEUX - TELEGRAPH HILL Switch.

5. Billeting party consisting of Lieut. YATES, 2 representatives per company and H.Q. and 1 for transport will meet representative of the Brigade at the Road Junction on the main ARRAS - SAVY Road immediately west of the E in E TRUN at 9.30am (Ref.sheet LENS 11)

6. 2 motor lorries are allotted for 2 journeys. The Q.M. will send guide to Bde H.Q. at 7.30am to bring lorries to camp. The Q.M. is responsible for guiding lorries to destination and for providing loading and unloading parties. First lorry not to arrive Y Huts until 10.am.

7. Bde Dump for storage of surplus kit and stores is at Billet No.27 MONT ST ELOI F.8.d.3.7. Floor space will be allotted under Bde arrangements.
   Following guard will report at Bde H.Q. at 7.30am. with rations for 24th and 25th inst. and in possession of blankets - Corpl.J.H.Haigh, Pte. Popplewell A., Pte Wilkinson T.H.
   The Q.M. will arrange for surplus stores to be dumped. Officers will stack their surplus packages outside officers quarters by 8.30am. Q.M. will prepare complete list in triplicate of stores dumped.
   Lorries to carry out move to new area will be used in first place for conveyance of stores to the dump.

8. All valises and blankets will be ready by 8.30am. Blankets to be rolled in bundles of 10 and placed at entrance to camp.
   T.O. will arrange collection of stores etc. to go on regimental transport during morning.

9. Time and place of refill will be notified later. Unless notification is sent, rations will be delivered by train transport to our present waggon lines.

(Sd) K.SYKES..............Capt.& Adjt.
5th.Duke of Wellington's Regiment.

24.3.18.

Secret.

5th Duke of Wellington's Regt
Operation Orders   No. 9
by Lt. Col. J Walker.   1-4-15

Ref. Map 57.D.N.E. 1/20000

1. The Battalion will be relieved to-night by 13th K.R.R. 37th Div. On relief the Battalion will march to billets at HENU.

2. Each Coy will send one guide per platoon and one for Coy Hdqrs to be at Batt Hdqrs at 6.45 pm. These guides will proceed to FONQUEVILLERS E.26.c.9.1 to be there by 8 pm. and guide incoming Unit to the trenches. They will be under Lt Waters.

3. Coys will report relief complete at once to Batt. Hdqrs. On relief Coys will march off independently to HENU. Route:– ESSARTS. GOMMECOURT ROAD. GOMMECOURT. FONQUEVILLERS, E.26.c.9.1 SOUASTRE – HENU

4. 1 Limber per Coy and one for Batt. Hdqrs have been ordered to be

2.

at Ration Dump at 9-30 p.m. Lewis Guns etc will be put on these limbers.

Each company will detail a N.C.O. to go with their limber and be responsible for its load. All petrol tins will be taken back on the limbers to Waggon lines.

Coy Commander's horses have been ordered to be at E.26.c.9.1. at 11 p.m.

5. On arrival in new area the battalion will be prepared to move at one hour's notice.

6. Movement to be by platoons as far as FONQUEVILLERS.

7. It is hoped that arrangements will be made for hot soup or stew at FONQUEVILLERS and hot tea on arrival at HENU.

(SD) K. SYKES Capt Adjt
5. D. of W. Regt.

1.4.18
Copies to :-
1. Adjt.
2. OC HdQrs Coy
3. OC A Coy
4. OC B.
5. OC C.
6. OC D Coy
7. S.Or 2dh
8. Officers Copy
9. War Diary
10. "

62nd Division
186th Infantry Brigade.

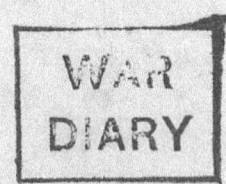

5th BATTALION

THE DUKE OF WELLINGTON'S REGIMENT

APRIL 1918

ORIGINAL

Army Form C. 2118.

5TH. DUKE OF WELLINGTON'S REGT.
WAR DIARY
or
INTELLIGENCE=SUMMARY.
(Erase heading not required.)

Instructions regarding War Diaries and Intelligence Summaries are contained in F. S. Regs., Part II. and the Staff Manual respectively. Title pages will be prepared in manuscript.

Place	Date	Hour	Summary of Events and Information	Remarks and references to Appendices
Ref.Map 57d.N.E. 1/20000. 5" 1.D.1/10000.	1918. April 1st.		Battalion in Support in trenches in E.30.b. At night the battalion was relieved by 13th. K.R.R., 37th. Division and on relief marched to billets at HENU.	
	2nd.		In billets at HENU. Fine and bright.	
	3rd.		Battalion reorganised and held inspections.	
	4th.		Reorganisation of battalion continued. Very wet.	
	5th.		Men all out on Working Parties on the CHATEAU DE LA HAIE Switch Line.	
	6th.		-- Ditto --	
	7th.		Very wet day. Battalion marched from HENU at 4.30pm. via SOUASTRE, BIENVILLERS, HANNESCAMPS, ESSARTS, to the Line. Men had hot tea at HANNESCAMPS en route. The Battalion relieved the 1/6th. Manchester Regiment and 2 companies 1/8th. Manchester Regiment (42nd. Division) in shell hole positions near ABLAINZEVILLE about F.22.d.7.8., F.29.a.2.9., F.28.b.9.8. to F.28.c.8.8. The relief was a long one on account of bad state of tracks and muddy and indifferent guides. Completed by 4.pm. on April 8th. The positions were very wet and muddy for with no shelter accommodation for the men. "D" Company was on the left front and "B" Company on the right with "A" Company in Support and "C" Company in Reserve. Battalion H.Q. was established in dugout in road about F.28.c.2.2.	
	8th.		A very wet day. Conditions very bad. Enemy very quiet. "A" Company had to take over a further company front on the right of "B" Company and extend our line to the Railway Line (grid line between F.28.a. and c.) At night 2 prisoners were captured by "B" Company carrying important despatches, which showed that the 90th Fusilier Regiment were to be relieved on the 9th/10th inst. by another Division and that a further attack on BUCQUOY and DIERVILLE FM. was contemplated. A very dark night. Ration carrying to the front line was a great difficulty.	

Army Form C. 2118.

ORIGINAL

5TH. DUKE OF WELLINGTON'S REGT.
WAR DIARY
or
INTELLIGENCE SUMMARY.
(Erase heading not required.)

Instructions regarding War Diaries and Intelligence Summaries are contained in F. S. Regs., Part II. and the Staff Manual respectively. Title pages will be prepared in manuscript.

Place	Date	Hour	Summary of Events and Information	Remarks and references to Appendices
Ref.map SHEET 57d.N.E. 1/20000.	1918. April 9th.		A foggy damp day. Enemy artillery was chiefly active on AYETTE - BUCQUOY Road and on DIERVILLE FM. Battalion H.Q. at F.22.c.1.2. was also shelled during the day. A very dark night. No signs of suspected enemy relief were seen. Artillery on both sides were very busy with harassing fire on lines of communication to front line. Some rain during the night. During the night H.Q. Personnel dug a line of new posts from F.28.a.1.9. to F.22.c.5.5.	
	10th.		A brighter day. Enemy artillery again active during morning firing on to AYETTE - BUCQUOY Road and on to DIERVILLE FARM. Trench Mortar Ammunition Dump was blown up on AYETTE - BUCQUOY Road during afternoon causing us 12 casualties to platoon located there. A quiet night.	
	11th.		A fine day with some haziness. Enemy artillery particularly active all morning in neighbourhood of Battalion H.Q. in F.22.c. During the night the Battalion had to side slip and take over more line from 2/5th. West Yorks Regiment on our right. On completion of the relief our line ran approx. F.28.b.8.6. to F.28 central to F.28.c.4.0. to L.3.b.5.8. "A" Company were on the left with 3 platoons in front line posts and one platoon in support. "D" Company were in the centre with 2 platoons in front posts and 2 posts in Support. "C" Company were on the right with 2 platoons in front posts (including Village Posts in houses) and 2 platoons in support.	
	12th.		A very bright clear day. Enemy had 24 balloons up and many enemy aeroplanes were seen. Much transport movement was observed in the neighbourhood of ACHIET le PETIT and was engaged by our heavies. Enemy artillery became very violent at night and lines of communication were badly shelled all night. The battalion changed its Head quarters to F.26.d.9.9. There was just one poor damp dugout. H.Q. Personnel had to be in the trench.	
	13th.		Very misty until 12 noon - then much brighter but very cold. Hostile artillery rather subdued. A very dark night. A strong Officer's Fighting Patrol went out from Centre Company into area F.28.d. to endeavour to secure an identification. No enemy were seen or	

Army Form C. 2118.

5TH. DUKE OF WELLINGTON'S REGT.
WAR DIARY
or
INTELLIGENCE SUMMARY.
(Erase heading not required)

Place	Date	Hour	Summary of Events and Information	Remarks and references to Appendices
Ref.Map. SHEET. 57d.N.E. 1/20000.	1918. April 14th.		encountered. Very heavy hostile artillery fire just in rear of our front line at 6.am. Several casualties were caused to Support Platoons of "D" Company located about F.27.b.5.5. A cold raw day with poor visibility. Rather quieter during the day.	
	15th.		A quiet day altogether. Cold and dull. Patrols out at night but no enemy seen.	
	16th.		A fine day. A very quiet day. Rather more active at night, with some little gas shelling.	
	17th.		Artillery more active during the morning on both sides. A wet afternoon. The Battalion was relieved by the 2/7th. West Yorks Regiment at night. The relief was carried through well and was completed by 12 midnight. On relief the Battalion moved into the PURPLE SYSTEM and became Battalion in Brigade Reserve to the Reserve Brigade. Dispositions were approximately as follows – "B" Company in old British Trenches in Square E.28. "A" Company in old British Trenches in square E.22. "C" Company in old British Trenches E.21 and 22. "D" Company were in Battalion Reserve in cellars and dugouts in FONQUEVILLERS. Battalion H.Q. was established in a cellar at FONQUEVILLERS.	
	18th.		Wet morning – fine gusty afternoon. Men all very tired but morale quite high. They were busy making themselves shelter accommodation and improving the trenches all day.	
	19th.		The battalion was employed all day under orders of O.C. 9th. Durham Light Infantry (Divl. Pioneer Battalion) in wiring on the outskirts of the village of FONQUEVILLERS.	
	20th.		– Ditto –	
	21st.		– Ditto –	
	22nd.		– Ditto –	
	23rd.		– Ditto –	
	24th.		The battalion was relieved by the 6th. Bedford Regt., 112th. Inf. Brigade, 37th. Division at night. On relief the battalion marched via SOUASTRE to billets at ST.LEGER les AUTHIE.	

ORIGINAL

Army Form C. 2118.

5TH. DUKE OF WELLINGTON'S REGT.
WAR DIARY
or
INTELLIGENCE SUMMARY.
(Erase heading not required.)

Instructions regarding War Diaries and Intelligence Summaries are contained in F. S. Regs., Part II. and the Staff Manual respectively. Title pages will be prepared in manuscript.

Place	Date	Hour	Summary of Events and Information	Remarks and references to Appendices
Ref. Map. SHEET 57d.N.E. 1/20000 57d. 1/10000	1918. April 25th.		Men all had baths at AUTHIE. Remainder of day was spent in Kit Inspections etc.	
	26th.		Wet and sultry. Battalion was engaged on working party on the RED LINE about J.13.c.	
	27th.		Battalion did training in I.6.c. and I.12.a. during the morning. Recreational games in the afternoon.	
	28th.		There was a Divisional Church Parade on the N.W. edge of BOIS DU WARNIMONT (I.17.a.) during the morning. The Divisional Commander and Brigadiers of 186th and 187th Inf. Brigades were present. Recreational Games were played in the afternoon and inter company football matches.	
	29th.		The battalion took part in a Brigade Tactical Exercise during the morning in conjunction with the 2/4th. Duke of Wellington's Regiment and 2/7th. Duke of Wellington's Regiment in the area I.18., I.17 and I.23. In the afternoon all men with leather equipment in the battalion interchanged with 2/4th. Duke of Wellington's and 2/7th. Duke of Wellington's for web equipment. Dull morning with some rain, but fine in afternoon.	
	30th.		A wet day. Battalion was engaged on Work on the RED LINE about J.13.c.	

J. Mackin ....Lieut.Col.

Commdg.5th.Duke of Wellington's (W.R.) Regt.

ORIGINAL.

5TH.DUKE OF WELLINGTON'S REGT.
WAR DIARY
or
INTELLIGENCE SUMMARY.
(Erase heading not required.)

Army Form C. 2118.

A P P E N D I C E S.   Summary of Events and Information

CASUALTIES etc.

Lieut. W. YATES - To England, 6 months' Light Duty. 3.4.18.
2/Lieut. H.D. FORREST - Killed 7.4.18
2/Lieut. A. WALKER - Wounded 9.4.18. Died of Wounds 15.4.18.
2/Lieut. R.J. MACHIN - WOUNDED and remained, 14.4.18.
Major F. BROOK - To Hospital sick, 12.4.18.
Capt. T.P. CROSLAND - To Hospital sick, 16.4.18.
Lieut. J.F. WATERS - To Hospital sick, 21.4.18.
Lieut. E.H. ARMITAGE - To Hospital sick 8.4.18. To England - 15.4.18.

    Killed.   16 other ranks.
    Wounded.   41 other ranks.
    S.I.Wounds.   2 other ranks.
    Wounded & remd. 1 other rank.

DRAFTS etc.

Capt. F.A. SYKES - Joined Battalion 5.4.18.   19 other ranks. 5.4.18.
Capt. W.S. CAULFIELD - Joined Battalion 19.4.18. 7 other ranks. 8.4.18.
2/Lieut. E.C. CHAPMAN) Joined Battalion 13.4.18. 7 other ranks. 9.4.18.
2/Lieut. G.H. APPLEBY)   35 other ranks. 12.4.18.
Capt. J.B. COCKHILL M.C. - Joined battalion 24.4.18. 87 other ranks. 13.4.18.
Lieut. E.G. WATKINSON - Joined Battalion 28.4.18. 10 other ranks. 15.4.18.
Capt. A.V. BROADBENT M.C. - Taken on strength 26.4.18. 3 other ranks. 17.4.18.
                                                         18 other ranks. 25.4.18.

PROMOTIONS etc.

Lieut. A.R. HAIGH is promoted captain with precedence from 1st Decr. 1917.

Army Form C. 2118.

ORIGINAL
5th Duke of Wellington's Regt.

WAR DIARY
or
INTELLIGENCE SUMMARY.
(Erase heading not required.)

Instructions regarding War Diaries and Intelligence Summaries are contained in F. S. Regs., Part II. and the Staff Manual respectively. Title pages will be prepared in manuscript.

Place	Date	Hour	Summary of Events and Information	Remarks and references to Appendices
			APPENDICES (continued).	
			PROMOTIONS etc. (contd.)	
			MAJOR F. BROOK relinquishes the acting rank of Major on ceasing to be employed as Second in Command on Headquarters dated 12.4.18. Capt. T.P. CROSLAND relinquishes the additional rank of captain on being evacuated sick dated 16.4.18. CAPT C.G.H. ELLIS will relinquish the acting rank of Captain on ceasing to command a company Lieut. C.G.H. ELLIS is appointed acting Captain (additional) vice Capt. T.P. CROSLAND dated 31.4.18. Capt. W.S. CAULFEILD is appointed acting Major vice Major F. BROOK dated 19.4.18.	
			HONOURS & AWARDS.	
			No. 9323 a/R.S.M. Earle B. awarded the BRONZE MEDAL for Military Valour (Italian) for gallantry and devotion to duty.	
			APPRECIATION During the month Sir Douglas Haig in his despatches made the following mention of this Division.:- " In the fierce fighting at the end of March and early in April around BUCQUOY and ABLAINZEVILLE the 42nd (East Lancashire) Division (T) and the 62nd (West Riding) Division (T) beat off many attacks and contributed greatly to the successful maintenance of our line in this important sector."	

SECRET.   Copy No.. 9.
                5TH. DUKE OF WELLINGTON'S REGT.
                     Operation Order No.10.
- -

Ref. Map. Sheet 57.d.   7th. April 1918.

1.   The Battalion will relieve a Battalion of the 127th. Inf.
   Brigade in the Left Section, 42nd Divisional Front to-night.
          The Battalion will be prepared to march from billets
   any time after 8.30pm. to-day.

2.   Our waggon lines will be taken over from 1/5th. Manchester
   Regiment in D.2 central.
          The nucleus personnel will be accommodated at VALLEY
   CAMP, BOUZINCOURT.
          All valises, packs, etc. will be dumped in one central
   dump per company by 3.pm. to-day and will be collected by
   the T.O.
          Further details of relief will be issued later.

                                    ...K.Sykes...Capt. & Adjt.
                                    5th. Duke of Wellington's Regiment.

Copies to -

        A, B, C, D and H.Q. Companies.
        T.O.
        Q.M.
        War Diary (2).
        Adjutant.
        Office.

Secret   Copy No 8

Operation Order
by Lt Col J Walker Comm'g
5 Duke of Wellingtons Regt d/17.4.18

1. The Battalion will be relieved tonight
by the 2/7 West Yorks Regt.
On relief the Batt. will move to
positions in the PURPLE SYSTEM
of trenches vacated by 2/7 West
Yorks Regt.
Batt HQ will be in FONQUEVILLERS

2. One NCO + 1 man per Coy will report
to Lieut MOORE at 5am to go
and reconnoitre new area.
One Officer per Coy from Rear
Batt HQ has been ordered to
meet this party at Cross Roads
E 27 b 2.6. The Officer and
Other Rank representative per Coy
will ascertain accommodation &
Battle Positions in PURPLE SYSTEM
They will be prepared to guide
their Companies to their new
positions after relief. When
accommodation has been
ascertained the Officer and
private per Coy will come back
to their Coys at dusk to

guide them out.

2/Lt MOORE will be responsible for reporting to OC 2/7 West York's Regt early to take over work in progress on the PURPLE SYSTEM

3) Transport arrangements, Routes out of line and Guide arrangements will be notified later.

4) All Aeroplane Photographs, Trench Stores etc will be handed over. Lists in duplicate to be sent to Orderly Room by 11am tomorrow.

5) Completion of relief to be reported at once AT ONCE by Runner. Arrival in Reserve Area to be reported by Runner.

6) Work in hand and contemplated will be carefully handed + taken over in each area

7) The troops will be careful to out of the line complete in ammunition, Reserve Grenades, pos, mais Very Lights and Aeroplane Flares.

Deficiencies (if any) should also be made up.

All empty Petrol Tins must be brought down to Batt HQ by 8.30 pm without fail

& Acknowledge

Khyber Capt & Adjt
5 Duke of Wellington's Regt

Copies to A B C D Coy
HQ Coy
Rear Bn HQ
War Diary (2)
2/Lt Moore

Secret.   Copy No 11
                    Operation Order.
              5th Bn. Duke of Wellington's Regt.
                        23.4.18.

1. **Relief**   The Battn. will be relieved
   tomorrow night by the 6th Bedford Regt.
   in Bde Reserve.
              On relief the battn. will take
   over accommodation from 1st Essex
   Regt in billets at ST. LEGER les AUTHIE

2. **Route**.   Route on relief - SOUASTRE-
   crossroads D.21.b.2.0 - Road junction
   J.1.b.0.2 - Road junction J.1.d.4.7 -
   ST. LEGER les AUTHIE
   All movement East of the grid line
   between D and E Squares will be
   by platoons

3. **Guides**   Each Company will send
   1 guide per platoon and 1 for Coy HQ
   and Battn HQ. 2 guides to report to
   2/Lieut. GADSBY at Battn HQ at 9.15 p.m.
   All guides to be in possession of
   written instructions
      2/Lieut Gadsby will collect guides
   at Battn HQ. and take them to
   guide rendezvous at junction of

Tracks at E.21.d.9.4 (about 200 yds N. of Bde HQ.) Brigade have made themselves responsible for placing a guide at FONQUEVILLERS CHURCH to direct incoming unit to the rendezvous.

4. **Advance Party.** Advance party consisting of Capt. W.S. CAULFIELD, Lieut. C.E. MORIER and representatives from each Company and Battn. HQ (taken from Rear HQ or nucleus) will proceed to ST. LEGER tomorrow to take over accommodation etc. under arrangements being made by the Staff Captain.
Transport lines will be located at about I.11.d.5.4.

5. **Transport.** The T.O. will arrange for one limber to be at Battn. HQ FONQUEVILLERS at 6pm tomorrow to take Officers Valises etc. and take to ST. LEGER. One limber per Coy will be sent up to each Company HQ at 10pm tomorrow for Lewis Guns and Petrol Tins etc. ~~A Coy will send 2 guides each to FONQUEVILLERS CHURCH at 9.30pm to guide their limbers to where they~~

~~require them~~

Each Company's Lewis Gun limbers will be accompanied by a guard of 1 N.C.O and 3 men who will be responsible for the custody of the guns. Riding Horses for C.O, Adjt, M.O, and Coy Commanders will be sent to fork road D.24.c.0.1 on SOUASTRE FONQUEVILLERS ROAD at 11.30pm.

6. <u>Food Arrangements</u>. The QM will arrange for Cookers to be on the FONQUEVILLERS – SOUASTRE Road about D.23.d. and D.24.c. at 11.30pm. and for hot cocoa to be issued to the troops.

7. <u>Handing over</u>. All defence schemes, aeroplane photographs, trench maps and sketches and trench stores will be handed over to relieving unit and receipt obtained. Copy of receipt to be forwarded to Orderly Room as soon as possible after relief.

8. <u>Reports</u>. Completion of relief will be reported at once to Battn. H.Q. by wire if possible or by runner by

using the code word "SPADES".
Coys will report 'Settled in Billets'
on arrival in the new area.

9. Acknowledge by wire.

Issued at 7-10 pm

                    K Syber Capt & Adjt
                5th Duke of Wellington's R.

Copies to
  1-5.   A B C D & H.Q. Coys.
   6.   Rear H.Q.
   7.   Capt. Canefield.
   8.   Q.M. & T.O.
   9.   6th Bedford Regt (for infm)
  10.   186th I.B. (for infm)
  11-12. War Diary
  13.   Office

CONFIDENTIAL

WAR DIARY

- of -

(W.R)
5TH. BN. DUKE OF WELLINGTON'S REGIMENT

1st to 31st MAY 1918.

(Volume 4).

J. Walker Lieut-Colonel.
Commanding. 5th Bn. Duke of Wellington's (W.R) Regt.

Original.

Army Form C. 2118.

5TH. BN. DUKE OF WELLINGTON'S REGIMENT

WAR DIARY
or
INTELLIGENCE SUMMARY.

(Erase heading not required.)

Instructions regarding War Diaries and Intelligence Summaries are contained in F.S. Regs., Part II. and the Staff Manual respectively. Title pages will be prepared in manuscript.

Place	Date	Hour	Summary of Events and Information	Remarks and references to Appendices
Ref.Map. 57.D. 1/40000	1918. May. 1st.		Battalion still in billets at ST.LEGER-les-AUTHIE. Training was done in area. I.6.c. during the morning. In the afternoon C.Coy did Musketry on range at AUTHIE and were inspected by the Army Commander (General Sir. Julian Byng), the Corps Divisional and Brigade Commanders.	
	2nd.		Fine and bright. The battalion took part in a Brigade Tactical Scheme near the BOIS DU WARNIMONT, I.18., I.17 & I.23.	
	3rd.		Fine, sunny and warm. Battalion had baths and did training remainder of day.	
	4th.		Battalion did training in morning. Recreational games in afternoon.	
	5th.		A showery day with fine intervals. Usual Church Parades during the morning for respective denominations.	
	6th.		Training morning and afternoon. A Brigade Horse Show was held near AUTHIE during the afternoon.	
	7th.		Very wet. Specialist training and lectures were held in billets.	
	8th.		Training morning and afternoon. Very fine and bright.	
	9th.		Companies did training in the morning. A ceremonial parade of the Brigade less Transport and 2/4th Duke of Wellington's Regt was held on training ground I.6.c. during the afternoon at which the Divisional Commander (Major General W.P. Braithwaite, C.B. presented medal brooches to recipients of recent honours in the Brigade. Thirty-three recipients were on parade from this Battalion.	
	10th.		The battalion had baths at AUTHIE. Two companies fired on the range during the afternoon.	
	11th.		Training during the morning. A boxing tournament was held in the evening.	
	12th.		Various Church Parades were held during the morning. Cool and showery.	

Army Form C. 2118.

5TH. BN. DUKE OF WELLINGTON'S REGIMENT

WAR DIARY
or
INTELLIGENCE SUMMARY.
(Erase heading not required.)

Instructions regarding War Diaries and Intelligence Summaries are contained in F. S. Regs., Part II. and the Staff Manual respectively. Title pages will be prepared in manuscript.

Original

Place	Date	Hour	Summary of Events and Information	Remarks and references to Appendices
Ref. Maps. 57.D. 1/40000 57 D.N.E. 1/20000	1918. May. 13th.		A very wet day. Training continued in billets.	
	14th.		A fine day. Two companies on the Range in morning. Remaining two Companies did Specialist Training in vicinity of training ground, I.6.c. In the afternoon there were Regimental Sports on the Training ground.	
	15th.		The day was treated as a holiday for the battalion. Recreational games were held. Very hot day.	
	16th.		A very hot day. The battalion left ST.LEGER-les-AUTHIE in lorries at 6-45 p.m. and debussed at SOUASTRE. From there the battalion marched by Platoons to the line via BIENVILLERS, HANNESCAMPS and ESSARTS. The battalion relieved the 8th (S) Battalion Somerset Light Infantry (63rd Inf. Bde, 37th Division) in Brigade Support. West of ABLAINZEVILLE and BUCQUOY. The relief was carried through fairly quietly and was completed by 1-50 a.m. A.Company had bad luck as they arrived, being caught by a few shells which wounded 2 Officers and 10 men. Dispositions of the battalion on relief were as follows:- D.Company, 4 platoons and Coy Hdqrs. in TOP TRENCH, F.21.b.&d. C.Company, 1 platoon in TOP TRENCH, F.21.c, 2 platoons in PRUSSIAN AVENUE F.20.d. and 1 platoon in HALIFAX TRENCH, F.20.d. Coy Hdqrs in same dug-out as Battalion Headquarters F.21.c.5.7. A.Company in BRADFORD and HALIFAX TRENCHES in F.20.b & d with Company Headquarters in same dug-out as Battalion Headquarters F.21.c.5.7. B.Company in HENLEY TRENCH in F.20.d. Company Headquarters at F.20.d.4.4.	
	17th.		A very hot day. Companies all employed on improving the trenches and making new fire bays. Hostile shelling not very great in the Battalion area. A good deal of shelling on both sides in back areas.	
	18th.		A quiet day. Hostile aircraft very busy.	
	19th.		A very hot day. Artillery quiet. Whole Battalion worked on widening TOP TRENCH F.21.c & d during night. Enemy gas shelled HENLEY TRENCH intermittently during night (F.20.d).	

Army Form C. 2118.

WAR DIARY
or
INTELLIGENCE SUMMARY

5TH. BN. DUKE OF WELLINGTON'S REGIMENT

(Erase heading not required.)

Place	Date	Hour	Summary of Events and Information	Remarks and references to Appendices
Ref.Maps. 57.D. 1/40000 57.D.N.E. 1/20000	1918. May. 20th.		A very warm day. Situation quiet. Enemy aircraft very bold. The Battalion relieved the 2/4th Duke of Wellington's Regiment in the Left sub-sector in front of ABLAINZEVILLE at night. Relief was carried through without hitch and was completed by 1-40 a.m. Dispositions were as follows:- Left front line Company ("C") held a series of posts in trench on grid line between Square 22 and 23, from the Divisional boundary F.23.a.00.85 to a point F.23.c.00.60. All four platoons were in the front line with 1 platoon of Left Support Company ("A") in close support. Company Headquarters was in the front line about F.22.d.8.6. Right Front Company ("B") held a series of posts from F.23.c.00.60 to F.28.b.5.2. All four platoons in front line with 1 platoon of Right Support Company ("A") in close support. Company Headquarters at F.22.d.4.1. The Right Company cannot be visited by day but the Left front Company can. Left Support Company ("A") lives partly in a small length of trench about F.22.b.10.20 with fire positions commanding the BUCQUOY-AYETTE Road. Company Headquarters at F.22.d.1.1. remainder occupy BADEN TRENCH in F.22.a. Right Support Company ("D") lives in dug-outs and shelters in sunken road between F.28.a.1.8 and F.22.c.50.95. In case of attack they man isolated pieces of trench and T.saps on the Eastern bank. Company Headquarters at F.22.c.4.8. Battalion Headquarters and details are in TOP TRENCH F.21.d.1.8.	
	21st.		The night was quiet. Enemy seemed to be very uneasy at "Stand To" between 3-30 a.m. and 4 a.m. and shelled our front area. Patrols were out during the night endeavouring to Secure an identification but no enemy was seen. A very hot day.	
	22nd.		Another very hot day. Artillery and aircraft on both sides were active during the morning.	
	23rd.		A fine day. Wind changed to S.W. Quiet day on the whole with usual Artillery activity on both sides. Enemy did rather more shelling on our forward positions. During the afternoon B.Coy Headquarters were French Mortared at intervals from direction S.E. of ABLAINZEVILLE. This was continued during the night and retaliation was obtained from our artillery.	

Army Form C. 2118.

5th. BN. DUKE OF WELLINGTON'S REGIMENT

WAR DIARY
or
INTELLIGENCE SUMMARY.
(Erase heading not required.)

Instructions regarding War Diaries and Intelligence Summaries are contained in F. S. Regs., Part II. and the Staff Manual respectively. Title pages will be prepared in manuscript.

Original

Place	Date	Hour	Summary of Events and Information	Remarks and references to Appendices
Ref.Maps. 57.D. 1/40000	1918. May. 23rd.		At 11 p.m. the enemy set up a big barrage over whole Battalion area. Front line posts, Support Line and Battalion Headquarters all came in for attention. We suffered 11 casualties.	
57.D.N.E. 1/20000	24th.		A very wet day. Rained practically all day and trenches soon became very bad. Artillery on both sides much quieter.	
	25th.		Fine again. Artillery less active then usual. Companies inter-relieved at night. After relief D.Company were in the Right Front Posts and A.Company on the left, with B & C Coys in Right and Left Support respectively. The enemy tried to rush one of our left posts of the Right Company during the night but were driven off by Lewis Gun fire.	
	26th.		Fine and bright. Enemy artillery was very active. Enemy tried to rush another of our posts in the Right Company but was driven off without loss to ourselves. During the morning between 11 a.m. and 1 p.m. the enemy bombarded D.Company's Front Posts very heavily and they had one post obliterated with the garrison all killed or wounded. . Remainder of day was quiet. Enemy aircraft very active in the evening.	
	27th.		Very heavy gas shelling on back areas about "Stand To" (3 a.m.) in the morning with whizz banging of our front line posts. Some Trench Mortaring of the front line during the day.	
	28th.		A quiet day on the whole until evening. Between 10-25 p.m. and 11-10 p.m. the enemy put down a very heavy barrage over whole battalion area and on the right and left. This was effectively replied to by our Artillery. No enemy raid resulted from the bombardment.	
	29th.		A quieter day. Enemy aircraft particularly active during the day. The battalion was relieved at night by the 2/7th Duke of Wellington's Regiment. The relief was carried through quietly and was complete by 12-30 a.m. The Battalion then became Brigade Support and was disposed similarly to 8 days previously.	
	30th.		A very fine day. Men employed on "improving" existing trenches and shelter accomodation. At night dug-outs were worked on in TOP TRENCH (F.21.d) and wiring in front of posts in	

Original

Army Form C. 2118.

5TH. BN. DUKE OF WELLINGTON'S REGIMENT

WAR DIARY
or
INTELLIGENCE SUMMARY.

(Erase heading not required.)

Instructions regarding War Diaries and Intelligence Summaries are contained in F. S. Regs., Part II. and the Staff Manual respectively. Title pages will be prepared in manuscript.

Place	Date	Hour	Summary of Events and Information	Remarks and references to Appendices
Ref.Maps. 57.D. 1/40000	1918. May. 30th.		F.21.A & B. TOP TRENCH was also worked on - deepened and widened.	
57.D.N.E. 1/20000	31st.		Quiet day.	

Waller
Lieut-Colonel.
Commanding, 5th Bn. Duke of Wellington's (W.R) Regt.

Army Form C. 2118.

5TH. BN. DUKE OF WELLINGTON'S REGIMENT

WAR DIARY
or
INTELLIGENCE-SUMMARY.

(Erase heading not required.)

Place	Date	Hour	Summary of Events and Information	Remarks and references to Appendices
			A P P E N D I C E S	
			CASUALTIES, ETC	
			2/Lieut. A.L. LORD - To England. 5-5-18.	
			2/Lieut. C.W. HEAWOOD - Posted to 186th T.M.Battery .30-4-18.	
			Lieut. J.F. WATERS - To England.Sick. 28-4-18.	
			Lieut. C.E. MORIER - Wounded. 16-5-18.	
			2/Lieut. R.B. Hill.- Wounded. 16-5-18.	
			Lieut. T.P. CROSLAND - To England. Sick. 19-5-18.	
			Killed. 4 Other Ranks.	
			Wounded. 45 " "	
			Wounded & remd. 2 " "	
			DRAFTS, ETC	
			Lieut. G.E. McKILLOP - Attached from 2/4th D.of W.Rgt. as Transport Officer - 24-5-18.	
			60 Other Ranks. 3-5-18. 8 Other Ranks. 19-5-18.	
			2 " " 3-5-18. 6 " " 23-5-18.	
			9 " " 5-5-18. 6 " " 25-5-18.	
			2 " " 9-5-18. 2 " " 27-5-18.	
			5. " " 11-5-18. 7 " " 30-5-18.	
			4 " " 16-5-18.	
			RELINQUISHMENT	
			Lieut. (A/Capt). F.H. WAITE relinquishes the acting rank of Captain on ceasing to command a Company dated 14-5-18.	

Original

Army Form C. 2118.

5TH. BN. DUKE OF WELLINGTON'S REGIMENT

WAR DIARY
or
INTELLIGENCE SUMMARY.
(Erase heading not required.)

Instructions regarding War Diaries and Intelligence Summaries are contained in F. S. Regs., Part II. and the Staff Manual respectively. Title pages will be prepared in manuscript.

Place	Date	Hour	Summary of Events and Information	Remarks and references to Appendices
			APPENDICES (CONTINUED)	

HONOURS AND AWARDS
   Decorations as under have been awarded to the following Officers and Non-commissioned officers for gallantry during operations which commenced on 25th March 1918.

Major (A/Lieut-Colonel). J. WALKER.   Distinguished Service Order.
Lieut.(A/Major). F. BROOK.   "
Lieut. B. MOLLETT, M.C.   Bar to the Military Cross.
Captain. G.L. TINKER.   Military Cross.
Lieut. W. YATES.   "
T/2nd Lieut. G.H. DODD.   "
T/2nd Lieut. T.R. MORTON.   "
1st Lieut. J.W. SHERRICK, (U.S.M.C.)   "
240358 C.S.M. W. Fisher.   Distinguished Conduct Medal.
240464 L/Cpl. H. Fawcett.   "
240101 C.S.M. H. Schofield.   "
265094 Cpl. H. Shires.   "
15807 Sergt. J. Hemshaw.   Military Medal.
10666 L/Cpl. J. Fairbairn.   "
306466 Cpl. A.E. Parker.   "
241549 L/Cpl. J. Armitage.   "
240604 Cpl. G.E. Ingram.   "
241320 L/Cpl. W. Whiting.   "
241565 Pte. C. Bonner.   "
204034 L/Cpl. H. Batty.   "
305308 Sgt. W. McNay.   "
240954 L/Cpl. R.M. Nedderman.   "
12886 Sgt. J.R. Greaves.   "
242392 Pte. H. Brook.   "
205353 L/Cpl. W. Wilkinson.   "
241956 Pte. A. Looking.   "
241688 L/Cpl. G.G. Robinson.   "
242472 Pte. T. Baker.   "
25101 Pte. A. Lee.   "
241860 Cpl. H. Lockwood.   "

Army Form C. 2118.

5TH. BN. DUKE OF WELLINGTON'S REGIMENT
WAR DIARY
or
INTELLIGENCE SUMMARY

APPENDICES (CONTINUED)

HONOURS & AWARDS (CONTINUED)

11013	Pte. J. Grogan.	Military Medal.
11099	Cpl. C. Wilman.	"
242683	Pte. P. Beardsley.	"
242067	Pte. R. Taylor.	"
240222	C.S.M. G.V. Jones.	Distinguished Conduct Medal.
241337	Sgt. B. Siswick, D.C.M.	Bar to Distinguished Conduct Medal.
14870	Private. J. Watson.	Distinguished Conduct Medal.

The following Officers and Warrant Officers were mentioned in Sir Douglas Haig's Despatch dated April 7th published in the London Gazette May 24th.1918.

Lieut-Col. J. WALKER, D.S.O.
Capt. & Adjt. K. SYKES, M.C.
Capt. T. GOODALL, D.S.O, M.C.
Lieut. H.S. JACKSON, D.S.O.
Capt. C.S. MOXON, D.S.O.
240389 Coy.Sgt.Mjr. G. Gannon.

Original.

[illegible] Copy No.......

[illegible] DUKE OF WELLINGTON'S REGT.

Battalion Order No. 14. 15.8.18.

Ref. Maps ... Sheet 57 ... 1/20,000.

1. RELIEF. The Battalion will relieve the 6th. Somerset Light Infantry in Brigade Support in the left sector of the Corps Front tomorrow night 16/17. [illegible] Companies will take over from corresponding Companies.

2. ROUTES etc. The Battalion will move via [illegible] - [illegible] - [illegible] to the point where the old British Front Line crosses the [illegible] Road at [illegible], where they will be met by platoon guides (under an officer) of 6th. Somerset L.I. All movement east of [illegible] will be by platoons at 200 yards distance. The head of [illegible] of the Regt. will not pass [illegible] till [illegible]. [illegible] of the Regt., [illegible] Battery and [illegible] of [illegible], will follow in order named.

3. TACTICAL COMMAND. During relief [illegible] of the line [illegible] - [illegible] the Battalion will be under the tactical command of the Brigadier in whose section it is moving.

4. TIME OF [illegible] etc. Busses have been applied for to carry out the move, and arrangements will be notified later. Time and mode of starting from [illegible] will be issued later as Appendix "A". The Q.M. will arrange for 2 cookers to provide tea for the troops en route on the [illegible] side of [illegible].

5. TRANSPORT. The T.O. will arrange for one limber to report to [illegible] Coys. at their convenience to carry Lewis Guns to the forward area. Coys. will supply a guard of at least 1 N.C.O. and 2 men for their Lewis Guns. 1 limber will also accompany Battalion H.Q. Personnel.

6. DEFENCE SCHEMES. All defence schemes, programmes of work, aeroplane photographs, trench maps etc. will be carefully taken over on relief. [illegible] will be handed over to relieving unit of [illegible] Inf. Bde.

7. ADVANCE PARTIES. Advance parties of 1 officer and 1 N.C.O. per platoon, and 1 N.C.O. and 4 runners for battalion H.Q. will be sent up to the line early tomorrow as already detailed.

8. DRESS & RATIONS. Dress for trenches - battle order - muzzle protectors on rifles. Rations for 17th inst. will be carried on the man.

9. REPORTS. Completion of relief will at once be reported [illegible] per runner by sending the word [illegible].

10. REAR HEADQUARTERS. Rear battalion headquarters will be established [illegible]. Transport Lines will be in [illegible] Camp. [illegible].

11. Acknowledge.

[illegible] Capt. & Adjt.
[illegible] Bn. Duke of Wellington's Regt.

Copies to :-

[illegible]
[illegible]
Adjutant.
[illegible]
[illegible]
[illegible] Somerset L.I. (for info)
[illegible] Inf. Bde. (for info.)
[illegible] (2).
File.

Original

APPENDIX "A".
to be attached to Operation Order No.14.

(a). 23 lorries are allotted to the battalion for the move as far as SOUASTRE. Embussing point will be at Billet No. 1 ST. LEGER. Order of embussing - D,C,H.Q., A,B. Time 6.15pm. Capt. Ellis will act as embussing officer and will report to a Brigade Staff Officer at above rendesvous at 6.0pm.

(b). On debussing at SOUASTRE the battalion will march by platoons to a point about L.25.a.2.7. on BIENVILLERS Road where B and C Coys. Cookers will provide hot tea for the battalion.

(c) Transport. Lewis Gun Limbers will report to respective Coys. at 4.pm and 1 Limber to Battalion H.Q. Each company will take 6 full petrol tins of water with them to the line in their limbers. Limbers and 2 cookers will leave ST. LEGER at 5.pm and halt at point L.25.a.2.7. where each company will take its own limber on. The O.M.S. will accompany it as detailed in par. b.

Packs, Blankets, Valises etc. to be ready to-day by 4.pm. To be put in one dump per company and collected by Q.M.

..........Kkyber..........Capt.& Adjt.
8th.Duke of Wellington's Regiment.

15.8.18.

Secret   Original   Copy No. 9

5th Duke of Wellington's Regt.
Operation Order No. 15.   19.5.18
Ref. Map. 57 D N.E. 1/20000

1. **Relief.**

    The battalion will relieve 2/4 of Duke of Wellington's Regt in the left sub section tomorrow night May 20/21st.

2. **Dispositions.**

    Coys will relieve as follows:-
    B Coy. 5th D of W Regt will relieve B Coy 2/4 D of W. in Right front posts.
    C Coy. 5th D of W Regt will relieve C Coy. 2/4 D of W Regt in Left front posts.
    D Coy 5th D of W. Regt will relieve A Coy. 2/4 D of W Regt in Right Support.
    A Coy 5th D of W Regt will relieve D Coy. 2/4 D of W Regt in Left Support.

3. **Guides.**

    Platoon guides will be provided by 2/4 D. of Wellington's Regt at the junction of PRUSSIAN and TOP Trenches at the following times.
    Left Front Company.   10 pm
    Left Support Company.   10.15 pm.
    Right Front Company.   11 pm
    Right Support Company.   11.15 pm
    H.Q. Coy   11.30 pm (no guides)

- 2 -

4. Rations.
Rations will be at point where road crosses the trench about T.21.b.9.7. at 11 pm. to-morrow.
Companies will each fetch their own rations from this point. B Coy will take their rations with them into the line picking them up "en route".

5. Defence Schemes, etc.
All defence schemes, programmes of work, aeroplane photographs, trench stores, etc will be carefully handed over and taken over.
Sketch disposition maps will be sent to Bn H.Q's. by Coys by 9 am. 21st inst.

6. Reports
Completion of relief will at once be reported by wiring the "THANKS"

7. Acknowledge by wire.

Rhys Capt & Adjt
5th Duke of Well. Regt.

1. A Coy   6. 2/4 D. of W. (for inf)
2. B   7. Rear H.Q.   11. Office
3. C   8. 156 T.B. (for inf)   12. Adjutant.
4. D   9. War Diary
5. M.O.   10. " "

Secret   Original   Copy No 6

5th Duke of Wellington's Regt.
Operation Order No. 16.

1. Relief

The Battn. will be relieved in the Left Subsector by 2/7th Duke of Wellington's Regt. on the night 29/30 May.

2. Order of Relief etc.

C Coy (5th) will be relieved by C Coy (2/7th) relief to commence at 9 pm. No guides.
B Coy (5th) will be relieved by A Coy (2/7th)
A Coy (5th) will be relieved by B Coy (2/7th)
D Coy (5th) will be relieved by D Coy (2/7th)

3. Guides

O.C. ABD Coys will provide platoon guides for 2/7th D. of W's Regt. to be at junction of TOP and PRUSSIAN Trenches at the following times tomorrow. The guides will all report to Lieut. I.M. TOD

    B (Right Support)   9.30 pm
    D (Right Front)   10 pm
    A (Left Front)   10.15 pm

D Coys guides with a N.C.O in charge will come out of the line tonight and be accommodated by B Coy for tomorrow.

4. <u>Dispositions on relief.</u>
On relief the Battn. will go into Brigade Support. Dispositions as follows:-

C Coy in TOP Trench.
D " " PRUSSIAN AV. (Coy HQ in B.H.Q dugout)
A + B Coys. Same as last time.

These areas will be reconnoitred during the day tomorrow and troops led back from the line under Company arrangement.

5. <u>Advance Party.</u>
Advance party of 1 Officer per Coy. and 1 N.C.O per platoon from 2/4th D. of W's will be attached to Coys tonight. Guides for this party will be provided by Battn. HQ

6. <u>Rations</u>
The T.O. will bring rations up tomorrow night to be at respective Ration rendezvous at 12.30 am. Coy Q.M. Sergts. to personally hand over rations in each case. Coys will be careful to bring all Petrol tins out of the line

7. Reports etc.

(i) Trench Stores, aeroplane photographs Defence Schemes, Work in hand will be carefully handed over and receipts obtained. Copies to be sent to BHQ by 10 am on 30th inst.

(ii) Relief complete will be reported by wire at once in BAB Code. Arrival in new area to be reported by runner.

8. Acknowledge.

Issued at 2.40 pm

Klyber Capt & Adjt
5th D. of W's Regiment.

Copies to:-
   HBcoD&HQ Corp
   Rear HQ.
   Adjutant
   186th IB (for infm)
   2/4th D.o.W's (for infm)
   1st Bn. Grenadier Guards (for infm)
   War Diary (2)
   Office

ORIGINAL
9/8/18

Maker Lieut Colonel.
Commanding 5 Duke of Wellington Regt. 7.6.54.
31 sheets

CONFIDENTIAL.

WAR DIARY.

- of -

5TH. DUKE OF WELLINGTON'S (W.R.) REGT.(2.F.)

1st to 30th June, 1918.

(Volume 5.).

SECRET

Army Form C. 2118.

Original

WAR DIARY
or
INTELLIGENCE SUMMARY.
(Erase heading not required.)

Instructions regarding War Diaries and Intelligence Summaries are contained in F. S. Regs., Part II. and the Staff Manual respectively. Title pages will be prepared in manuscript.

CONFIDENTIAL.

WAR DIARY

-of-

5TH. DUKE OF WELLINGTON'S (W.R.) REGT.(T.F.)

1st to 30th. June, 1918.

(Volume 5.).

[signature] ...Lieut.Col.
Commdg. 5th. Duke of Wellington's (W.R.) Regt.

ORIGINAL.

Army Form C. 2118.

5TH. DUKE OF WELLINGTON'S (W.R.) REGT. T.F.

WAR DIARY
or
INTELLIGENCE SUMMARY.

(Erase heading not required.)

Instructions regarding War Diaries and Intelligence Summaries are contained in F. S. Regs., Part II. and the Staff Manual respectively. Title pages will be prepared in manuscript.

Place	Date	Hour	Summary of Events and Information	Remarks and references to Appendices
Ref. Map. 57.d.N.S. 1/20,000.	1918. Jan. 1st.		Battalion in Brigade Support to BUCQUOY - ABLAINZEVILLE Sector. Men engaged on working parties day and night, widening and deepening TOP TRENCH in F.21.b. and d. Making Company H.Q.'s and Platoon dugouts in TOP TRENCH. Wiring 4 new posts in F.21.a and c. A quiet day on the whole. Usual reciprocal artillery fire, and aeroplane activity.	
	2nd.		At 2.30am. the enemy put down a very heavy Gas Bombardment chiefly phosgene in area F.14, F.20 and F.21. This lasted about 40 minutes and was most intense. The battalion area soon became full of gas and Box Respirators had to be worn for a couple of hours. The Battalion was relieved by 2/7th. West Yorkshire Regt. at night. On relief the battalion moved into Divisional Reserve and occupied positions as follows - A. & D. Coys. in old German Trenches in E.30.a and b. B and C Coys. in old British line in E.22.b. and d. Battalion H.Q. in a dugout in old German Front line in E.23.c. The relief was a quiet one and no untoward incident occurred.	
	3rd.		A very fine day. Vicinity of Battalion H.Q. shelled a little in the early morning. B and C Coys. were employed on carrying parties for 479 Tunnelling Coy. R.E. in FONQUEVILLERS A and D Coys. were employed in their own areas clearing trenches, making fire bays etc.	
	4th.		Fine and bright. Work continued the same as previous day. Some little shelling of Battalion H.Q. about 12.noon. News was received that Lieut.Col. Walker D.S.O. had been awarded a bar to his D.S.O.	
	5th.		Fine and bright. A and D Coys. were shelled at intervals during the day and had one casualty. The work was continued the same as the previous day. News was received that Major E. Brook D.S.O. and R.S.M. Earle E. had been awarded the Military Cross.	
	6th.		Very fine and bright. Some shelling of the battalion area throughout the day. Battalion Headquarters shelled lightly at 8.45pm. Work continued as on the previous day.	
	7th.		Bright day but cloudy in the evening and a shower of rain about 10.30pm. Quiet in the battalion area. Work continued as usual on the lines of previous day. Battalion H.Q. lightly shelled at 8.45pm.	
	8th.		Very fine and bright. Quiet day on battalion area. Work as on previous day. Our Artillery very active.	

ORIGINAL.

5TH. DUKE OF WELLINGTON'S (W.R.) REGT.
WAR DIARY
or
INTELLIGENCE SUMMARY.
(Erase heading not required.)

Army Form C. 2118.

Instructions regarding War Diaries and Intelligence Summaries are contained in F. S. Regs., Part II. and the Staff Manual respectively. Title pages will be prepared in manuscript.

Place	Date	Hour	Summary of Events and Information	Remarks and references to Appendices
Ref. Map. SHEET 57.d. N.E. 1/20,000.	June. 9th.		Enemy artillery very active during the morning in the neighbourhood of Battalion H.Q. A bright morning but signs of rain in the afternoon which however were not fulfilled. The rear companies (B and C.) had a few gas shells near their area. Work continued as on previous day.	
	10th.		A little rain fell during the morning and a short heavy shower during the afternoon. All was quiet in the battalion area in the PURPLE SYSTEM. The battalion moved out of the PURPLE SYSTEM at dusk and relieved the 2/4th. York and Lancaster Regt. in the left front line positions of the right section. The relief was carried out quietly and was completed at 1.am. The dispositions were - "B" Coy - right front line with 2 platoons in outposts on the S.W. outskirts of BUCQUOY L.3.c. and 2 platoons in HEDGE TRENCH L.2.b. "C" Coy. left front line with 2 platoons in outposts amongst the houses in the S.W. corner of BUCQUOY L.3.a. and 2 platoons in HEDGE TRENCH L.3.c. "A" Coy in support in CROSS TRENCH F.26.d. and "D" Coy. in reserve in BUCQUOY AVENUE and trench running N. from F.26.a.70.05. (F.26 central). Five officers and 27 other ranks of the 2/4th. Hampshire Regt. were attached to the battalion for instruction in trench warfare.	
	11th.		A fine day. Quiet on the battalion front. All companies worked on improving the wire in front of posts and trenches. Digging was also done on new posts and trenches were cleared.	
	12th.		A bright sunny day. B and C Coy. H.Q. in the CHATEAU, BUCQUOY were shelled from 9.45am to 10.45am with 5.9s otherwise nothing of importance occurred. Work was continued on the posts - wire put out and trenches deepened.	
	13th.		A fine day. Quiet on the battalion front except for active machine gun fire during the night. A patrol of B Coy. were bombed and fired on by machine guns by an enemy post but no casualties resulted. Work of wiring the forward posts and deepening trenches was continued by all companies.	
	14th.		Very quiet day. Fine and bright.	
	15th.		Fine. Quiet day. A little trench mortaring of forward Coy. H.Q. at BUCQUOY CHATEAU about 3.pm.	

ORIGINAL.

5TH. DUKE OF WELLINGTON'S Regt.

WAR DIARY
or
INTELLIGENCE SUMMARY.

(Erase heading not required).

Army Form C. 2118.

Place	Date	Hour	Summary of Events and Information	Remarks and references to Appendices
Ref. Map. SHEET. 57.d.N.E. 1/20,000.	June. 15th.		One of our patrols at night saw 4 of the enemy in the village but failed to capture them after a good chase.	
	16th.		Fine and bright with exception of one shower of rain at 12 noon. A reorganisation of the battalion sub-section took place at night resulting in the thinning out of the forward area, on completion the battalion was roughly disposed as follows. Two companies in front system with 2 platoons each in HEDGE TRENCH in L.2.b. L.3.a. and F.27.c. These two companies had 1 platoon each in forward posts in BUCQUOY about 300 yards in front of the HEDGE TRENCH LINE. Each company had one platoon in Reserve in CROSS TRENCH in L.2.b. and F.26.d. Remaining two companies occupied BUCQUOY AVENUE, LEEDS TRENCH, RETTEMOY AVENUE, BRIDGE TRENCH in F.26.a. and c., and F.25.b, c, d.	
	17th.		A quiet day. A patrol of 9 other ranks under 2/Lieut. R.J. Machin went out at "S" Post in BUCQUOY (L.3.a.8.4.) at 1.30am. They stopped out until 5.pm. No enemy were captured owing to operations being out short through our own trench mortars firing short and wounding 4 of the patrol. An enemy post was located at L.3.b.2.3. Houses, cellars, and dugouts in Orchard L.3.b.15.30. to L.3.a.95.50 were searched and found to be unoccupied. 2/Lieut. Machin took out another patrol of 6 other ranks from S. Post at 10.15pm. with the object of waylaying any enemy patrol and locating enemy posts and working parties. On leaving "S" Post an enemy party was reported in house at L.3.a.8.4. Stick bombs had been thrown about 2 minutes before. The patrol went to the house and after throwing 12 bombs inside they heard the enemy retiring at the double. Egg bombs were thrown after them and the vicinity was thoroughly searched for any enemy but none found. During the night "A" and "C" Coys. of 2/4th. Hants Regt; relieved "D" and "B" Coys. 5th. Duke of Wellington's. On relief "D" and "B" Coys. went into Brigade Reserve. "D" Coy. occupied area GOMMECOURT TRENCH and BRIDLINGTON S.P. in E.30.b., F.25.a. and E.24.d. "B" Coy. were in trenches N. of RETTEMOY FARM in E.30.b. The 2/7th. Duke of Wellington's Regt. ceased to be a unit in the Brigade to-day on being disbanded and posted as drafts to other units. The 2/4th. Hants Regt. took their place as third battalion in the Brigade.	
	18th.		At 1.am a projector gas attack was carried out on BLAINZEVILLE by the Brigade on our left. 1000 gas projectors were discharged and an artillery and M.G. Barrage was put down at the same time. It evoked very little retaliation from the enemy.	

ORIGINAL.

Army Form C. 2118.

Instructions regarding War Diaries and Intelligence
Summaries are contained in F. S. Regs., Part II.
and the Staff Manual respectively. Title pages
will be prepared in manuscript.

5TH. DUKE OF WELLINGTON'S REGT. (T.F.).

WAR DIARY
or
INTELLIGENCE SUMMARY.

(Erase heading not required.)

Place	Date	Hour	Summary of Events and Information	Remarks and references to Appendices
Ref. Map. SHEET.57.d. N.E. 1/20,000.	June. 18th		Remainder of Battalion and Hd.Qrs. were relieved at night by 2/4th. Hampshire Regt. On relief the battalion became Brigade Reserve. Battalion H.Q. was in PIGEON WOOD E.30.a. "A" Company was in GOMMECOURT TRENCH Posts. 2,3,4 an E.30.a. "C" Coy. was in LA BRAYELLE AVENUE E.24.c.	
	19th.		Men rested during the day. At night "C" Coy. was employed in putting out a double apron wire fence in front of RUM TRENCH between LA BRAYELLE Road and LA BRAYELLE Trench in E.24.c. "B" Coy. deepened and widened CYCLE TRENCH in L.1.b. "A" Coy. widened and deepened Posts 1,2,3,4 in GOMMECOURT TRENCH in E.30.a. and "D" Coy. dugout and made fire bays in RIFLE TRENCH in E.24.d. It was a very wet morning but became fine in late afternoon.	
	20th.		At 2.am the enemy heavily gas shelled PIGEON WOOD in the vicinity of Battalion H.Q. and a few men were gassed. PIGEON WOOD was intermittently shelled during the day but no casualties were caused. After fine weather up to 6.pm rain fell for a few hours. Work was done on improving trenches during the day. No work was done at night	
	21st.		A fine day till about 8.pm when there was a slight downfall of rain. PIGEON WOOD and the battalion area in its vicinity were shelled lightly at intervals. Work was continued on the trenches occupied by the companies by day – no work was done at night. 2/Lieut. Machin and 2/Lieut. B———— were commended by the Brigade Commander for good patrol work and ———— work. by the Divisional Commander also.	
	22nd.		The day was fine but not very sunny- rain fell in the early morning. PIGEON WOOD was intermittently shelled during the day. "B" Coy. situated between GOMMECOURT TRENCH and RETTEMOY FARM had 4 casualties by the shelling of their positions. Work was done in the daytime only on improvement of trenches in the battalion area.	
	23rd.		The day was fine but dull on the whole. All remained quiet in the battalion area. A number of men had to go to hospital suffering from a high temperature and general weakness Work was continued on the trenches in the battalion area during the day.	

Army Form C. 2118.

ORIGINAL

5th. DUKE OF WELLINGTON'S (W.R.) REGT.

WAR DIARY
or
INTELLIGENCE SUMMARY.
(Erase heading not required.)

Instructions regarding War Diaries and Intelligence
Summaries are contained in F. S. Regs., Part II.
and the Staff Manual respectively. Title pages
will be prepared in manuscript.

Place	Date	Hour	Summary of Events and Information	Remarks and references to Appendices
Ref. Map. SHEET 57.d.N.E. 1/20,000.	1918. June 24th.		A fine day and quiet in the vicinity of the Battalion. PIGEON WOOD was shelled from 11.am to 1.pm. The Battalion was relieved by the 13th. X.R.R. 111th. Inf. Brigade, 37th. Division during the night. Relief started at 11.30pm and went smoothly, being completed at 1.am. The Battalion then marched to SQUASHED by platoons where a half was made during which tea was issued. Buses then conveyed the battalion to THIEVRES and companies were settled in billets at this place by 5.30am.	
	25th.		The companies were disposed in THIEVRES as follows - A and B Companies in billets on the THIEVRES - ORVILLE Road. "C" Company were billetted on the main THIEVRES - FAMECHON Road one hundred yards north of the Church. "D" Company were billetted in the south of the village and H.Q. Company in a farm just west of the Church. All the billets were barns and very comfortable. The day was spent in resting and distributing packs.	
	26th.		A fine day. The companies were engaged in reorganisation cleaning up and inspections.	
	27th.		A fine day. Reorganisation of companies was continued. 2/Lieut. Machin and Sergt. Hepworth were granted leave for daring and initiative in action, during last tour in the trenches.	
	28th.		A fine warm day. The companies completed their inspections and a battalion parade under the R.S.M. completed the programme of training. The 4th. Corps Boxing Competition was held at MARIEUX in the afternoon.	
	29th.		A bright and sunny day. The Battalion received word at 7.30am to man their battle positions in the RED LINE. Having been warned of this, breakfast was served at 6.30am and the companies moved off to their positions by 8.am. The battalion was in support to the other two battalions of the 186th. Brigade. A, C, D Companies being in position in D.26.d. and D.27.a. with B Company and Battalion Headquarters in the vicinity of ROSSIGNOL FARM J.3.c.6.5. The forming up was complete by 10.30am. Orders were then received to form up in new positions in D.18 and this operation was carried out by 12.30pm. when the battalion was ordered to march back to billets which were reached at 3.30pm.	
	30th.		A very fine day. Voluntary divine services for the men of Church of England and Non-conformists denominations were held in the open. Mass for Roman Catholics was held in the Church THIEVRES.	

ORIGINAL.

Army Form C. 2118.

5TH. DUKE OF WELLINGTON'S (W.R.) REGT. T.F.
WAR DIARY
or
INTELLIGENCE SUMMARY.
(Erase heading not required.)

Instructions regarding War Diaries and Intelligence Summaries are contained in F.S. Regs., Part II. and the Staff Manual respectively. Title Pages will be prepared in manuscript.

Place	Date	Hour	Summary of Events and Information	Remarks and references to Appendices
			HONOURS, AWARDS etc.	
			Decorations as under have been awarded to the following for bravery and devotion to duty in the Field.	
			Lieut. Col. J. WALKER. DSO. BAR to D.S.O.	
			Major F. BROOK. DSO. M. C.	
			9383 R.S.M. Earle B. M. C.	
			240358 C.S.M. Fisher W. DCM. BAR to D.C.M.	
			240101 C.S.M. Scrofield H. DCM. BAR to D.C.M.	
			240545 Sergt. Collins E. MERITORIOUS SERVICE MEDAL.	
			268909 Pte. Denton T.A. M. M.	
			J. Walker. Lieut. Col. Commdg. 5th. Duke of Wellington's Regiment.	

ORIGINAL.

Army Form C. 2118.

5TH. DUKE OF WELLINGTON'S (R.) REGT.
WAR DIARY
or
INTELLIGENCE SUMMARY.
(Erase heading not required.)

Instructions regarding War Diaries and Intelligence Summaries are contained in F.S. Regs., Part II. and the Staff Manual respectively. Title Pages will be prepared in manuscript.

Place	Date	Hour	Summary of Events and Information	Remarks and references to Appendices
			CASUALTIES etc.	
			Capt. A.R. Haigh. Wounded. 4.6.18. To England. 10.6.18.	
			2/Lieut. G.E. Dodd MC. Wounded (gas). 6.6.18. To England. 18.6.18.	
			2/Lieut. J. Thompson MC. To England (injured). 29.5.18.	
			2/Lieut. G.H. Appleby. To Hosp. (Sick) 13.6.18. To England 20.6.18.	
			Lieut. E.C. McKillip (atta.). To England, sick.	
			Lieut. W.H. Chambers. Posted to 1/7th. West Riding Regt. 28.6.18.	
			2/Lieut. W. Barber. To Hospital, sick. 20.6.18.	
			" E.P. Dunsmee. " " " 24.6.18.	
			" T. Chapman. " " " 24.6.18.	
			" R.O. Stead. " " " 27.6.18.	
			" C.L. Gadsby. " " " 25.5.18.	
			Wounded. 14 other ranks.	
			Wounded (gas). 12 other ranks.	
			Wounded at duty. 3 other ranks.	
			Died of wounds. 1 other rank.	
			DRAFTS etc.	
			Major F. Brook DSO, MC. Rejoined from Hospital. 31.5.18.	
			Lieut. C.E. Morier. Rejoined from Hospital (wounded). 11.6.18.	
			2/Lieut. F.R. Barnes. ⎫	
			2/Lieut. L. Brock. ⎬	
			2/Lieut. G.F. Clay. ⎪ Joined Battn. 9.6.18. Posted from 2/5th. West Yorks Regt.	
			2/Lieut. H. Greenwood.⎬	
			2/Lieut. A.E. Lowe. ⎪	
			2/Lieut. L.F. Walker. ⎭	
			Capt. C. Lockwood. ⎫	
			2/Lieut. E.R. Storry. ⎪ Joined Battn. 14.6.18. Posted from 2/7th. Duke of	
			2/Lieut. E.W. Taylor. ⎬ Wellington's Regiment.	
			2/Lieut. B.M. Milnes. ⎭	

ORIGINAL.

5TH. DUKE OF WELLINGTON'S (W.R.) REGT. B.E.F.

WAR DIARY
or
INTELLIGENCE SUMMARY.

(Erase heading not required.)

Army Form C. 2118.

Place	Date	Hour	Summary of Events and Information	Remarks and references to Appendices
			APPENDICES (continued).	

DRAFTS etc. (continued).

Lieut. T.H. Chambers.   } Joined Battn. 17.6.18. Posted from 2/7th. Duke of
Lieut. E. Tanner M.C.   } Wellington's Regiment.

Major E. Senior.   ) Joined Battn. from England 25.6.18.
Lieut. H.D. Wraith.   )

2/Lieut. D. A.S. Haigh.   Rejoined from Hospital. 26.6.18.
2/Lieut. W. Barber.   ditto. 28.6.18.

Lieut. R.G. Irvine.   Posted to Battn. from 1/7th. West Riding Regt.

```
37 other ranks.         4.6.18.
 4     "     "          5.6.18.
 4     "     "          7.6.18.
 4     "     "         10.6.18.
 6     "     "         11.6.18.
 1     "     "         12.6.18.
 2     "     "          9.6.18.
 4     "     "         16.6.18.
16     "     "         20.6.18.
 2     "     "         23.6.18.
132    "     "         17.6.18.
 6     "     "         27.5.18.
13     "     "         28.6.18.
```

PROMOTIONS, APPOINTMENTS, RELINQUISHMENTS etc.

Capt. (a/Major) F. BROOK DSO, MC, assumed appointment of Second in Command d/ June 1st.1918.
Capt. (a/Major) W.S. CAULFEILD relinquished the acting rank of Major on ceasing to be employed as Second in command dated 31st MAY 1918.
Lieut.(a/Capt.) C.G.H. ELLIS relinquished the acting rank of Captain on being superseded dated 25.5.18.

Secret.   Copy No 8
               5 Duke of Wellington's Regt
                  Operation Order No 14
Ref Map. 57d N.E 1/20,000.   June

1. Relief:
        The Battn. will be relieved in
Bde Support to the Left Section on the
night June 2/3rd by 2/7th West Yorkshire
Regt.
        On relief the Battn. will go into
Divisional Reserve in the Right Sub-
Section PURPLE SYSTEM at present
occupied by 2/5th West Yorkshire Regt.

2. Method of Relief etc:
        Our Companies will be relieved
by Coys of 2/7th West Yorks Regt. as
follows:-
Our C Coy in TOP Tr. by D Coy 2/7th W.Y.R.
 " D "   TOP & PRUSSIAN Trenches by B
Coy 2/7th W.Y.R.
Our A Coy in Left Rear Position by 'C' Coy
2/7th W.Y.R.
Our B Coy in Right Rear Position by
A Coy 2/7th W.Y.R.
Platoon Guides and 2 guides for Battn
H.Q. will meet incoming unit at
York Road F.2.O.b.45.60 at 10.15 p.m
tomorrow. All guides will report to
2/Lieut. Appleby at the rendezvous and
each will have a written docket

stating where they are to guide.

3. Advance Parties
   Advance parties of 1 Officer per Coy and 1 N.C.O. per platoon from 1/7th West Yorks Regt. will come up to respective Companies early tomorrow.
   Advance party of 1 Officer per Coy and 1 N.C.O. per platoon will proceed to 1/5th West Yorks Regt. for attachment early tomorrow leaving Lippars' line not later than 8 am. Our party will take over similar parts of 1/5th W.Y.R. ie A Coy from A Coy etc.

4. Dispositions in Reserve Area
   Headquarters in Reserve line are as follows:-
   Batt HQ. E.23.c.65 A Coy. E.30.a.66
   B Coy. E.22.d.2.4   C Coy E.22.d.15.90
   D Coy E.30.a.00.60.

5. Route
   Unless further ordered Coys will leave the Pushpool area by the following route:- Fork Roads F.20.b.45.60. Cross Roads F.20.b.00.94. Crucifix F.19.c.8.2 to PIGEON WOOD and LA BRAYELLE Road. This route will be carefully reconnoitred in daylight tomorrow by A and B Coys in morning

2nd & C and D Coys in afternoon.

6. Transport & Rations
The T.O. will send 1 complete
limber to each of present rendezvous
of A B C D HQ Coys tomorrow night
at 11 p.m. for conveyance of Lewis
guns, petrol tins etk. Rations for the
TANK detachment for consumption
on June 3rd to be brought up on one
of these limbers.

The T.O. will deliver rations and
water to respective Coys and Bttn
HQ in new area by the same limbers
which come for Lewis guns. Coy QMS
will hand over their rations
personally to an Officer of each Coy.
Each Coy will detail a guard of
1 N.C.O. and 3 men to accompany
their Lewis Guns.

7. Defence Schemes etc.
All Defence schemes, sets of
photographs, maps of the Section
programmes of work and trench
stores will be handed over to off'r
W.Y. Reg't.
Defence scheme etc. of 2/5th West
Yorks Reg't will be taken over on
relief

List of French stores handed over and taken over will be forwarded to Battn HQ by 9am on June 31st.

8. Reports

Confirmation of relief will be notified by BAB code or runner at once.

Arrival in new area will be notified by BAB code and runner.

9. Acknowledge.

Issued at 9.15 pm

K Sykes. Capt & Adjt
5th D. of Wellington's Regt.

Copies to :-
1-5   ABCD HQ Coys
  6   Adjt.
  7   TO & QM.
  8   Rear HQ
  9   186th I.B. (for infm)
 10   2/5th W.Y.R (" ")
 11   2/4th W.Y.R (" ")
12 13 War Diary
 14   Office

12.

Copy. 2nd Bn Manchester Regt
Operation Order No 18

1. Map Sht NE Ypres. 9.6.18

1. Relief.
The Batt. will relieve the 2/4th
York & Lancaster Regt in the Left Sub-sector
of the Right Section tomorrow night 3/4th.

2. Dispositions.
Coys. & Coys will behave as
follows:-
B Coy 5th Bn. We will relieve B Coy 1/4th
Y & L in the left front line.
A Coy 1st Bn. We will relieve C Coy 1/4th
Y & L in left front line.
C Coy 5th Bn. We will relieve D Coy 1/4th
Y & L in right front line.
D Coy 5th Bn. We will relieve A Coy 1/4th
Y & L in Reserve.

3. Guides.
Platoon guides will be provided
by 4th Y & L. Coy platoons will form
(ditto) will be at the bend of BETHUNE
AVENUE and BRITISH STREET at
E.28.d.2.9. at 9.45 p.m.

4. Order of Relief
   "C" Coy leaving their present position 9.0 p.m.
   "B"   "   "   "   "   "   9.10 p.m.
   H.Q.   "   "   "   "   "   9.30 p.m.
   "A"   "   "   "   "   "   9.50 p.m.
   "D"   "   "   "   "   "   9.50 p.m.
   Movement by platoons at 250 yds intervals.

5. Route
   LA BRAYELLE Road to BEARER POST
   E.23.d.35. thence by STOUT trench to
   E.23.b.5.4. (for B, C & H.Q. Coy) LA BRAYELLE
   AVENUE to E.30.a.S.H. CONNECTICUT
   trench - KETTENDY AVENUE - BRIDGE Trench
   (F.5.d.2.9. for Companies) where guides
   will be met.

6. Advance Party.
   An advance party of 1 Officer
   1 N.C.O. and 1 N.C.O. per platoon per
   Company will be attached to 2/4th
   & to be sent night 9/10th to reconnoitre new
   positions

7. Rations
   Rations and water of B, C & A
   Coys will be at CROSS in F.H.d.U.U.
   at 12 midnight.
   D Coy 5 Hqrs. Rations and water will

at the orch of [illegible] and ESSARTS
BLOUGUY ROAD at F.24.c.20.65 at 12
midnight.

7. Water Guards
    [illegible] will be carried on by the
    [illegible]

9. Defence Schemes etc.
    Defence Schemes, map of [illegible]
    photographs, maps of the sector,
    programme of work and a [illegible] sheet
    will be [illegible] taken over from 2/4th
    Yorks.
        Defence scheme if found any
    will be handed over the [illegible] [illegible]
    12th & 5th.
        [illegible] [illegible] handed over and
    [illegible] be forwarded to Batt. HQ
    by 9 a.m. 11th inst.

10. Reports
    Completion of relief will be
    reported [illegible] by wiring the word
    CERTAINLY
        [illegible] dispositions etc
    [illegible] [illegible] [illegible] will be sent by
    [illegible] to Battn. HQ by 9 a.m.
    11th inst.

Acknowledge
Send at 11:15 p.m.

I.M. Doe
Lieut. [?]
O. of Washington Rifles

Capacity –
1-5   M.B.A. & & Capt.
6   Lieut. M.G.
7   adjutant
8   [illegible]
9   156th Y.B. ([illegible])
10-11 Non Com'y
12   Officer

Secret   Copy No.
5th Duke of Wellingtons (WR) Regt
Operation order No 19
Ref Sheet 57 D.N.E./20000

1 Reorganisation
The divisional sector is being reorganised so as to reduce the number of troops in the front system, i.e. the trenches in front of the PURPLE SYSTEM
The front system will be held on the principle of outposts in open warfare, viz A picket line, a support line and a reserve line.
The troops in the Picket and Support line should not always occupy the same post, or even the same trench, but should change their positions periodically so as to deceive the enemy as to the strength in which the line is held, and the dispositions of our troops.

2 New dispositions etc.
The battalion will move into new positions tonight (16/17 June) as follows:-
A Coy will occupy the Picquet Line in HEDGE TRENCH garrisoning Posts 5 6 8 9 10 with 3 platoons. From these platoons they will find garrisons for the front posts K L M N O P. The officer on duty in front

posts will be provided by each of these platoons in turn.

The 4th platoon will be in Coy Reserve in CROSS TRENCH and garrison posts 1. 2. 3. 5. 6.
Coy HQ will move to present Support Coy HQ in CROSS TR occupied by B Coy.

D Coy will occupy the Picquet Line in HEDGE TRENCH garrisoning posts 12. 13. 14. 16. 17 with 3 platoons. From these platoons they will find garrisons (1 N.C.O. & 6) for the front line Posts U. T. Q. Front platoon HQ (S) will be occupied by the officer on duty, his orderly, and 4 men provided by the platoon supplying the officer and changed daily. The left platoon will garrison U post in front and Posts 16 & 17. The Centre platoon will garrison T post in front and No 14 post. The Right platoon will garrison Q Post in front and No 12 & 13 post.

The 4th platoon will be in Company Reserve in CROSS TRENCH and garrison posts 7. 8. 9. 10.

Company HQ will remain at the CHATEAU.

C Coy will remain in their present locations and will become Company in battalion Support. In case of alarm they will occupy the posts in F 26. a.

B Coy will move into battalion Reserve and will relieve the left Company of 2/4th Hants

Regt occupying dugouts, shelters etc in
BUCQUOY AVENUE, LEEDS TRENCH and
BRIDGE TRENCH.
Company HQ in LEEDS TR in F.25.b

3. Order of Move etc.
B Coy will move into new positions
immediately, after ~~dusk~~ the arrival of front line Reserve Platoons
A & D Coys will arrange their new dispositions
as soon as darkness allows. The 2 night
front posts of A Coy not ~~are~~ being disturbed
before 12.30 am.
Coys will report completion of reorganisation
by wiring the Code Words "names for leave
NIL".

4. Reconnaissance
Advance parties of one officer and one N.C.O
per platoon will reconnoitre their new
positions during daylight today. They
will then act as guides for their Coys
tonight.

5. Rations.
Rations will arrive at usual time tonight.
B Coys Rations will be dumped at HQ
Ration Dump at junction of BRIDGE TRENCH
with BUCQUOY Road. Other Coys as usual.

6. Trench Stores.

Trench Stores will be taken over in situ. Coys will forward lists of trench stores remaining in possession and taken over in their areas (in duplicate) by 10 am tomorrow 17th inst.

7. Acknowledge.

       K. Sykes. Capt & Adjt.
        5 Duke of Wellingtons

Copies to
- 1-4 A. B. C. D Coys
- 5 Adjt's office.
- 6. 186 Inf Bde (for inf)
- 7 2/4 Duke of Wellingtons (for inf)
- 8 2/4 Hants Regt (for inf)
- 9.10. War Diary

Secret/- Ref O.O. 19 para 2.

The instructions regarding
C Coy are cancelled and
the following substituted:-
C Coy will move to
NETTIEMORE AVENUE and
BRIDGE STREET in F 25 b,c,d
and F 26 c

               K Byles Capt & Adjt
               5 West Rid Regt

Copies to:-
1 - 4   A B C D Coy
5   Adj Office
6   K.O.Y.L.I. (for inf)
7   D of W (for inf)
8   Hants Regt (for inf)
9 + 10   War Diary

Secret.   Copy No 12
         5 Duke of Wellingtons Regt.
           Order No 20 d/ 16.6.18

1. Relief
  The 2/4 Hants Regt will relieve the
  Battn in the left sub-section on the
  nights of 17/18th and 18/19th
  Reliefs will take place as follows:-
  Night 17/18 June
     A Coy 2/4 Hants Regt will relieve D
  Coy 5 D of Well Regt in left front area
  C Coy 2/4 Hants will relieve B Co 5th
  D of Well. in Reserve Area.
  Night 18/19th June
     B Coy 2/4 Hants Regt will relieve A Co
  5th D of Well. Regt in right front area
  D Coy 2/4 Hants Regt will relieve C Co
  5th D of Well Regt in Reserve area.
  OC 5 Duke of Wellingtons Regt will
  remain in command of the Sub-
  Sector till completion of relief
  on the night 18/19th June
  On Relief Coys. of 5th Duke of Wellingtons
  will move to area vacated by
  Coys of 2/4 Hants Regt which relieve
  them, in Brigade Reserve.

2/ Guides
D + B Coys will provide platoon guides under a NCO to report to Lieut TOD on night of 17 June at Batt HQ at 8.45 pm. They will meet incoming Companies of the 2/4th Hants. Regt at junction of RETTEMOY AV. and GOMMECOURT TRENCH about F 25 a 2.7 at 9.30 pm

A + C Coys will provide platoon guides under a NCO + Batt. HQ 2 Guides to report to Lieut TOD on night June 18th at BHQ at 10.45 pm. They will meet incoming troops at same rendezvous at 11.30 pm

3/ Advance Parties
Advance Parties of 1 Officer per Coy and 1 NCO per platoon and a proportion of Signallers + Runners will be sent up by 2/4 Hants Regt 24 hours previous to relief.
Coys of 5 D of W. will each send 1 NCO per Platoon + 1 Officer and 1 Runner to reconnoitre new area on morning of relief.

4) **Rations**
Rations for A & C Coys 2/4 Hants Regt
will come up to Ration Dump of our
D & B Coys on night of 17th June.
The T.O will provide the necessary
guides.
Rations for D & B Coys will be sent
up to E 30 b 70 99 and E 30 d 5.9
to be at these rendez-vous by
12 midnight
D & B Coys will carry their Lewis
Guns by hand to new area
Ration arrangements for night
of 18th June will be notified later.

5) **Trench Stores &c**
All trench stores &c will be handed
and taken over most carefully.
Lists to be forwarded to Batt. H.Q
the morning after each relief.
Defence Schemes work in hand
and contemplated to be handed
over and taken over.

6) **Reports**
D & B Coys will notify Relief
Complete on night 17/18 by wiring
the word "SEVENTEEN"
A & C Coys will notify Relief Complete
on night 18/19th by wiring the word

"EIGHTEEN"

J. Acknowledge.

K. Sykes.
Capt & Adjt
5 West Rid? Regt

Copies to :-
1 - 5   A. B. C. D. HQ Coy
   6   Adjutant
   7   186? I B (for inf)
   8   2/4? Hants Regt (for inf)
   9   2/4? D of Well. Regt (for inf)
  10   TO + QM
  11   Rear HQ + Office
  12 + 13 War Diary

15/6/18

5/6?ure? Warwickshire Regt.
Battalion Order No. 24 d/23.6.18
Ref Map 57D 1/40000   57D NE 1/20000

1/ Reld? The Batt will be relieved in Reserve
   to the right Sector by the 13 KRRC on
   night of 24/25 of June.
     Bn Reld? The Batt will occupy
     Trenches vacated by the 13 KRRC ? at
   INTERVES?

2/ Relief Relief? Coys will be relieved by
   Companies in the following order:-

   A C   13 KRRC Platoons   MG C 5D/W/Regt
   AB   "   "   "
   BA   "   "   "
   DC   "   "   "
   DC   "   "   "

3/ Guides Platoon Guides at 9.2 B.M.Q? will
   report to M/C strong at Post JNQ at 9.45pm
   on 24/25 to Guide in Platoons of 13 KRRC C/OA
   Guides must be in possession of a route
   sketch showing their lines of relief. Each
   Guide ? will lead old guide to
   Junction of LA BRAYVEILLE Rd + STOUT
   tRENCH (E 23 c 7) & be there by 10.15pm

4/ Advance Party of 1 Officer per Coy + 1 NCO per

1. Report on the 13 KRCE will be up Corp Tonight outside of the 23/24 to accommodate their crew over. All those parties will be asked by 20 ladies from BSHO 1 at Duncans HO at 9:30 Pm 23rd at the Junction & E30 a 5) before City Sunday will proceed from there polices to be append at HQ.

5/ January 26/10 will escort a Plunder to escort City to the PoRTION to collect Firearm Contact liaison Peter Jone at Anonsly Thu K THIEVES

Please ensure this to at usual City during 21 11 pm 24th.

Conf: insure Little to team of THE ORCHARD

E 15/a La to There by 12 Analmity 24/25 Moreso Pn Back NO finish to eat the same lunch of 1AM 25th

C) Bolene Scheme All Bojhece scheme Atmosphere Police Preliminary & work throwh charges of the Kipti Seth, will be founder over lots of Silver houses over will be Jamemden La B NO THIEVES by la own asplace

7/ Compelling 1 Party will ask to collect to BSHD by doing dock loads NIL RETURN

6) Completion of Relief will be notified to HQ by wiring the Code Words "NIL RETURN"

7) Route on relief. On relief Coys will move out by Platoons at 100 yds interval by the following route
LA BRAYELLE RD - WILLOW PATCH TRACK - SOUASTRE - D.21 b 3.1 - COUIN - ST LEGER - AUTHIE - THIEVRES. Platoons will halt at a point between SOUASTRE & COUIN where hot tea will be prepared & issued to Coys will then cross [?] independently

8) Advance party under Maj. Brooke will arrange for billets, packs etc at THIEVRES.

9) Acknowledge

Sn Tod [?]
for Lieut [?] Adj
5th West Rgd. Regt

Cps to: 1-5 ABCD +HQ
6 186 Inf Bde
7 B K R R
8 TC + QM
9 Office
10 + 11 War Diary.

CONFIDENTIAL.

WAR DIARY

- of -

5TH. DUKE OF WELLINGTON'S REGIMENT.

1st to 31st July 1918.

(Volume 5.).

J Walker
Comdg.5th.Duke of Wellington's Regiment.
Lieut.Col.

186th Brigade,

62nd Division.

5th Bn. DUKE OF WELLINGTON'S (W.R.) REGT.

J U L Y, 1 9 1 8.

Army Form C. 2118.

WAR DIARY
or
INTELLIGENCE SUMMARY.
(Erase heading not required.)

Instructions regarding War Diaries and Intelligence Summaries are contained in F. S. Regs., Part II. and the Staff Manual respectively. Title pages will be prepared in manuscript.

Place	Date	Hour	Summary of Events and Information	Remarks and references to Appendices
Bat. Hqs. SERET. N.d.	1918. July 1st.		A bright hot day. "A" Company were on the range in C.25.c. Where the company fired 4 practices and did section and platoon training. "B" & "D" Companies did section and platoon work in a field in I.7.c. and "C" Company similar work in the vicinity of HURKNISS FARM. Games of cricket were played in the afternoon.	
	2nd.		A bright warm day. Training in section and platoon work was done by three companies in the morning, and one company was firing on the range C.25.c. morning and afternoon. Games were played during the afternoon and evening.	
	3rd.		Rather a dull day. Training continued by three companies in section and platoon work in the morning and one company on the range morning and afternoon. Games of the Battalion Cricket League were played off in the afternoon and evening.	
	4th.		Fine day. Training continued - one company on the range and three companies doing section and platoon work during the morning. The company on the range continued their work during the afternoon - the remainder played games. Cricket matches between companies were also played in the evening.	
	5th.		A bright day. Usual training was carried out - one company on the range morning and afternoon, and the three remaining companies on the training grounds in the morning only. Games were played in the afternoon and evening.	
	6th.		The usual training programme was continued with one company on the range and the remainder doing section and platoon work. Games were played during the afternoon and evening and a concert was held in the evening.	
	7th.		Church services in the morning for various denominations. The 310th. Bde. R.F.A. held Sports in the village in the afternoon and were witnessed by the battalion.	

Original

5th. DUKE OF WELLINGTON'S REGT. T.F.

Army Form C. 2118.

WAR DIARY
or
INTELLIGENCE SUMMARY.
(Erase heading not required.)

Instructions regarding War Diaries and Intelligence Summaries are contained in F. S. Regs., Part II. and the Staff Manual respectively. Title pages will be prepared in manuscript.

Place	Date	Hour	Summary of Events and Information	Remarks and references to Appendices
	1918. July 8th.		Training continued in morning. Brigade sports were held at LENU during the afternoon. The Division provided lorries for the journey from THIEVRES to LENU for the men.	
	9th.		The very hot weather continued. Men all had baths at PAS during the day. "C" Coy. were on the range C.25.a.	
	10th.		Showery day but did not interfere with training. "B" & "C" Coys. practised "the attack" on ground in C.25.c. "D" Coy. were on the Range all day in C.25.a. and "A" Coy. did Company training on THIEVRES Football Ground I.7.a. at 12.30pm. the 186th. Inf. Bde. Trench mortar battery gave a Stokes Mortar demonstration to whole battalion on ground C.25. showing the barrage effect of Stokes Mortars on a strong point and its effect for anti-aircraft purposes.	
	11th.		Training continued. Games in the afternoon. Showery weather.	
	12th.		Ditto.	
	13th.		Ditto.	
	14th.		Usual Divine Services held during morning for different denominations. Orders were received for the 62nd. Division to move by strategical trains to a new area and to join the 22nd Corps. The battalion less "A" Coy. entrained at MONDICOURT STATION at 12 midnight accompanied by transport.	
	15th.		Battalion in the train all day. Went via AMIENS, BEAUVAIS, EPLUCHES, PARIS, MONTEREAU and ST. MORITIN (Ref. Maps. INMB 11 1/100,000, DIENS 17, BEAUVAIS 21). Halts of an hour each were made at EPLUCHES and MONTEREAU for meals. The troops were given an ovation by the French populace especially round PARIS. "A" Coy. travelled by train with 527th. Coy. A.S.C. from MONDICOURT at 9.am. A very hot day.	

Army Form C. 2118.

5TH BATT. OF WELLINGTON'S REGT. T.F.

WAR DIARY
or
INTELLIGENCE SUMMARY.
(Erase heading not required.)

Instructions regarding War Diaries and Intelligence Summaries are contained in F. S. Regs., Part II. and the Staff Manual respectively. Title pages will be prepared in manuscript.

Original

Place	Date	Hour	Summary of Events and Information	Remarks and references to Appendices
Ref.map. FRENCH MAP. 50 CHALONS & ARCIS No.67.	1918. July 16th.		Battalion (less "A" Coy.) arrived at MAILLY au CAMP at 10.a.m. After detraining the Battalion less transport embussed to ST. HILAIRE just N.W. of CHALONS where billets were obtained. Transport followed by march route.	
	17th.		Battalion (less "A" Coy. detached) moved by march route to APHIS via VANOUEUS and JALONS. Transport also moved by road. The battalion became part of the XXII Corps under the orders of the Fifth French Army. The battalion was entirely in the French area. News was received that "A" Coy. was bivouaced at MAILLY au CAMP. A very severe thunderstorm occurred during the night. Good news of the French and American counter thrust near SOISSONS during the day.	
	18th.		The battalion (less "A" Coy. detached) remained at ATHIS for the day. Inspections were carried out under company arrangements and all companies had a bathing parade to a pool near the village. The band played selections in the village square in the evening.	
	19th.		The battalion (less "A" Coy. detached) moved out of ATHIS at 6.35a.m. and moved to GERMAINE via MOURS-AVENAY. The destination was reached about 10.a.m. and companies fell out under the cover of the woods in the immediate vicinity of the village. The Commanding Officer, the Adjutant and company commanders reconnoitred the routes to COURMAGNON in the afternoon. About 8.p.m. news was received that the battalion would be required to attack on the following morning together with the remainder of the division. "A" Coy. arrived at GERMAINE in the afternoon having been brought from MAILLY le CAMP by motor lorry.	
Ref.Map. 1:Tac:3.G 1/50000. (French).	20th.		The battalion with the 62nd. (W.R.) Division concentrated at GERMAINE in preparation to attacking enemy positions N.W. of COURMAGNON on the following day in conjunction with 51st. British Division and the 22nd. French Colonial Division. At 12 midnight the battalion marched to forming up positions on the western edge of FORET DE LA MONTAGNE just E. of COURMAGNON CHATEAU. Owing to great concentration of French transport on the road it was not until 4.am that the troops were in position. The Coy's. were accompanied by their Lewis Gun limbers and battalion H.Q. had 1 G.S.A. Cart and 1 bomb limber.	
	20th.		Zero hour for the attack was 8.am. The XXII Corps attacked with the 62nd. Division on the right and the 51st and the French troops cooperated in the attack on the left. Division on Night	

Original

5TH. DUKE OF WELLINGTON'S REGT. T.F.

WAR DIARY
or
INTELLIGENCE SUMMARY.
(Erase heading not required.)

Army Form C. 2118.

Instructions regarding War Diaries and Intelligence
Summaries are contained in F. S. Regs., Part II.
and the Staff Manual respectively. Title pages
will be prepared in manuscript.

Place	Date	Hour	Summary of Events and Information	Remarks and references to Appendices
	JULY 20TH.		and left. 2nd 187th. Inf. Bde. (on right) and 185th. Inf. Bde. (on left) attacked side by side and had as their objective a line just S. of MERY - FLESQUY - One kilometre west of JUBILLY - fork roads N. of BAROT - the 185th. Inf. Bde. attacked on a 3 battalion front each on a frontage of about 700 yards - 5th. Duke of Wellington's on the right, 2/4th. Hants Regt. in the centre and 2/4th. Duke of Wellington's on the left. The orders of the Brigade were to leap frog through the 185th. and 187th. Inf. Bdes 3rd to capture the final objective - a line one kilometre S.E. of MARION - Railway about 200 yds. S.E. of RAMENY STATION - to a point about 2 kilometres S.S.W. of MERY. In the event of the 185th and 187th. Inf. Bdes was only partially successful the Brigade had to be prepared to leap frog through and continue the advance, but had to be careful not to allow troops to become prematurely engaged during the earlier stages of the advance. Duke of Wellington's Regt. moved forward 400 yards in rear of the front at Zero hour 5th. Duke of Wellington's regt. moved forward 400 yards in rear of the front brigades accompanied by Lewis Gun Limbers and S.A.A. and Bomb carts. "A" and "D" Coys. were to capture the first objective - "A" Coy. on the left and "D" Coy. on the right. We left Coys. capturing MOULGRE VILLAGE and the 2nd Mt. Coy. the area N. of BOULGUE Village. "B" Coy. (left) and "C" Coy. (right) were to leap frog through and capture the final objective. The dividing line between the battalion and 2/4th. Hants regt. was a line between JUBILLY and BOULGUS both inclusive - western corner of wood about 1 kilo. south by west of MARION (exclusive) B.G and N.W. Boys. advanced in N.W. direction through the BOIS de CURIANCE to BOUSLA leap through the BOIS d'BOULLA to the Village of OUSNI. Here the position was found to be distinctly obscure and nothing definite could be ascertained of the advance of the 187th. Inf. Bde. although it was said they had captured JUBILLY. the enemy shelling was very intense in the BOIS D'ECHILLI and 2 OURNAS - Three Coys. and Battalion HQ suffering many casualties. A position was taken up short N.E.of the JUBILLY - BOIS D'ECHILI overlooking the village of CANIHAB and the Valley. "A" and "D" Coys. advanced behind the 185th. Inf. Bde. at Zero hour & as soon as along the COURBAYON - POUZEL Road and then in a N.W. direction through the BOIS de POURGY. On reaching the western edge of BOIS de POURGY they were subjected to heavy artillery fire and suffered 25% casualties. This Position in front of them was not clear. The next Machine Brigade advanced to the field in rear of CANIHAB and & BOIS de POURGY and would have got on. B. Coy. and "C" Coy. ... and "D" Coys. as soon as POURGY wood and the BOIS de POURGY took up a position and the two Wellingdalls and Hants and "A" and "D" Coys. took up a position W. of the JUBILLY - POURGY Road. These two	

Army Form C. 2118.

WAR DIARY
or
INTELLIGENCE SUMMARY.
(Erase heading not required.)

5th. BN. OF WILTSHIRE REGT.

Instructions regarding War Diaries and Intelligence
Summaries are contained in F. S. Regs., Part II.
and the Staff Manual respectively. Title pages
will be prepared in manuscript.

Place	Date	Hour	Summary of Events and Information	Remarks and references to Appendices
	July 20th		Coys. were out of touch with battalion H.Q. throughout the day. During the evening the battalion received instructions to attack the villages of ARRAUX and MEROY from the N. and W. and to consolidate them after capture. This attack was considered necessary as elements of various regiments in shell holes between country were in advance of being cut off by the enemy. This attack was to be made in artillery formation and timed for 8 p.m. The orders were only received at 6.45 p.m. and as the battalion was not in touch with "A" and "D" Coys. a scheme was prepared to attack with B & C Coys. and H.Qrs. from the N.W. edge of BOIS DE PETITS CHAMPS using the N.E. of TINE and extreme S. edge of BOIS DE PETITS CHAMPS. The difficulty of finding positions through the wood without previous reconnaissance of elements of the battalion did not reach the position in ground until zero hour. Company Commanders and P.C. staff went forward to reconnoitre and found an almost impossible position. The two villages lay in the bottom of a valley and attacking troops would have to cross the open for 800 yards under a withering M.G. barrage from the front and from a strong M.G. nest at S.E. corner of BOIS DE PETITS CHAMPS. Touch was obtained with 2do H.V., and the attack was cancelled. B and C Coys. and H.Qrs. then returned to their positions overlooking GOURNAY.	
	21st		Bettn. H.Q. obtained touch with A and D Coys. on the western edge of BOIS DE POURCY during the morning. On obtaining touch the tactical positions of the battalion were reorganised. A and D Coys. remained on the western edge of BOIS DE POURCY. "B" Coy. remained on the western edge of BOIS D'ECUEIL overlooking GOURNAY. "C" Coy. and Battalion H.Q. moved to a point about 200 metres N.W. of X in ARFEAUX at northern end of BOIS DE POURCY. There the battalion remained all day. Orders were received during the afternoon that the battalion had to attack the BOIS DU PETITS CHAMP (part of which was still in enemy hands) next morning. During the day the battalion was subjected to heavy enemy shelling.	
	22nd		The battalion received orders to capture the BOIS DU REIMS part of the BOIS DU REIMS as far west as the track between GOURNAY and CHAUMUZY, the idea of the attack being for "A" & "D" Coys. to advance along the north and for B and C Coys. along the south limits of the objective on a one platoon front of 50 yards. The leading platoons to endeavour to push forward to the furthest limit of the objective, one platoon to be dropped from the rear of the attacking columns at distances of 300 metres. These platoons to form strong points capable of all round defence. After the strong points had been established by platoons the	

Original

Army Form C. 2118.

5TH. DUKE OF WELLINGTON'S REGT. T.F.

WAR DIARY
or
INTELLIGENCE SUMMARY.
(Erase heading not required.)

Instructions regarding War Diaries and Intelligence Summaries are contained in F.S. Regs., Part II. and the Staff Manual respectively. Title pages will be prepared in manuscript.

Place	Date	Hour	Summary of Events and Information	Remarks and references to Appendices
	1918. July 22nd.		latter to send out section patrols to search the wood for any enemy posts or personnel between themselves and adjoining posts. The attack was covered by an artillery barrage which came down at zero about 250 yards in front of the existing front line (roughly N. and S. line through the wood N. of D. in BOIS de REIMS. The barrage remained stationary for ten minutes and then crept forward at the rate of 100 yards inten minutes till clear of the final objective. The heavy artillery bombarded selected areas during the advance. Machine Guns assisted the advance by direct fire on the southern slopes of the hill and south of it and French machine guns covered the northern slopes of the hill. Company commanders and Battalion H... Staff carefully reconnoitred the jumping off positions in liaison with the French who were holding the existing front line on the eastern edge of BOIS de REIMS CHAMPS early in the morning. Troops were all in position by 11.30am and zero hour was at 12.15pm. Almost immediately the right company ("A") met with slight opposition and captured one prisoner and were able to get about 250 yards into the wood before they encountered a strong point held by the enemy consisting of 4 machine guns and about 2. personnel. After a severe struggle the resistance was overcome and the garrison and M.G's captured. After proceeding another 200 yards they met with similar opposition and captured another 6 machine guns and a further batch of 30/35 prisoners. In this latter operation the right company ("A") were assisted by the supporting Coy. ("D") as casualties had been heavy. They then pressed on almost another 300 yards capturing several isolated machine gun posts for the most part consisting of single machine guns, until they met with really serious opposition from a strong point about the centre of the wood whose exact position was difficult to locate. Having suffered serious casualties they withdrew 300 yards and consolidated their position in a series of posts from the N. edge of the wood to about the centre. By patrols these two companies ("A" & "D") endeavoured to gain touch with the two companies ("B" & "C") operating on the southern edge of the wood. They were assisted in the consolidation by two platoons of 1/5th. Battn. Devon Regt. sent up by brigade to reinforce. On the south edge of the wood, opposition was encountered immediately from a strong Point about 50 yards from the jumping off point just outside the wood. This held up the advance for some time but was finally encircled from both flanks and captured with the help of the rear company ("B")	

5th.D.of WELLINGTON'S REGT.T.F.

Army Form C. 2118.

WAR DIARY
or
INTELLIGENCE SUMMARY.

(Erase heading not required.)

Instructions regarding War Diaries and Intelligence Summaries are contained in F.S. Regs. Part II. and the Staff Manual respectively. Title pages will be prepared in manuscript.

Place	Date	Hour	Summary of Events and Information	Remarks and references to Appendices
	1918. July 22nd.		8 Machine Guns and 50 enemy garrison were captured. A series of 5 enemy strong points were encountered at the S. edge of the wood all of which were quickly dealt with and the machine guns and garrisons captured. These yielded about 20 Machine Guns and 80 prisoners. Isolated small posts were met with and easily overcome, the forward company ("C") finally reaching its objective at the N.W. edge of the wood after having suffered heavily after having reached its objective "C" Coy. was threatened with envelopement by a very strong counter-attack which the enemy launched from the North. "C" Coy. were eventually surrounded. The enemy captured the most forward post held by 2/Lieut. STORRY. He then charged the other two posts of "C" Coy. with fixed bayonets. A Lewis Gun was put into action and caused great damage amongst the enemy compelling him to retire temporarily. They came on again using stick bombs freely and got so close and in superior numbers that the position became untenable. Capt. J.B. COGHILL M.C. withdrew his few remaining men into a shell hole in the open on the S. edge of the wood where they were subjected to rifle and machine gun fire from the wood and from the valley at QUITROM. A shell burst in the shell hole putting the Lewis Gun out of action and no other means was open but to retire further. This was done in a westerly direction followed closely by the enemy, and finally the elements of the company - 2 officers and 6 other ranks fought their way out to "B" Coys. posts. "B" Coy. in the meantime had made a strong point about 700 yards in the wood away from the jumping off point and with the assistance of a company of the 1/5th. Devon Regt. they consolidated a line from the S. edge of the wood to meet "A" & "D" Coys. The total prisoners taken were 2 officers and 206 other ranks and 41 machine guns. The prisoners belonged to 53rd. Prussian Regt. Our artillery barrage was very accurate and caused many casualties. The troops who were attacked were taken completely by surprise and had only just completed a relief an hour before zero hour. After the attack was launched the enemy artillery reply was negligible but as the afternoon wore on and he became aware of the situation the edges of the wood and all approaches were subjected to a heavy counter bombardment. The new line was consolidated by nightfall and held by the battalion with the help of 1/5th. Devons. During the night the enemy pushed out strong reconnoitring parties to locate and endeavour to surprise our line but on each occasion was repulsed. Our casualties during the operation were 5 officers and approximately 150 other ranks. The battalion was heartily congratulated by the Corps, Divisional and Brigade Commanders on a particularly fine night which had had the effect of greatly reducing the enemy's power of resistance. The whole operation was carried	

Army Form C. 2118.

5th. BAT. DUKE OF WELLINGTON'S REGT. A.I.F.

WAR DIARY
or
INTELLIGENCE SUMMARY.
(Erase heading not required.)

Instructions regarding War Diaries and Intelligence Summaries are contained in F. S. Regs., Part II. and the Staff Manual respectively. Title pages will be prepared in manuscript.

Place	Date	Hour	Summary of Events and Information	Remarks and references to Appendices
	July 23rd.		through with great vigour and all commanders led their men with great dash and determination. In conjunction with attacks on right and left the 8th. West Yorks Regt. at 6.am attacked from our new front line in BOIS DU PETIT CHAMP with the object of clearing the wood completely. This attack was only partially successful. They took a few more prisoners and machine guns. The battalion continued to hold the line captured the previous day. Enemy artillery fire throughout the day was very heavy.	
	24th.		The battalion was ordered to round up the enemy strong point which was still holding out just on the spur immediately south of BOIS DU PETITS CHAMPS. The enemy had been very quiet during the night and suspicious were entertained that he had cleared away from the BOIS DU PETITS CHAMPS. The Commanding Officer (Lieut. Col. J. Walker D.S.O.) led a patrol at 6.am along the south edge of the wood to reconnoitre the strong Point. Encountering no opposition the patrol went forward and walked into the strong point which was found unoccupied. Two enemy trench mortars and a search light were captured in the strong point. Patrols were sent forward during the day and the whole of BOIS DU PETITS CHAMPS was found to be clear of the enemy. Later in the day the 186th. Inf. Bde. front was readjusted. The battalion moved on to the slope of the hill S. of BOIS DU PETITS CHAMPS overlooking GUEUDOT Hamlet and became support battalion to 9th. Durham Light Infantry who were holding a line in front of GUEUDON. The enemy was very active with his artillery between 7.pm and 10.pm. Much gas being used in the valleys.	
	25th.		Quiet day on the battalion front. Heavy fighting in progress on the french front north of us.	
	26th.		Quiet day on battalion front. Hostile artillery aggressive but chiefly in the woods.	

Army Form C. 2118.

WAR DIARY
or
INTELLIGENCE SUMMARY.
(Erase heading not required.)

Place	Date	Hour	Summary of Events and Information	Remarks and references to Appendices
	July 27th		Wet day. Heavy showers of rain. At 1.P.M. patrols of the 1/6th. Inf. Bde. followed by stronger forces, advanced from the line just in front of VITENCH and MARAUX and occupied a line from BOIS DE LOUVROY(west of Cl. DE RETS) exclusive, along ridge in a S.W. direction to River ARDRE near GUMURY. This battalion followed, behind 2/4th. Duke of Wellington's Regt. on the right, 2/4th. Leeds Regt. (in front) and 9th. Durham Light Infantry (in support) on the left. No opposition was encountered and the line was gradually advanced. Towards evening the boys Bayed?? came into action and set held up by strong enemy opposition in front of BLIGNY.	
	28th		The Brigade was ordered to continue the advance and to occupy the old French front line north of the village of BLIGNY from the west edge of BOIS DE REIMS to the River ARDRE. The advance was continued about 5 a.m. Very little progress was made owing to intense enemy artillery fire which was most accurate. Machine gun fire was also encountered from ridges to right and left. Our Divisional artillery probably owing to the sticky roads and tracks after the rain had not got into new positions in following up the advance and were not able to give counter artillery resistance. The 2/4th. Hants Regt. and 2/4th. Duke of Wellington's Regt. endeavoured many times to get forward but suffered many casualties under the enemy barrage fire. During the evening both battalions gained their objectives and found safety closer of the enemy. The battalion was still in support to the 2/4th. Duke of Wellington's Regt. and followed them up during the day in close liaison. We suffered some casualties from enemy artillery during the day which was very intense at times. At night the brigade was relieved by 187th. Inf. Bde.	
	29th		At 2.3.a.m. the battalion was relieved by 2/4th.King's Own Yorkshire Light Infantry. On relief the battalion became Divisional Reserve and took up a line about 300 yards in front of MARAUX with battalion H.Q. at VIENCH. The men were all utterly worn out, are exhausted after 3 days of very hard fighting in most difficult country. Their morale was still high but they were physically exhausted. The casualties to the battalion in the weeks fighting had been particularly heavy - about 15 officers and 400 other ranks, leaving only a composite company of about 150 fighters.	
	30th		The battalion rested all day. The battalion remained in Divisional Reserve in front of MARAUX.	

(Original)

5th. DUKE OF WELLINGTON'S REGT. T.F.

Army Form C. 2118.

WAR DIARY
or
INTELLIGENCE SUMMARY.
(Erase heading not required.)

Instructions regarding War Diaries and Intelligence Summaries are contained in F.S. Regs., Part II. and the Staff Manual respectively. Title pages will be prepared in manscript.

Place	Date	Hour	Summary of Events and Information	Remarks and references to Appendices
	July.			
	30th		During the evening the battalion marched back to bivouacs in a point just south of second M of GOURNAMON. Battalion extremely tired but in good spirits.	
Bed. Aug. CINGIS, 1/100,000	31st.		A very fine day. Battalion marched on to new bivouacs near ST. IMOGES. The General Officer commanding XIII Corps - Lieut. General Sir A.. Godley K.C.B., K.C.M.G. visited the battalion and was introduced to representatives of companies and battalion H.Q. who had taken part in recent operations.	

Special order of the day by Lieut Genl commanding 4 Lord Rawly xx " Rosdick Corps

C.O.T (W.R) Durham in [signature] in [illegible]

[signature] Lieut. Col.
Commdg. 5th. D.of W. (Duke of Wellington's Regiment.

Original

5th. DUKE OF WELLINGTON'S REGT. T.F.

Army Form C. 2118.

WAR DIARY
or
INTELLIGENCE SUMMARY.
(Erase heading not required.)

Instructions regarding War Diaries and Intelligence Summaries are contained in F. S. Regs., Part II. and the Staff Manual respectively. Title pages will be prepared in manuscript.

Place	Date	Hour	Summary of Events and Information	Remarks and references to Appendices
			APPENDICES.	
			CASUALTIES etc.	
			Major F. Brook, D.S.O., M.C. Transferred to 2/4th.Hants regt. 14.7.18.	
			Lieut. A. Brown. do. 9.7.18.	
			2/Lieut. C.A. Eason. do. do.	
			" A.E. Lowe. do. do.	
			" H.L. Burgood. do. do.	
			Capt. E.A. Dykes. wounded. 20.7.18.	
			" V.V. Horrey's M.C. do. 22.7.18.	
			" A.V. Broadbent M.C. hospital – sick. 22.7.18.	
			Lieut. L. Renner M.C. wounded. 21.7.18.	
			" F.H. White. do. 20.7.18.	
			2/Lieut. D.R.W.L. Thorpe. wounded (gas). 24.7.18.	
			" L.B. Moore. wounded.(Remained at duty) 20.7.18.	
			" L.A.B. Haigh. do. 20.7.18.	
			" F.H. Barnes. do. 22.7.18.	
			" H. Greenwood. do. 22.7.18.	
			" L.T. Walker. do. 22.7.18.	
			" B.H. Storry. missing. 22.7.18.	
			" L. Brook. hospital – sick. 14.7.18.	
			" G.R. Lunshee. do. (at duty) 14.7.18.	
			Capt. & Adjt. C.H.W. Culliff (wounded at duty) 22.7.18.	
			OTHER RANKS.	
			Killed. 44.	
			Died of wounds. 8.	
			Wounded. 268.	
			Wounded at duty. 4.	
			Missing. 38.	

5th. DUKE OF WELLINGTON'S REGT. B.E.F.

Army Form C. 2118.

WAR DIARY
or
INTELLIGENCE SUMMARY.
(Erase heading not required.)

Place	Date	Hour	Summary of Events and Information	Remarks and references to Appendices
			A P P E N D I C E S (contd.)	
			D R A F T S etc.	
			Lieut. A. Chelsey.)	
			Lieut. W.C. Sidders.) Joined Battalion. 27.7.18.	
			2/Lieut. J. Forritt.)	
			2/Lieut. E.R. Dunshee. Retd. from Hospital. 6.7.18.	
			" T.R. Norton ..S. do. 4.7.18.	
			" F. Chapman. do. 4.7.18.	
			2 other ranks. 10.7.18.	
			30 other ranks. 11.7.18.	
			3 other ranks. 12.7.18.	
			111 other ranks. 25.7.18.	
			6 other ranks. 25.7.18.	

J Walker. Lieut.Col.
Commdg. 5th. Duke of Wellington's Regiment.

Vme Armée

Etat-Major
3me Bureau

No. 1863/3

Q. G., le 30 Juillet 1918

ORDRE GENERAL No. 63

Au moment où le XXII C.A. Britannique est appelé à quitter la Vme Armée, le Général Commandant l'Armée lui exprime toute la reconnaissance et toute l'admiration qu'ont mérité les hauts faits qu'il vient d'accomplir.

A peine débarqué, tenant à honneur de participer à la contre offensive victorieuse qui venait d'arreter la furieuse ruée de l'ennemi sur la MARNE et commençait à le rejeter en désordre vers le Nord, précipitant ses mouvements, réduisant à l'extrême la durée de ses reconnaissances, le XXII C.A. s'est jeté avec ardeur dans la Mêlée.

Poussant sans répit ses efforts, harcelant, talonnant l'ennemi il a, pendant 10 jours successifs d'âpres combats, fait sienne cette vallée de l'ARDRE largement arrosée de son sang.

Grâce au courage héroïque et à la ténacité proverbiale des fils de la GRANDE-BRETAGNE, les efforts continus et répétés de ce brave Corps d'Armée n'ont pas été vains :

21 Officiers, plus de 1300 soldats prisonniers, 140 mitrailleuses 40 canons enlevés à l'ennemi, dont 4 divisions ont été successivement malmenées et refoulées,
la haute vallée de l'ARDRE reconquise avec les hauteurs qui la dominent au Nord et au Sud.
tel est le bilan de la participation Britannique à l'effort de la Vme Armée.

ECOSSAIS de la MONTAGNE, sous le Commandement du Général CARTER-CAMPBELL, Commandant la 51me Division,
Enfants du YORKSHIRE, sous le Commandement du Général BRAITHWAITE, Commandant la 62me Division,
Cavaliers NEO-ZELANDAIS et AUSTRALIENS,
Vous tous, Officiers et soldats du 22me C.A., si brillamment commandés par le Général Sir A. GODLEY, vous venez d'ajouter une page glorieuse à votre histoire.

MARFAUX, CHAUMUZY, MONTAGNE de BLIGNY, ces noms prestigieux pourront être écrits en lettres d'or dans les annales de vos régiments.

Vos amis Français se souviendront avec émotion de votre brillante bravoure et de votre parfaite camaraderie de combat.

LE GENERAL COMMANDANT LA Vme ARMEE,

' BERTHOLOT '

SPECIAL ORDER

By

Lieutenant-General Sir A. J. GODLEY, K.C.B., K.C.M.G.,

Commanding XXII Corps.

The following Order of the Day by General Bertholet commanding Fifth (French) Army, together with the Corps Commander's reply to it, are published for the information of all ranks.

The Corps Commander wishes this Order to be distributed as widely as possible, and to be read out on Parade, and takes this opportunity of expressing to the Commanders, Staffs and all Ranks of the 51st (Highland) and the 62nd (West Riding) Divisions, and all the Corps Troops, his thanks for the loyal assistance and support that he has had from them during the recent arduous operations.

He takes this opportunity of again expressing his admiration of the conspicuous valour and endurance of the troops and trusts that it may be his good fortune to have them again under his command in any future operations.

Alix de la Voye

Headquarters,
31.7.1918.

D.A. & Q.M.G.

and will form up as close to their objectives as possible.

7. Lewis Gun Limbers, Pack Animals, S.A.A. Carts will accompany Batt. H.Q. and Coys as far as practicable. Tools will be issued by R.S.M. to Coys at the Starting Point (COURTAGNON). These are to be given to Riflemen.

8. The general direction of attack is N.W.

9. Reports will be sent to Batt. H.Q. as often as possible. Reporting of capture of objectives or villages to be done at once.

10. Battalion H.Q. at commencement of operation will be huts in front of COURTAGNON CHATEAU. Batt. H.Q. will be marked by a Blue & White Signal Flag.

1) 1 Section of Machine Gun Battalion is attached to Battalion. 2 Guns will support the Right of the attack and 2 Guns the left.

Khyber Capt Adjt

Copies to A. B. C. D. H.Q. Coys.
   Adjutant
   War Diary (2)
   2/4 Hants Regt
   2/4 D. of Well Regt
   Office

Secret.   Copy No. 7

5th Duke of Wellington's Regt
Operation Order No. 126.

Ref. Maps. French Map REIMS 1/80000.

1. The Battalion is taking part in an attack by the 62nd (W.R) Division on enemy positions N.W. of COURTAGNON. A French Colonial Division is attacking on the right of this Division and the 51st British Division on the left.
   The first stage will be captured by 185th Bde (Right) and 187th Bde (Left).
   The second stage will be captured by 186th Bde.

2. Areas of attack are marked on maps issued to Coys.
   5th Duke of Wellingtons is attacking on the right of 186 Inf. Bde with 2/4 Hants Regt on left and the French on the right

3. A & B. Coys will capture first objective – A. Co. on the right – B. Coy on the left – the left Coy

capturing BOULEUS village and the right boy. The area N of BOULEUS village to the Divisional northern Boundary bounded by the "Ride" N.W. of the triangular Wood about 500 yards N of BOULEUS village – Wood inclusive.

C & D. Coys will capture the second objective each on a 350 yards frontage (approximately) D. Coy. on the left and C. Coy. on the right. Objectives as marked on the maps already issued.

4. Coys will attack on a three Platoon frontage with one Platoon in Reserve.

5. Zero hour is 8 am on 20th July 1918.

6. The Battalion will form up in the wood just S of COURTAGNON-CHATEAU N of COURTAGNON-POIRY Road.
   At Zero hour Coys will move by previously reconnoitred routes 4000 yards in rear of leading Brigades

TRANSLATION

Vme Armée
————————
Etat-Major
3me Bureau
————————
No. 1863/3

Q. G., July 30th, 1918.

ORDER OF THE DAY No. 63.

      Now that the XXII British Corps has received orders to leave the Fifth (French) Army, the Army Commander expresses to all the thanks and admiration which the great deeds, that it has just accomplished, deserve.

      The very day of its arrival, feeling in honour bound to take part in the victorious counter-attack which had just stopped the enemy's furious onslaught on the Marne, and had begun to hurl him back in disorder to the North, the XXII Corps, by forced marches and with minimum opportunity for reconnaissance, threw itself with ardour into the battle.

      By constant efforts, by harrying and by driving back the enemy for ten successive days, it has made itself master of the Valley of the ARDRE, which it has so freely watered with its blood.

      Thanks to the heroic courage and proverbial tenacity of the British, the continued efforts of this brave Army Corps have not been in vain.

      21 Officers and 1300 Other Ranks taken prisoners, 140 Machine Guns and 40 Guns captured from an enemy, four of whose Divisions have been successively broken and repulsed; the Upper Valley of the ARDRE, with its surrounding heights to the North and South, reconquered; such is the record of the British share in the operations of the Fifth Army.

      Highlanders under the orders of General Carter-Campbell, commanding the 51st Division; Yorkshire lads under the orders of General Braithwaite, commanding the 62nd Division; Australian and New Zealand Mounted Troops; all officers and men of the XXII Army Corps, so ably commanded by General Sir A. Godley, you have added a glorious page to your history.

      MARFAUX, CHAUMUZY, MONTAGNE de BLIGNY---all these famous names will be written in letters of gold in the annals of your regiments.

      Your French comrades will always remember with emotion your splendid gallantry and your perfect fellowship in the fight.

      ' BERTHOLOT '

      le General Commandant,
      la Vme Armée.

Headquarters,
XXII Corps, 30th July, 1918.

My dear General,

I have received your most kind letter of farewell and Order of the Day addressed to me and the XXII Corps, and both on my own behalf and on behalf of all the officers, non-commissioned officers and men of the Corps I thank you most deeply.

That we have been fortunate enough to participate under your Command in this, the Second Battle of the Marne, will ever be a source of great pride to us all, and we count ourselves lucky to have been so closely associated with you and our gallant French comrades of your Army.

It is with deep regret that we leave your Command, where we have been very happy and where we hope we have made many friends.

Your Order will be highly valued by us all. I am having copies made which will be circulated to all Regiments before they leave and will be read to the troops, so that all will know that their efforts have been appreciated and will be aware of the high praise you have been good enough to bestow.

I would like to take this opportunity of asking you to convey to your Staff our great appreciation of all the help they have given us. No trouble has been too great for them to take on our behalf and everything possible has been done for us.

In the name of the XXII Corps I wish the Fifth Army and its Commander continued success and prosperity, and we all hope that the best of good fortune may attend you till the final victory is assured.

Yours sincerely,

(sd.) ALEX. J. GODLEY.

- - - - - - - - - - - - - - - - - -

SPECIAL ORDER OF THE DAY
by
Major General W.P. BRAITHWAITE, C.B.
Commanding 62nd (West Riding) Division.

31st July 1918.

The operations which commenced on the 20th July, were brought to a successful termination at midnight on the 30th July.

During the whole of this period the 62nd (West Riding) Division has had continuous fighting, manoeuvring, and marching in new and, hitherto, unknown country of a character entirely different from anything in which it has operated before during this campaign. Especially have the densely wooded slopes of the BOIS DE REIMS been a difficulty for troops unaccustomed to Wood Fighting.

But neither the difficulty of the country, nor the determined and bitter resistance of the enemy, have militated against the victorious operations of the Division.

The Division made a great name for itself at the Battle of CAMBRAI. It enhanced that reputation at BUCQUOY where it withstood the attacks of some of the best of the German troops up to that time flushed with success. It has, in this great battle, set the seal on its already established reputation as a fighting force of the first quality.

During the period it has been fighting with its comrades of the French Army and side by side with the 51st (Highland) Division, the 62nd (West Riding) Division has utterly defeated the 123rd German Division, which had to be withdrawn on the 22nd instant, and the 50th German Division (an assault Division of the first rank) shared a similar fate a few days later.

The fortitude, steadfastness and valour of all ranks has been beyond praise.

MARFAUX, CUITRON, BOUILLY, the clearing of the BOIS DU PETIT CHAMP, attest your gallantry, while ESPILLY, NAPPES, the advance up the ARDRE VALLEY and the capture of BLIGNY and the MONTAGNE DE BLIGNY, are evidence of your sustained valour.

To every Officer, Warrant Officer, Non-commissioned Officer and Private Soldier I tender my grateful thanks and express my unstinted admiration of their victorious efforts. They have gloriously upheld the highest traditions of the British Army.

It is with intense pride that, once again after a great victory, I have the honour to sign myself as Commander of the 62nd (West Riding) Division.

Walter Braithwaite
Major General

The Divisional Commander has the honour to publish to the Division the attached Order of the Day of the Commander of the 5th French Army together with the forwarding Order of the Commander of the XXIInd, British Corps.

31.7.1918.

Lieut Colonel,
A.A.& Q.M.G. 62nd (West Riding) Division.

ARCIS.

ARCIS.

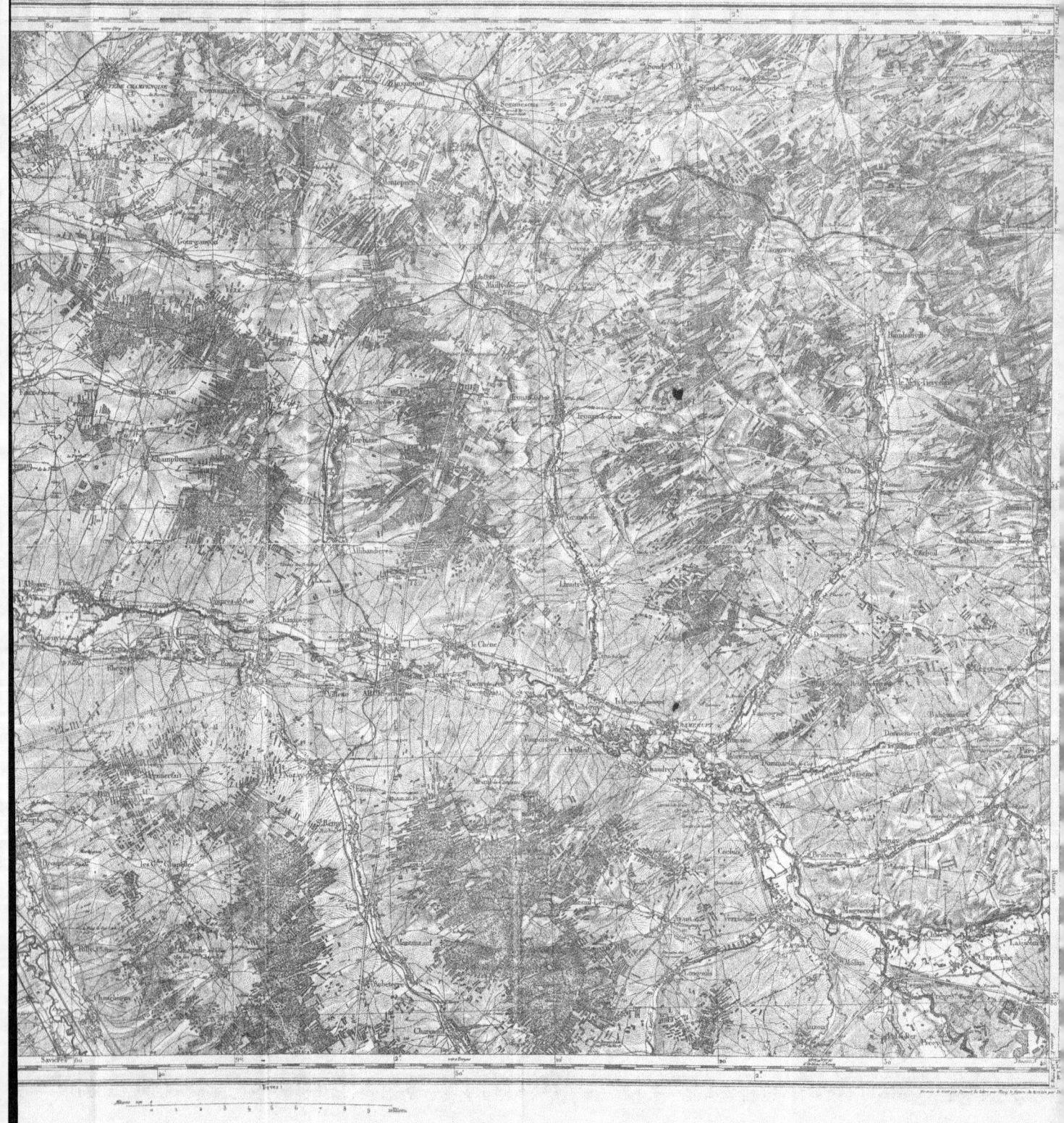

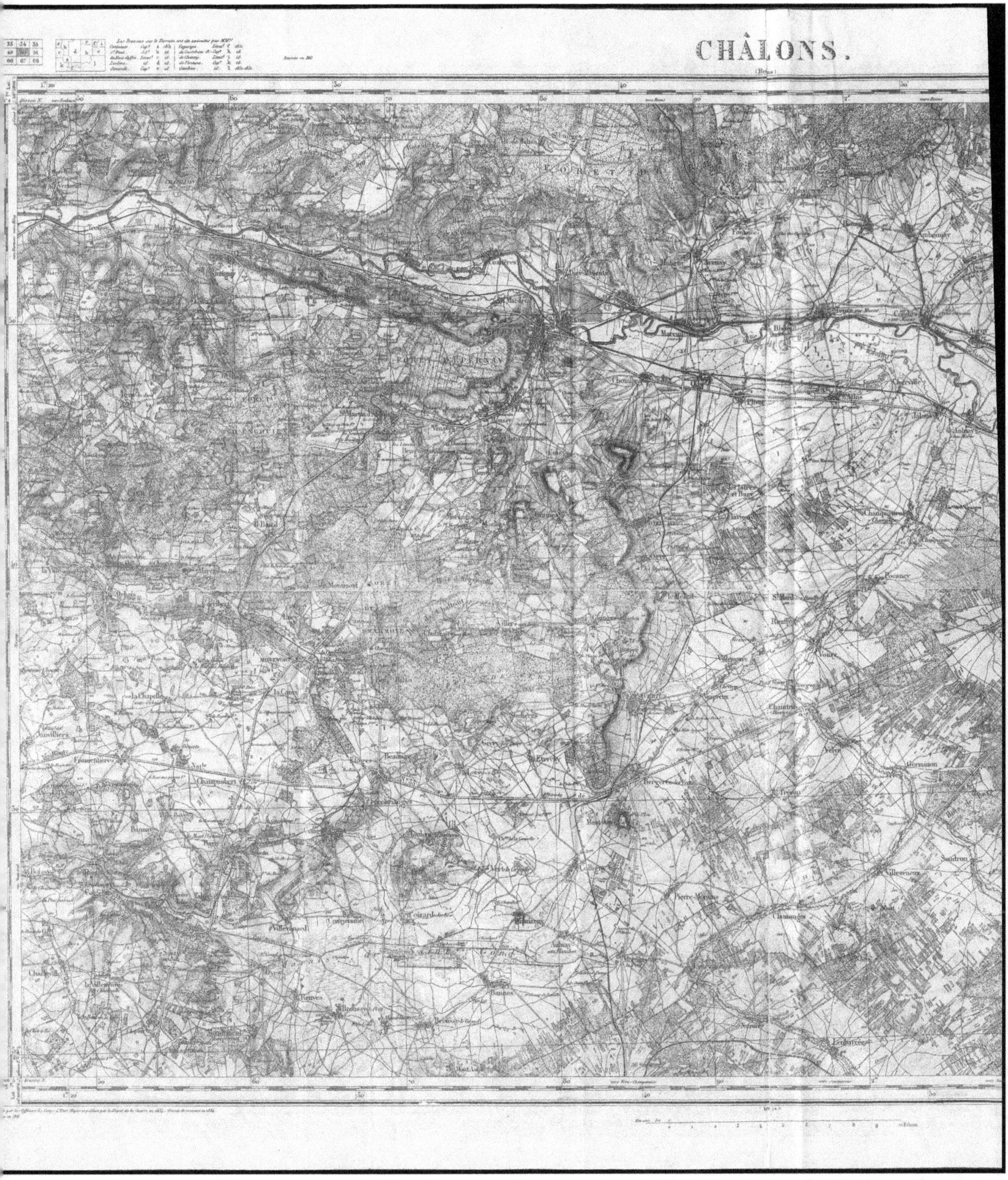

CHÂLONS.

CHÂLONS.

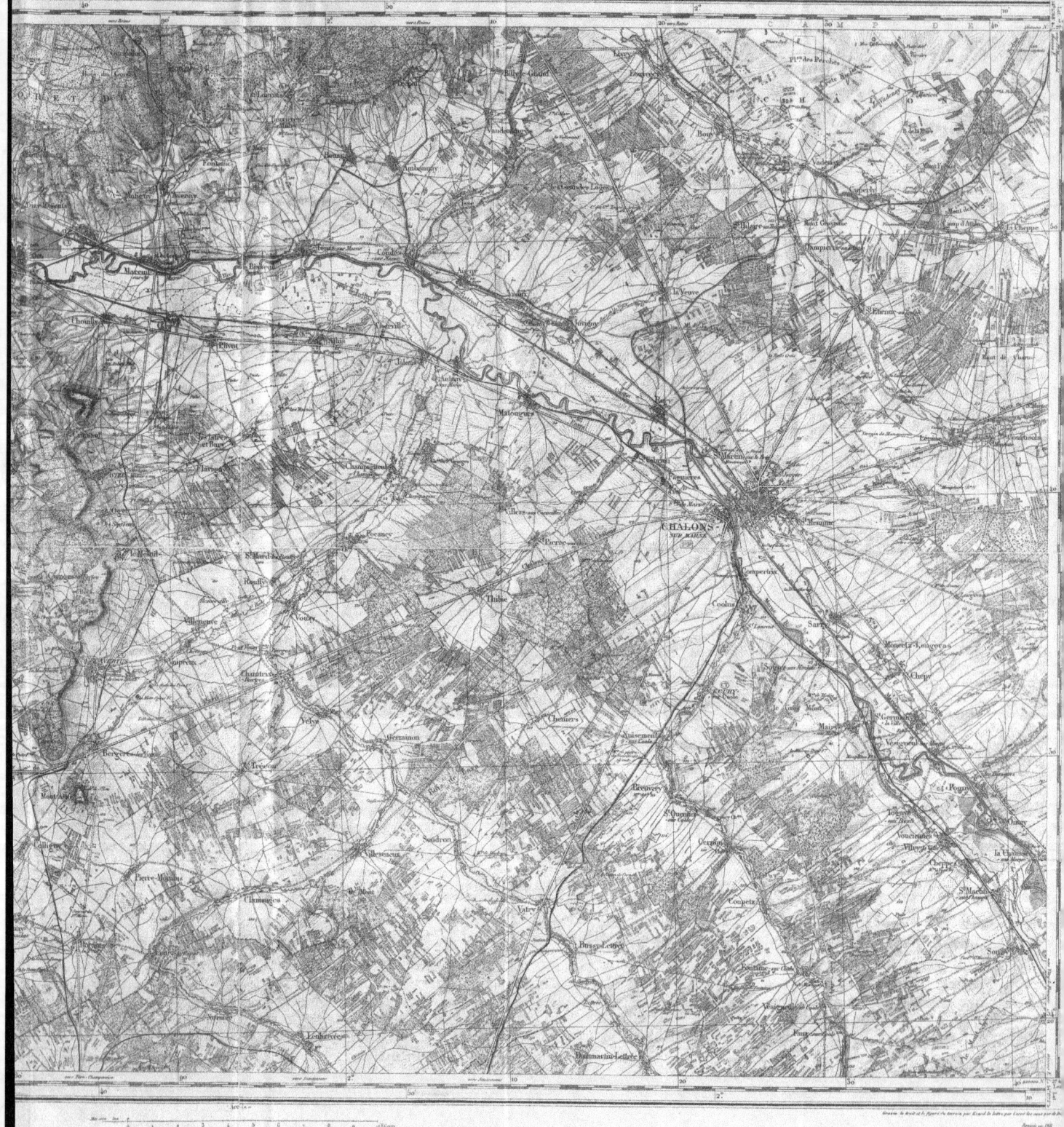

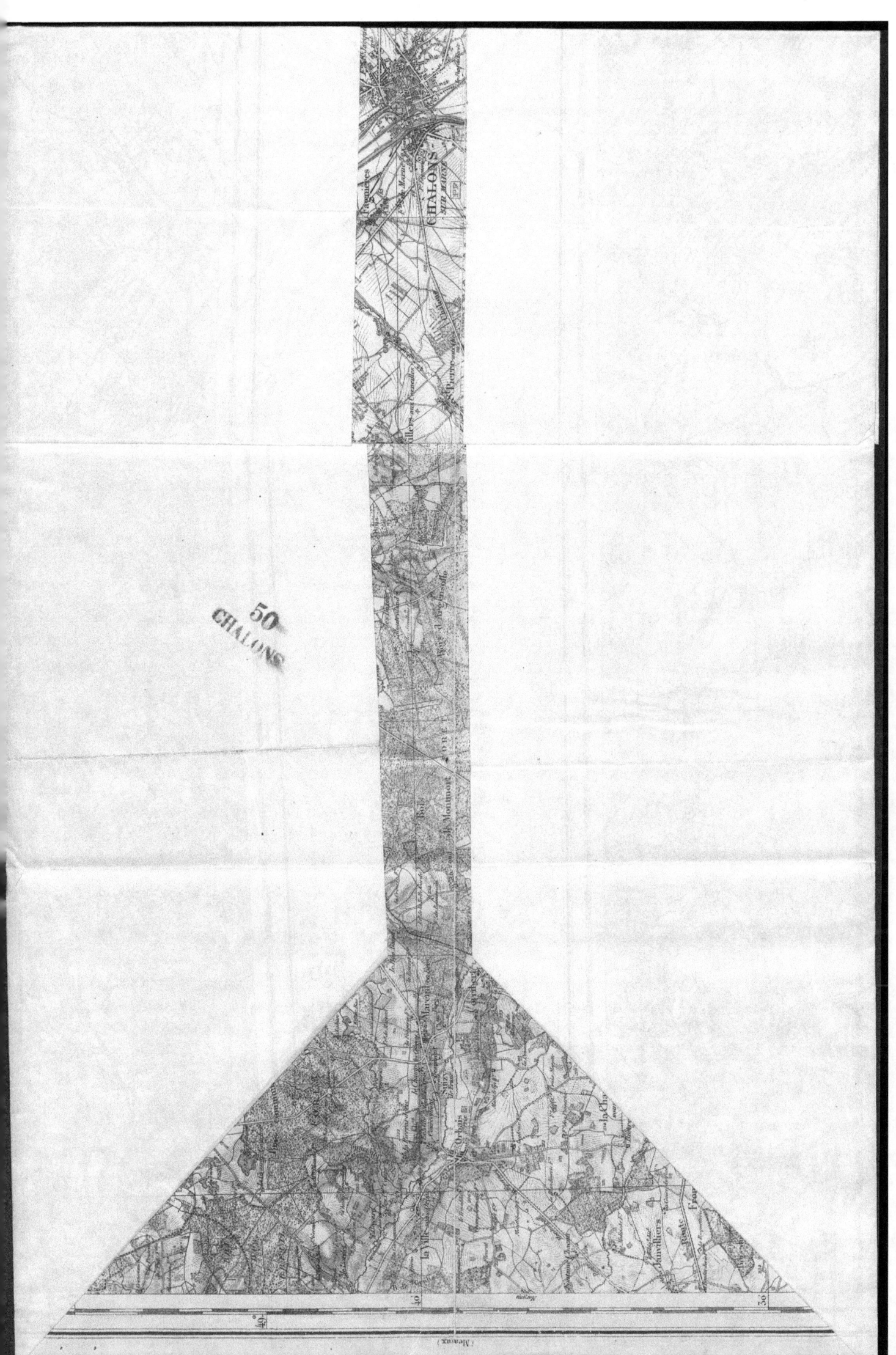

ORIGINAL.

CONFIDENTIAL.

WAR DIARY

- of -

5TH. DUKE OF WELLINGTON'S REGIMENT.

1st to 31st Augt.1918.

(Volume 6)

SECRET.

Vol 20

..................Lieut.Col.
Commdg.5th.Duke of Wellington's Regt.

Army Form C. 2118.

5th. Duke of Wellington's Regt.

WAR DIARY
or
INTELLIGENCE SUMMARY.

(Erase heading not required.)

Instructions regarding War Diaries and Intelligence Summaries are contained in F.S. Regs., Part II. and the Staff Manual respectively. Title pages will be prepared in manuscript.

Place	Date	Hour	Summary of Events and Information	Remarks and references to Appendices
Ref.Map. CHALONS (French) 1/80000.	1918. Augt. 1st.		The Battalion left the bivouac area in Foret de Reims near ST. IMOGES at 9. am and marched to CHOUILLY S.E. of EPERNAY via CHAMPILLON and EPERNAY. En route at DIZZY MAGENTA the 186th Infantry Brigade Group marched past the Commander of the Fifth French Army (General Berthelot). Massed Bands of the Brigade and the Divisional Band played during the March Past. The Battalion was congratulated on a very smart turn out, especially the Regimental Transport. The battalion bivouaced in a small wood about 1½ kilometres due south of CHOUILLY Village.	
	2nd.		A Very fine day. At night enemy bombing aeroplanes were over in the vicinity but none were dropped in the battalion area.	
	3rd.		A wet day. Battalion rested in its bivouac area.	
	4th.		Another wet day with fine intervals. Troops prepared to move at night from French area.	
Ref. Map. 57.d. 1/40,000.	5th.		Battalion marched to OIRY Station and entrained in one Strategical Train at 4.30pm. in very wet weather. Whole battalion entrained on one train complete with transport. Train went via MARLES (at 3.pm.) PARIS (at 7.30pm.) and EPLUCHES (9.pm.) The battalion was greatly cheered by the French populace in the environs of PARIS. Journey continued via AMIENS (at 8.am) CANDAS to DOULLENS where the battalion detrained After dinners on the road side the battalion marched in pouring rain via ORVILLE and THIEVRES to a Camp at AUTHIE (I.16.d.) Everyone thoroughly drenched and camp very wet.	
	6th.		Still very wet. The men cleaned up and dried themselves as well as possible. A large draft of 282 men arrived chiefly men from 4th, 12th, and 13th, Yorkshire Regts.	
	7th.		Men all had baths. Remainder of day was spent in re-organisation.	
	8th.		Finer. The G.O.C. Brigade (Brig. Genl. J.G. Burnett DSO) inspected the new draft in the morning. The battalion then did platoon training on ground near ST. LEGER (I.6.c.).	

Army Form C. 2118.

5th. Duke of Wellington's Regt.

WAR DIARY
or
INTELLIGENCE SUMMARY.
(Erase heading not required.)

Instructions regarding War Diaries and Intelligence Summaries are contained in F.S. Regs. Part II. and the Staff Manual respectively. Title pages will be prepared in manuscript.

Original

Place	Date	Hour	Summary of Events and Information	Remarks and references to Appendices
Ref. Map. 57.d. 1/40,000.	Augt. 9th.	M	Games in the afternoon. Fine day.	
			The Divisional Commander (Major General W.P. Braithwaite C.B.) visited the battalion and inspected 430 of the new drafts. In addressing the battalion he congratulated it on its great achievements in the recent Second Battle of the Marne and said he was very proud to have such a unit under his command. The battalion did specialist and platoon training in the vicinity of the Camp during the day.	
	10th.	M	A very fine day. Platoon and Specialist training near camp in the morning. "B" Coy. were on the Range. Games in the afternoon.	
	11th.	M	Church parade of a Thanksgiving Character was held in Camp at 10.am. Very fine and bright.	
	12th.	M	Platoon Training and usual specialist classes took place on training ground near ST. LEGER in I.6.b. Games in the afternoon and evening.	
	13th.	M	Very fine and hot. Platoon training and specialist classes near Camp I.16. Games, lectures etc. in afternoon.	
	14th.	M	Usual Platoon Training on the ST.LEGER Ground I.6.c. Games in the afternoon.	
	15th.	M	Platoon and Specialist Training near Camp I.16 during morning. Very fine.	
	16th.	M	Training near Camp I.16 during the day. Men all had baths at Divisional Baths on AUTHIE - ST. LEGER Road. The 54th. Heavy Artillery Brigade Concert Party "The Heavies" gave an admirable Concert to the battalion during the evening.	

Army Form C. 2118.

5th. Duke of Wellington's Regt.
WAR DIARY
or
INTELLIGENCE SUMMARY.
(Erase heading not required.)

Place	Date	Hour	Summary of Events and Information	Remarks and references to Appendices
Ref. Map. 57.d. 1/40,000.	1918. Aug. 17th.		Training in morning. Half holiday in afternoon.	
	18th.		Church parades in morning. Holiday remainder of day. Fine and bright.	
	19th.		Battalion struck the Camp at AUTHIE (i.16.d.) during the day. At night the battalion moved with remainder of Brigade from IV Corps Area to VI Corps Area The Brigade marched in one column via PAS, MONDICOURT, HUMBERCOURT. This battalion was accommodated in a tented Camp in the Chateau Grounds at SAULTY. Bde. H.Q. and 2/4th. Duke of Wellington's Regt. went to SOMBRIN and 2/4th. Hampshire Regt. to WARLUZEL. On account of congested state of roads, and the long column, and the difficulty of transport taking the hills, the march was an unpleasant and wearisome one. The battalion left AUTHIE at 8.45pm. and arrived at TENT CAMP, SAULTY at 3.am. on 20th inst. It rained all night.	
	20th.		Battalion rested at SAULTY all day. Very bright and fine.	
	21st.		A little training was done during the morning in the Camp. At 8.30pm. the battalion marched from SAULTY to BILLETS at THIEVRES via GOUTERELLE, PAS and FAMECHON. On completion on move battalion was in the IV Corps again.	
	22nd.		Very hot day. Specialist Training during the afternoon near billets. Lieut.Col.J. Walker. DSO. went to Brigade as Brigade Commander during the absence of Brig. Genl. J.G. Burnett DSO.on leave.	
	23rd.		The battalion did Company Training on Area C.25 (Ref. Sheet 57.d.) near HURTEBISE FARM during the morning. The Divisional and Brigade Commanders visited the battalion during training. Intensely hot day again.	

Army Form C. 2118.

5th. Duke of Wellington's Regt.
WAR DIARY
or
INTELLIGENCE SUMMARY.
(Erase heading not required.)

Instructions regarding War Diaries and Intelligence Summaries are contained in F. S. Regs., Part II. and the Staff Manual respectively. Title pages will be prepared in manuscript.

Place	Date	Hour	Summary of Events and Information	Remarks and references to Appendices
	1918. Augt. 23rd.		The battalion was moved from IV Corps Area to THIEVRES to VI Corps area SAULTY at night. Soon after arrival at TENT CAMP, SAULTY orders were received for a move forward and most of the night was spent in forming dumps of surplus kit etc.	
	24th to 31st.		See narrative attached.	

J Walker, Lieut.Col.
Commdg. 5th. Duke of Wellington's Regiment

Army Form C. 2118.

5th. Duke of Wellington's Regt.

WAR DIARY
or
INTELLIGENCE SUMMARY.
(Erase heading not required.)

Instructions regarding War Diaries and Intelligence Summaries are contained in F.S. Regs. Part II. and the Staff Manual respectively. Title pages will be prepared in manuscript.

Place	Date	Hour	Summary of Events and Information	Remarks and references to Appendices

A P P E N D I C E S.

D R A F T S etc.

Capt. C.H. Lockwood.
2/Lieut. H. Drabble.
" J.T. Boardman.
" W. Saunderson.   Joined Battalion 6.8.18.
" W.J. Lloyd.
" T. Briggs.
" W. Walker.
" G.G. Hoyle.

2/Lieut. L. Brook – Rejd. from Hospital 9.8.18.

282 other ranks.   6.8.18.
 52   "   "   8.8.18.
  8   "   "   12.8.18.
 20   "   "   13.8.18.
  2   "   "   14.8.18.
 30   "   "   19.8.18.
  1   "   "   17.8.18.
  3   "   "   22.8.18.
  4   "   "   24.8.18.

C A S U A L T I E S etc.

2/Lieut. C.W. Mellalieu.   Wounded.   25.8.18.
2/Lieut. F. Chapman.   do.   do.
2/Lieut. R.J. Machin.   do.   do.
2/Lieut. W. Walker.   Died of Wds.   25.8.18.
2/Lieut. J.T. Boardman.   Wounded.   29.8.18.
2/Lieut. H. Drabble.   do.   do.
Capt. E.G. Watkinson.   Wounded at duty.   30.8.18.
Lieut. G.F. Clay.   do.   29.8.18.
Lieut. E.W. Taylor.   To Hosp. sick.   8.8.18.
2/Lieut. L. Brook.   do.   14.8.18.
2/Lieut. R.O. Steed.   To England,
                            struck off.   18.8.18.
2/Lieut. E.R. Dunshee.   Died of Wds.   11.8.18.
Capt. W.S. Caulfeild.   Crossposted
                            to 2/4th. Duke   21.8.18.
                            of Wellington's
                            Regt.

Other ranks.

Killed.   26
Died of Wounds.   6
Wounded.   171.
Wounded (Gas)   36.
Wounded at duty.   5
Missing.   5

5th. Duke of Wellington's Regt.

WAR DIARY
or
INTELLIGENCE SUMMARY.

Army Form C. 2118.

(Erase heading not required.)

APPENDICES (contd).

APPOINTMENTS, RELINQUISHMENTS etc.

Lieut. C.G.H. Ellis appointed acting Captain dated 4.8.18.
Lieut. C.E. Morier   "   "   "   "   "
Lieut. E.G. Watkinson   "   "   "   "   "
Lieut. (a/Capt.) G.V. Bernays relinquishes the acting rank of captain dated 23.7.18.
Major Genl. C.P. BRAITHWAITE, C.B. relinquished command of the 62nd.(W.R.) Division 27.8.18.
and was succeeded by Maj.General Sir R.D. Whigham K.C.B., D.S.O.

HONOURS, AWARDS etc.

The following Officers, Warrant Officers, Non-commissioned Officers and men have been awarded decorations as stated against their names for bravery and devotion to duty in the Field.

Capt. J.B. Cockhill M.C.		D.S.O.
1st.Lieut. G.S. Osincup. (M.O.R.C.)		M.C.
2/Lieut. F. Chapman.		M.C.
" P.R. Barnes.		M.C.
" R.J. Machin.		M.C.
" L.F. Walker.		M.C.
240598 C.S.M. Waterhouse C.E.		D.C.M.
12775 C.S.M. Handby K.		D.C.M.
242879 Sergt. Hazle R. MM.		Bar to M.M.
240088 Sergt. Merriman H.S. MM.		do.
240433 Pte. Crosland W.D. MM.		do.
12886 Sergt. Greaves J.R. MM.		do.
241688 L.Cpl. Robinson G.G. MM.		do.
242439 Pte. Raistrick T. MM.		do.
265782 Dvr. Walker M. MM.		do.
242392 Pte. Brook H. MM.		do.
242683 Pte. Beardsley P. MM.		do.

5th. Duke of Wellington's Regt.

WAR DIARY
or
INTELLIGENCE SUMMARY.

Army Form C. 2118.

APPENDICES (contd.)

HONOURS, AWARDS etc. (contd.).

240156	Sergt. Ware G.A.W.	M.M.
240219	L/Sergt. Field R.	M.M.
241704	Sergt. Dyson B.	M.M.
242367	Pte. Raynard J.	M.M.
15002	Sergt. Judson M.	M.M.
242759	L.Cpl. Pearce G.W.	M.M.
265691	Pte. Butterfield J.	M.M.
240763	Sergt. Hepworth T.	M.M.
242466	Pte. Wray E.G.	M.M.
23901	Pte. Holroyd B.	M.M.
17052	Dmr. Moran P.	M.M.
240832	Cpl. Cox A.F.	M.M.
242859	Pte. Ibbetson P.	M.M.
29495	Pte. Strafford T.	M.M.
241978	Pte. Hartley F.	M.M.
25262	Pte. Linsley B.	M.M.
266187	Pte. Whitham J.S.	M.M.
268050	L/Sergt. Spivey F.	M.M.
267955	Corpl. Pemberton P.	M.M.
241045	Pte. Dale E.	M.M.
240742	Pte. Tomlinson R.	M.M.
23773	L.Cpl. Chapman J.G.	M.M.
22602	Pte. Frank T.	M.M.
240159	Pte. Dobson G.B.	M.M.

SECRET.

5th. DUKE OF WELLINGTON'S REGT.

NARRATIVE OF OPERATIONS

August 24th. to Septr. 2nd.1918.

Ref. Map. 57.c. 1/40,000. 57.c.N.W. 1/20,000. ERVILLERS special 1/20,000.

August 24.

The battalion with remainder of 186th. Inf. Bde. assembled on the ARRAS - DOULLENS Road where the SAULTY - LA BAZEQUE Road crossed it, at 9.am and there embussed. Debussing took place at ADINFER about 12 noon. From there the battalion marched over the newly captured ground to the valley just west of the Village of COURCELLES about F.12.c. and became part of the Brigade in Divisional Reserve. The remaining two brigades of the Division went forward East of COURCELLES. At 9.pm the battalion moved further forward in A.14.c. and d. under orders from Brigade. The 2/4th. Duke of Wellington's Regt and 2/4th. Hampshire Regt. went forward East of GOMIECOURT and ACHIET LE GRAND respectively. The 187th. Inf. Brigade relieved the 99th and 6th. Infantry Brigades on the general line B.27.c.0.0. - B.27.a.8.7. - B.21.d.4.2. - B.21.b.4.0. - B.16.c.0.0. - B.10.c.4.0. during the night.

August 25th.

At 4.30am. instructions were given verbally by the Brigade for the battalion to move forward and attack at 9.am. The battalion moved off from A.14.d. at 6.30am and assembled on a jumping off line about B.25.c.0.2. - B.25.c.2.0. H.1.a.3.4. - H.1.c.0.8. The plan of attack was for "C" Coy. (left) and "B" Coy. (right) to advance through the villages of BEHAGNIES and SAPIGNIES and capture the line about B.27.d.1.2. - H.3.b.3.0. - H.3.d.a.0. Then for "A" Coy. (left) and "D" Coy.(right) to leap frog through and capture a final objective on the VRAUCOURT - BEUGNATRE Road about H.6.a.5.9. - H.6.c.3.0. Two companies of 2/4th. Duke of Wellington's Regt. were placed at the disposal of the battalion in support of the attack and were concentrated at G.6.d. At Zero Hour it was not known whether BEHAGNIES and SAPIGNIES wre cleared of the enemy. If not cleared the orders were to mop it up as a preliminary operation. Battalion H.Q. for the attack was established under the bank at G.6.b.9.8.

The attack was done under a barrage. The forming up was successfully accomplished and the troops moved off at zero hour. No opposition was encountered in BEHAGNIES or SAPIGNIES and the existing outpost line was found to be on the line of the BAPAUME - ERVILLERS Road. The attack went well but the enemy contested every bit of ground. The whole of the first objective was gained by about 10.30am. Very heavy machine gun fire was encountered from FAVREUIL and MORY which sprinkled the whole area of the attack causing us heavy casualties. In advancing through BEHAGNIES and SAPIGNIES the troops became a little disconnected and some loss of direction. The advance was steadily continued to a line in front of the Light Railway in H.9.b. and by 3.pm. ran about H.3.b.15.50, H.3.b.15.10 - H.3.b.20.10, H.3.d.4.7. - H.10.a.2.9. - H.10.a.4.2. Sniping by enemy artillery and machine guns continued to be troublesome, all day.

At 5.pm. the enemy put down an intense barrage with guns of all calibres over the whole area B.27, 26, H.1, 2, 3, 7, 8, 9. This continued until after 7.pm. At about 6.15pm. the enemy launched a powerful counter attack. About two companies of the enemy attacked frontally from the VRAUCOURT - BEUGNATRE Road. They were plainly seen by our troops on the left ("C" AND "A" COYS) As they were came down the slope of the hill they were met with rifle and lewis gun fire and when their officer who was seen to be vainly trying to get his men on, was shot, this attack collapsed and the enemy fled in disorder. The main attack, however came from the right. The enemy had concentrated five battalions in FAVREUIL WOOD and he attacked in great strength the right of our line where there was a gap between us and the IV Corps. Realising his danger Capt. C.G.H. ELLIS Commanding "D" Company made a prompt and accurate appreciation of the situation and slightly withdrew his line forming an offensive flank facing S.E. The attacking force came under our artillery barrage at the N. end of FAVREUIL and were badly shaken, as could be heard by the amount of shouting and groans. Those of his troops who emerged from the wood were met by a withering fire from rifles and Lewis Guns of our troops and he retreated in full disorder. Capt. ELLIS at once restored his original line at 8.pm.

The night was a comparatively quiet one and enabled us to advance our line to H.4.a.1.2 - H.10.a.2.9. - H.9.b.3.0. with posts in H.10.a. During this days fighting the battalion captured 1 officer and 40 other ranks prisoners, about 20 machine guns and considerable stores including a dump of 9 in. and 8 in. shells. Our casualties amounted to about 4 officers and 180 other ranks.

August 26th.

At 6.am. the 2/4th. Hampshire Regt. jumped off from our line about the MORY - FAVREUIL Road to capture the high ground in B.29 and H.5.a. The battalion reorganised itself during the day and was disposed in depth in H.4 in close support to 2/4th. Hants Regt. Battalion Headquarters moved to the bank H.2.c.7.5. during the day.

From 6.40pm. to 7.15pm. the enemy put down an intense barrage on our line of the road from H.4.a.05.00 to H.4.c.40.00. Enemy aerial activity at the time was most marked. No hostile infantry attack developed.

The night was a quiet one.

August 27th.

Orders were received during the night that pressure was to be maintained against the enemy during the day. The 187th. Brigade on our left were ordered to advance along the spur running N. of VRAUCOURT with objectives BANKS RESERVE and the Road running through B.24.b.. Zero hour was 7.am. The 2/4th. Hampshire Regt. in front of us were ordered by frequent patrols to keep in touch with any change in the situation. The dividing line between 186th and 187th. Brigades was B.29. cent. - N.end of VRAUCOURT.

At 6.am. the enemy again barraged our line in H. 4 very heavily causing us several casualties. It continued for $2\frac{1}{4}$ hours and became more intense as our attacking barrage opened at 7.am.

The remainder of the day was comparatively quiet on the battalion front.

During the day the following telegram was received from the Divisional Commander - "The Commander in Chief orders me to convey his congratulations to the Division on their fine performance".

August 28th.

Quiet day for the battalion. Companies were subjected to some shelling in H.4 with H.E. and Gas shells at intervals through the day. Much of our captured material was collected and removed to Waggon Lines. Preparations were made for an attack by "D" COMPANY on the two lines of trenches running from H.6.c.4.5. to I.7.a.6.0. and H.6.c.3.1. to I.7.a.6.0. but it was later cancelled.

August 29th.

Quiet day up to 5.pm. on the whole, with a little intermittent shelling in area H.3 and 4 from 3.pm to 4.pm. The battalion was ordered to make an attack at 4.pm in conjunction with an attack by the IV Corps on our right. The objective allotted was the trench system H.6.c.4.5. to I.7.a.6.0. and H.6.c.3.1. to I.7.a.6.0. The task was given to "D" Company under the command of Capt. C.G.H. Ellis with "A" Company also under his command in close support. The two companies successfully formed up in H.5.d. and H.6.c. at 3.30pm. Zero hour was then changed to 5.30pm owing to the troops on our right being unable to be ready in time for 4.pm. - having had two short notice. The artillery arrangements were as follows - A smoke barrage was put down on the N. side of the North Trench to screen the operation from direct observation. A creeping barrage 300 yards N. and S. of the trenches to commence at 5.30pm. and creep 100 yards in 4 minutes to finally rest in front of the apex of the final objective as a protective barrage covering the consolidation.

DISPOSITIONS. Two Bombing parties of 9 other ranks each to work down each trench towards the junction at I.7.a.6.0 A Lewis Gun with 4 men worked on each side of each trench over the open to deal with any enemy getting out of the trench and to keep heads low. These guns kept pace with the leading bombing teams. About 150 yards in rear of the bombing teams and down each trench the remainder of "D" Company working as two complete platoons follows, dropping section posts on the way as flank guards as the attack proceeded. "A" Company provided 4 Lewis Guns Teams working across the open about 100 yards in rear of "D" Company and about 50 yards N. and S. of each trench. The remainder of "A" Company working as two platoons moved down the trenches in rear of "D" Company with orders to immediately support "D" Company if necessary or to deal with any enemy posts between the two trenches or on either flank.

The operation was very successful, the men showing great dash. The enemy at first put up a stiff fight in the trench but the cross fire from our Lewis Gunners disorganised his bombers and at bayonet work our men were infinitely superior. There were a number of derelict huts between the two trenches with enemy posts dotted about which were dealt with by the support company (A).

When the final objective was reached the enemy opened a heavy fire from about the railway I.7. cent. but the immediate action of a small bombing party worked round and mopped up the post taking 20 prisoners. The success was due to the great dash with which the operation was carried out by all ranks. The attacking troops closely followed the barrage and prevented the enemy having time to grasp the situation. The artillery barrage was very good and the smoke barrage proved quite effective. The rapidity with which the Lewis Guns followed up and covered the attack prevented any organised resistance overground. By 6.30pm. all objectives had been gained and a post established on the normal gauge railway at about I.7.d.i.9. in touch with the Corps on our right.

At 8.pm. information was received that the enemy were preparing to counter attack from I.13.b. and I.13.d. and that parties of the enemy were seen in I.7.d. The artillery were informed and the enemy proved a good target.

The newly captured system of trenches was quickly consolidated during the evening. Our casualties during the days operations were slight, whereas 35 of the enemy were killed and buried by us, 93 prisoners, 15 machine guns and 1 trench mortar captured.

The night was a very dark one and rain fell.

The 2/4th. Hampshire Regt. (now on our immediate left) were relieved during the night by 2/4th. Duke of Wellington's Regt.

August 30th.

The general attack was continued and the battalion cooperated. The task for the battalion was as follows -
In cooperation with the 2/4th. Duke of Wellington's Regt. on our left the battalion had to take the line of the railway from about I.1.d.4.2. S. of VAULX VRAUCOURT to a point where the trench crosses the railway about I.7.d.1.9. as a first objective, and a line from I.8.a.7.8. to I.8.a.7.0. as a second objective, and a line from I.8.a.7.8. to I.8.a.7.0. as a second objective. The 2/4th. Duke of Wellington's Regt attacked on a similar line north of us. Zero hour was 5.am. The barrage came down on the line of the BAPAUME - ECOUST Rd and paused there for 3 minutes. Then moved forward at the rate of 100 yards in three minutes till it got to the first objective (the line of the railway). There it halted for 15 minutes until 6.25am. and then went on to the final objective at the rate of 100 yards in 6 minutes. Two tanks moved forward with the Brigade attacking troops, keeping well under the barrage and working independantly of the Infantry.

"A" & "D" Companies remained in their captured trenches of the day previous. "B" Company was detailed for the attack with "C" Company in close reserve. "B" company was organised into 3 platoons. One platoon advanced in one line to take the first objective, the two remaining platoons advanced in columns behind the leading platoon and leap frogged through them to take the second objective. At zero the leading platoon advanced, keeping well under the barrage. Very little opposition was met with and several prisoners were captured before the first objective was reached. After capturing the first objective the remaining 2 platoons extended and passed through to the second objective. Again no heavy opposition was encountered until nearing the objective when a hostile machine gun, became active. A Lewis Gun was set on and quickly silenced the enemy M.G. The consolidation was done without enemy interference. Our casualties were very light. One M.G. was captured and about 100 prisoners. Touch with both flanks was quickly gained and maintained throughout.

Towards the end of the day the battalion was disposed as follows -

One company holding the line I.8.a.7.5. to I.8.a.7.2. with 2 platoons and 2 platoons in support about line of railway in I.7.b. Two companies in trench system about H.6.c. and H.12.b. One company in Bank H.6.b. Battn. H.Q. shared the H.Q. of 94th. Inf. Bde at H.5.d.9.2.

August 31st.

Fine day again. The night had been quiet except for a little whizz banging on our forward posts. The S.O.S. went up on our right at 5.am and a hostile counter attack was completely repulsed. Our forward area in H. 6 was heavily shelled from 5.am to 8.am. Remainder of the day was quiet.

Orders were received for the battalion to be relieved by 5th.Battn.K.O.Y.L.I. at night and all arrangements were made. The orders were subsequently cancelled at 7.pm.

Men becoming very tired.

Septr. 1st.

The 8th. West Yorks Regt. assembled within our line during the night about I.7.b., this battalion being responsible for guiding them into position. At 6.am. they attacked the village of VAULX VRAUCOURT from the south. Hostile retaliation on our front was slight. Their objectives were eventually gained. Enemy aeroplanes flying very low fired into our trenches in H.6.c. and H.12.b. and 2.pm. They also dropped bombs.

Remainder of the day comparatively quiet.

Much cooler.

Septr. 2nd.

The 187th. Inf. Bde. plus the divisional Pioneer Battalion (9th. Durham Light Inf.) attacked through 186th and 185th. Inf. Bdes. at 5.30am. They had 3 objectives, their final one being the high ground E. of MORCHIES. At first their attack was successful but owing to the troops on right and left not getting forward as well, they were held up and partially driven back in places.

Towards evening the front line of 9th. Durham L.I. in front of this battalion ran through I.9. This battalion was ordered to move up on to the high ground in I.8. "B" Coy. was therefore moved forward with "A" Company on its right, in touch with the division on our right. "C" Company was moved from the Bank in H.6.b. to the line of the railway in I.7. "D" Company remained in its captured trench in H.6.c. and H.12.b.

At night the 62nd. (W.R.) Division was relieved by the 2nd. Division. This battalion was relieved by 2 companies and B.H.Q. of 1st. King's Liverpool Regt. The two remaining companies relieving 2/4th. D. of Wellington's Regt. Relief was completed by about 1.am on Septr. 3rd. On relief the battalion marched to dugout accommodation in Railway Embankment about A.22.b. E. of COURCELLES.

During the 9 days fighting the men acquitted themselves well and did all that was asked of them. Considering that the battalion just prior to going into action had received 450 men in new drafts they put up a very good fight. Some little difficulty was experienced at the commencement of operations with neither men nor officers knowing one another very well.

(5).

A shortage of trained Lewis Gunners was seriously felt throughout operations.

The casualties of the battalion during operations were as follows -

OFFICERS.

Died of Wounds.	1.
Wounded.	6.
Wounded at duty.	2.

OTHER RANKS.

Killed.	26.
Died of wounds.	6.
Wounded.	171.
Wounded (gas).	36.
Wounded at duty.	5.
Wounded & missing.	1.
Missing.	4.

The captures of the battalion amounted to -

Prisoners.	2 Off. 250 O.R.
Machine Guns.	55.
German Rifles.	175.
Trench Mortars.	6.
German Very Pistols.	15.
Belt cases.	70.
Anti-Tank Guns.	3.
Motor Headlight.	1.
German telephones.	3.
Daylight signalling lamp.	1.
German Bicycle.	1.

and large quantities of Gun ammunition, equipment etc. not recovered.

H.Qs. 62nd (W.R.) Division.

27th August 1918.

It is a matter of great regret to me that I cannot see this Battle out as Commander of the Division, but my orders are to hand over this afternoon and proceed to take command of an Army Corps.

I have commanded the Division since December 1915, so saying goodbye to it is no easy matter. I am, and always shall be, very very proud of the 62nd West Riding Division and the memories of its fighting at the ANCRE, BULLECOURT, CAMBRAI, BUCQUOY, the MARNE, and in the present Battle, can never fade.

I hope it may be my good fortune to have the Division under my command in the future, and until that time comes I must say goodbye.

I take this opportunity of thanking every Officer, Warrant Officer, N.C.O. and private soldier for their unfailing support and their matchless gallantry, which has made the Division what it is — a fighting force of the first rank.

Walter Braithwaite

Maj.Genl

Comdg 62nd (W.R.) Division

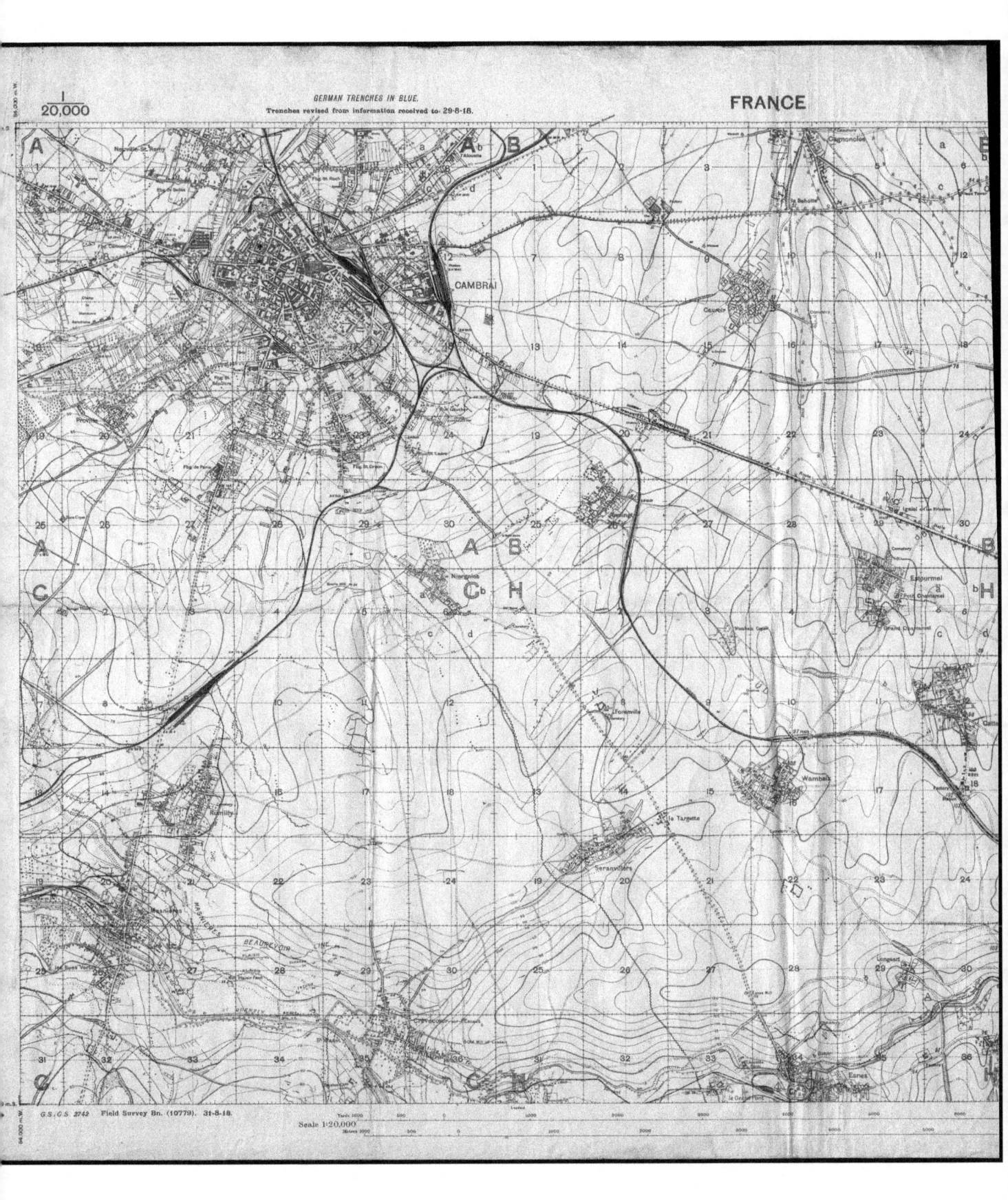

ORIGINAL.   CONFIDENTIAL.   SECRET.

WAR - DIARY

-of-

5TH. DUKE OF WELLINGTON'S (W.R.) REGT.

1st to 30th.Septr.1918.

(Volume 7).

J. Walker
Commdg.5th.Duke of Wellington's (W.R.) Regt.
.... Lieut.Col.

9521

WAR DIARY
or
INTELLIGENCE SUMMARY.
(Erase heading not required)

Army Form C. 2118

Instructions regarding War Diaries and Intelligence Summaries are contained in F.S. Regs., Part II. and the Staff Manual respectively. Title pages will be prepared in manuscript.

2nd Batt. of Wellington's (W.R.) Regt.

Place	Date	Hour	Summary of Events and Information	Remarks and references to Appendices
Ref. Map Sept. C7.C. 1918 .N.W. 1st. 1/20000.			The 8th. West Yorks Regt. assembled within our line during the night about 1.V.D., this battalion being responsible for guiding them into position. At 5.a.m. they advanced the village of VAULX VRAUCOURT from the south. Hostile retaliation on our front was slight. Their objectives were eventually taken. Enemy aeroplanes flying very low into our trenches, H.Q. and H.Q.L.D. at 6.a.m. They also dropped bombs. Remainder of the day comparatively quiet, much cooler.	
	2nd.		The 127th. Inf. Bde. plus the Divisional Pioneer Battalion (5th. Durham Light Infantry) attacked through 125th. Inf. Bde and 126th. Inf. Bde at 5.30am. They had 2 objectives, their first one being the high ground N. of MORCHIES. At first their advance E. of MORCHIES was successful but owing to the troops on their right not getting as far as they were held up, eventually driven back in places. Towards evening the 6th. Durham Light Infantry in rear of this battalion was through D.D. This battalion was ordered to move up close to the HALL ground in D.O. "B" Company moved forward with a Company on its right, in action for one mile up to our signal. "C" Company reached to its captured guns in H.S.a. on the line of the railway in M. "D" Company was relieved by the 2nd. Division. This battalion was relieved by 2 Coys Kings 3rd B.B.W. of 1st Kings Liverpool Regt. on relief the battalion marched to dugout accommodation in Railway Embankment about A.2..W.B. of COURCELLES.	
	3rd.		The battalion rested all day and improved its accommodation.	
	4th.		Large new drafts arrived. A little training was done.	
	5th.		The battalion all had baths at SAPIGNIES.	

5th BN DUKE OF WELLINGTON'S REGT.

WAR DIARY
or
INTELLIGENCE SUMMARY.
(Erase heading not required.)

Army Form C. 2118.

Instructions regarding War Diaries and Intelligence Summaries are contained in F. S. Regs., Part II. and the Staff Manual respectively. Title pages will be prepared in manuscript.

Place	Date	Hour	Summary of Events and Information	Remarks and references to Appendices
	1918. Sept. 13th.		post established. A similar post was made about 30 yards down LIN LANE. The enemy later tried to bomb his way back into SWING TRENCH but after a stiff fight lasting twenty minutes he retired in disorder leaving 1 M.G. and several dead. During these operations of the leading platoons one two remaining platoons consolidated a line of posts along the line of CHAP IRN SPUR ROAD. After one was a strong enemy counter attack, by bombing, was feared at K.34.s.9.0. One platoon was moved up into TANGANCO AVENUE. During the morning considerable numbers of the enemy were seen to be retiring over the ridge between T Wood in K.29.D. and TRIANGLE WOOD in K.36.B. They were fired on by Lewis Guns, and rifles and casualties were inflicted. Stiff fighting took place all morning before "B" Coy. obtained its final objective. Dugouts in SWING TRENCH were bombed and cleared after one operation. All objectives were consolidated in depth by midday. During the afternoon the enemy's artillery fire was very severe. The afternoon was comparatively quiet. Objectives on our right and left were held to be taken. During the night A and C Coys. relieved D and B Coys. who went back to W.O.C. Our casualties for the day amounted to about 1 officer and 100 other ranks. We captured 2 Machine Guns and 60 prisoners. At dusk the enemy counter attacked in strength at HAVRINCOURT on our left. This attack which was supported by a squadron of low flying aeroplanes was repulsed. A wet night.	
	13th.		The battalion was ordered to continue the attack and to capture the double trench system Hindenburg Part of the HINDENBURG Front line (K.34.c.99.60 - K.35.a.50.66 and K.34.a.99.85. - K.35.a.62.78). "B" Coy. was to endeavour to obtain a footing in HINDENBURG TRENCH on the north and centre on the south. By means of patrols "D" Coy. on the W. trench and "A" Coy. on the S. trench at same time. It was ascertained that the enemy was in occupation of the trench system. "D" and C Coys. made a bombing attack supported by Lewis Guns in the trench system without artillery assistance. Considerable opposition was met with. For the commencement, "C" Coy. being held up at Road about K.34.c.2.5. although one platoon got through and were detailed for some time. A Coy. after a stiff fight finally reached K.35.a.2.4. establishing a post there about 60 yards from the enemy. The whole area was swept by intense M.G. fire from each side and enfilade down the trenches. M.G's in T. Wood (K.35.c.) and TRIANGLE WOOD (K.33.a.3.) were very troublesome. The area K.34 centrals was closely filled by the enemy about 11.30 am.	

Army Form C. 2118.

WAR DIARY Regiment.
or
INTELLIGENCE SUMMARY.

(Erase heading not required.)

Instructions regarding War Diaries and Intelligence Summaries are contained in F. S. Regs., Part II. and the Staff Manual respectively. Title pages will be prepared in manuscript.

Place	Date	Hour	Summary of Events and Information	Remarks and references to Appendices
Ref. Map. S/20,000.	1918. Sept. 8th.		Training during the morning. A Memorial service was held at Divisional Cemetery at 2.30. for those who had fallen in recent operations belonging to the Division. The services conducted by the Senior Church of England Chaplain in the Division. This battalion provided a firing party.	
	7th.		Training in the morning. Athletics in the afternoon.	
	8th.		There was a Brigade Ceremonial Parade and March Past the Divisional Commander (Major Genl. R.D. Whigham. A.D.B. D.S.O.) in the morning. Recipients of honours gained on the Marne were presented by the Divisional Commander to recipients of honours gained on the Marne. Very dusty with rain in the afternoon.	
	9th.		Battalion rested all day in preparation for moving forward the battle area which was being demolished. Very wet.	

Army Form C. 2118.

5th Bn. DUKE OF WELLINGTON'S Regt.
WAR DIARY
or
INTELLIGENCE SUMMARY.
(Erase heading not required.)

Instructions regarding War Diaries and Intelligence Summaries are contained in F. S. Regs., Part II. and the Staff Manual respectively. Title pages will be prepared in manuscript.

Place	Date	Hour	Summary of Events and Information	Remarks and references to Appendices
Ref.Map 57.C. 1/40,000. 57.C.1.E. 57.C.3.B. 1/20,000.	1918 Septr. 10th.		The battalion with 150th. Inf. Bde. moved from COURCELLES AREA at 3.p.m. and marched via ACHIET LE GRAND, BIEFVILLERS, BAPAUME, BANCOURT, BERTINCOURT, RUYAULCOURT to S.E. corner of HAVRINCOURT WOOD. The battalion were there accommodated in huts evacuated first by the British in March 1918 and then by the Germans in Septr. 1918. Men marched in "battle order" and none fell out. Tea was served "en route".	
	11th.		Boisterous day with showers of rain. Officers all went forward during the day reconnoitring the N.E. edge of HAVRINCOURT WOOD preparatory to moving up at night. At dusk the battn. moved forward to forming up positions. B and D Coys. relieved a Company of the 6th. Somerset Light Infantry in the front line about QUEEN ST. BUTLER TRENCH and BUTLER SUPPORT in Q.5.B. and D. Forward Battalion H.Q. was established in the front line Coy.H.Q. about Q.5.C.1.1. A and C Coys. were located in the area Q.5.C. in HAVRINCOURT WOOD. This forming up was successfully accomplished by 11.p.m. with only one casualty. The night was a comparatively quiet one.	
	12th.		The 52nd.(W.R.) Division with 150th.Inf. Bde. on the right, and 149th. Inf.Bde. on the left and 186th. Inf.Bde. in Reserve made an attack on HAVRINCOURT. The front. of the 150th. Inf. Bde had two objectives. The first objective was the SHROPSHIRE SPUR ROAD as far North as Trench Junction K.4.a.9.6. Thence to the S.E. corner of HAVRINCOURT Village L.26.c.6.7. thence along the eastern edge of HAVRINCOURT Village to where RUTLEY TRENCH crosses K.32.c.5.1. Second objective was K.20.c.2.5. along Dunn Road to K.25.a.6.5. - Trench Junction K.25.a.9.5. - Trench Junction L.29.c.7.4. Thence along AMBER TRENCH to the One of K.22.d.4.4. The first objective on the right was alloted to this Battalion to be done with two companies. The 5/4th. Duke of Wellington's Regt. were in the centre and the 4/4th.Herts Regt. on the left of the Brigade front. Two companies of this Battalion remained in Brigade Reserve. The boundary between the Battalion and 2/4th.Duke of Wellington's Regt. was the most of the southern edge of the CHATEAU Grounds (inclusive to 2/4th. D. of Wellington's Regt.) thence to the junction of SWING TRENCH and KANGAROO AVENUE K.34.a.8.3.	

Army Form C. 2118.

5th BN DUKE OF WELLINGTONS REGT.
WAR DIARY
or
INTELLIGENCE SUMMARY.
(Erase heading not required.)

Instructions regarding War Diaries and Intelligence
Summaries are contained in F. S. Regs., Part II.
and the Staff Manual respectively. Title pages
will be prepared in manuscript.

Place	Date	Hour	Summary of Events and Information	Remarks and references to Appendices
	1918 Sept. 18th.		The attack of the battalion was given to D and B Coys. leaving A and C Coys. in Brigade Reserve located in 4.S.c. The general plan of the attack was for "B" Coy. to attack on the left on a two platoon front with one platoon in reserve having one objective (K.33 central at A.33.a.9.9.), the remaining platoon of this Company to be under the command of O.C. "D" Coy. for use in forming a defensive flank in rear of that on the SHROPSHIRE SPUR ROAD facing East by South, "C" Coy. to consolidate on a front facing north in touch with A.4th. Duke of Wellington's Regt. "D" Coy. to attack on a two platoon frontage with two objectives — the first objective being the two trenches running N. and W. between SHROPSHIRE SPUR ROAD and KNUCKLE TRENCH, the second objective being the line A.34.a.3.3. to A.34.a.5.5. This second objective to be taken by one platoon aided by bombing through the other two. The fourth platoon of "D" Coy. and attached platoon from "B" Coy. to be responsible for the security of the flank along SHROPSHIRE SPUR ROAD facing East (in K.34.c.). The attack took place with a creeping barrage which made a preliminary rest of three minutes on the line of QUEER STREET in K.3.a. and b. moving at the rate of 100 yards in 3 minutes until a rest of 10 minutes on the line A.34.c.4.5. — A.34.a.5.8. Zero hour of the attack was 5.25am.	
			NARRATIVE. When our barrage opened at Zero the Coys. moved forward close up to it. Within a very few minutes the enemy counter barrage came down and caused as many casualties, amongst the advancing platoons. The enemy's main barrage line seemed to be on our line of BUTLER TRENCH. Owing to the thickness of the shrub B Coy's progress was slow at first and men became rather mixed and involved. The objective of B Coy. was reached and consolidated and touch obtained with units on each flank. The first objective of D Coy. was gained in face of heavy machine gun fire. They then bombed their way down KANGAROO AVENUE in A.34.a. capturing 1 M.G. and 8 prisoners half way down besides inflicting casualties on the enemy. On reaching SWING TRENCH A.34.a.5.5. hostile bombing squads were met and driven along Eastwards towards the SWAY LINE, a number of the enemy being seen to retire into the valley towards HAVRINCOURT and were taken prisoner by 2/4th D. of W. on their right. On reaching the point A.34.a.5.5. a block was formed and a	

Army Form C. 2118.

5th BN DUKE OF WELLINGTON'S REGT.

WAR DIARY
or
INTELLIGENCE SUMMARY.
(Erase heading not required.)

Instructions regarding War Diaries and Intelligence
Summaries are contained in F. S. Regs. Part II.
and the Staff Manual respectively. Title pages
will be prepared in manuscript.

Place	Date	Hour	Summary of Events and Information	Remarks and references to Appendices
	1918. Sept.		At 3 p.m. it was decided not to continue the attack further but to hold on to the ground captured. 1 enemy M.G. was captured during the operation and many Germans were killed. Our casualties amounted to 2 Officers (1 killed) and 30 other ranks (5 killed) Most of these casualties were caused by M.G. fire. Throughout the day considerable movement of the enemy in small parties were seen trickling forward. These proved good sniping targets and it is claimed that many of the enemy were killed by us. The night was comparatively quiet with intermittent shelling and M.G. fire.	
	14th.		During the night the 2/20th. London Regt. 185th. Inf.Bde. formed up behind our line and that of the 2/4th. Duke of Wellington's Regt. in A.34.a. At 5.20am. they attacked under an artillery creeping barrage having as an objective the HINDENBURG LINE K.28.d.5.5. - TRIANGLE WOOD - KIMBER TRENCH to the Railway A.28.c.9.3. One hour before Zero this Battalion was ordered to withdraw all posts in the HINDENBURG LINE to West of the grid line between A.54.a. and b. Until the barrage had passed. A Coy. was therefore withdrawn to ANGLES TRENCH in A.35.d. and to BUTLERS TRENCH (C.S.A.) "C" Coy. formed up behind the leading wave of the 2/20th. London Regt. with orders after Zero to follow them and mop up the front and support trenches of the HINDENBURG LINE in A.34.a. and b. and after the objective had been gained to take over the line between K.35.a.5.5. and A.35.a.5.8. and establish a liaison post with 9th. Durham Light Infantry at K.35.a.5.0. By 7 a.m. it was ascertained that the 2/20th. London Regt. had cleared T Wood (in K.28.b.) and TRIANGLE WOOD (K.35.a.) of the enemy and were in KIMBER TRENCH, "C" Coy. successfully mopped up the trench system in A.34.a. and b. Without any casualties to themselves and captured 2 Machine Guns and 3 Officers and 73 other ranks prisoners in their area. The line was then established and consolidated from A.35.a.5.8. to A.35.a.5.4. in touch with 2/20th. London Regt. on the N. and 9th. Durham Light Infantry on the S. On obtaining their objective the 2/20th. London Regt. found themselves rather weak N. of the HINDENBURG LINE and we were asked to reinforce them. This was done by moving C Coy. up KEATINGS LANE in K.29.c. and extending our front northwards whilst they also closed up northwards.	

Army Form C. 2118.

5th BN DUKE OF WELLINGTON'S REGT.
WAR DIARY
or
INTELLIGENCE SUMMARY.
(Erase heading not required.)

Instructions regarding War Diaries and Intelligence Summaries are contained in F.S. Regs., Part II. and the Staff Manual respectively. Title pages will be prepared in manuscript.

Place	Date	Hour	Summary of Events and Information	Remarks and references to Appendices
	1918. Sept.		At night the Brigade front was readjusted and this Battalion took over the front area of the right sub-sector with a front line (C Coy. and half a platoon of B Coy.) extending from K.35.a.6.7. in touch with 2/4th. Duke of Wellington's Regt. along Sunken Road in K.35.b.C. to a point K.35.c.2.5. in touch with 7th. Division. "A" Coy. in support in HINDENBURG LINE about KUT LANE K.34.b. "B" Coy. from The TIP K.34.d.5.0. to A.34.d.95.40. "D" Coy. 1 platoon at junction of SWING TRENCH with KANGAROO AVENUE, 2 platoons in KNUCKLE TRENCH K.35.d. and 1 platoon in BUTLER TRENCH Q.5.a. Battalion H.Q. remained at Q.5.b.1.1. The night was quiet with exception of the usual intermittent artillery fire and Machine Gun fire.	
	15th.		During the night information was received that prisoners reported a possible counter-attack might take place this morning. Our artillery accordingly put down heavy counter preparation barrages at 4.45am, 5.30am and 6.30am. This drew heavy enemy retaliation. From dawn until 7.0am. the whole of the forward area was very heavily shelled and considerable casualties resulted. At 6.15am. the S.O.S. signal went up on our left. No hostile attack developed on the front of the battalion or on the battalion fronts immediately north and south. At night the battalion was relieved by the 1st. Herts Regt. 57th. Divn. The night was comparatively quiet and the relief was effected by 2.am. without many casualties. On relief the battalion very tired but cheery marched to Bivouacs at SEUGNY. During these operations extending from Sept. 14th. to 15th. the battalion suffered casualties:— 5 Officers 145 other ranks. 5 enemy machine guns were captured and 147 other ranks taken prisoner by the battalion.	

Army Form C. 2118.

1st Bn. 5th D. of Wellington's (W.R.)Regt.

WAR DIARY
or
INTELLIGENCE SUMMARY.
(Erase heading not required.)

Instructions regarding War Diaries and Intelligence Summaries are contained in F. S. Regs. Part II. and the Staff Manual respectively. Title pages will be prepared in manuscript.

Place	Date	Hour	Summary of Events and Information	Remarks and references to Appendices
Ref.Map. 57.c. 1/40000.	1918. Sept. 16th.		The Batt'lion marched from BEUGNY over cross country tracks via BARASTRE to near HAPLINCOURT (A.23.c.) There was practically no communication between the 20 Bivouac sheets. The men were therefore bivouaced in the open as it was raining.	
	17th.		A very violent thunderstorm occurred during the night. Practically all bivouacs were blown down and officers and men were all drenched besides having lost their equipment wet as well. Battalion left very busy during the day with reorganisation work. Getting dry and drawing up.	
	18th.		Aft' All day spent on activities. Reorganisation was continued. A.M.'s held a low ... to help us in making the men soldiers assured. Very stormy.	
	19th.		Battalion all ranks training in morning with close order drill at intervals.	
	20th.		- Ditto -	
	21st.		Wet day all day. Close line interval. Battalion in camp. By the wire in morning. Reoreation in the afternoon.	
	22nd.		Church Services for all denominations during the morning. Remainder of the day was observed as Sunday.	
	23rd.		Fine day but windier Sight. The Battalion did Battalion Attack practice during the morning. 'A' & 'D' Spec'list Training and Recreation as held in the afternoon.	

Army Form C. 2118.

5th. Duke of Wellington's (W.R.) Regt.

WAR DIARY
or
INTELLIGENCE SUMMARY.
(Erase heading not required.)

Instructions regarding War Diaries and Intelligence
Summaries are contained in F. S. Regs., Part II.
and the Staff Manual respectively. Title pages
will be prepared in manuscript.

Place	Date	Hour	Summary of Events and Information	Remarks and references to Appendices
Ref.Map. 57.c. 1/40000.	1918. Sept. 24th.		Battalion did a Battalion attack practice in the morning. Brigade Sports were held during the afternoon and all men did baths at SAPIGNIES.	
	25th.		Battalion made battle arrangements and dumped packs, Surplus Stores etc. Battalion moved from GOMIECOURT AREA at night and marched to FAVREUIL area. Battalion H.Q. was at B.27. central - 1 Company, at H.10.c. and 3 Companies and transport at H.5.b.	
	26th.		Battalion rested all day.	

5th. Duke of Wellington's (W.R.) Regt.

WAR DIARY
or
INTELLIGENCE SUMMARY.
(Erase heading not required.)

Army Form C. 2118.

Place	Date	Hour	Summary of Events and Information	Remarks and references to Appendices
Ref. Map. 57.c.N.E. 57.D.S.W. 1/10000.	1918. Sept. 25th.		The Battalion marched with transport of 186th. Inf. Bde. to BEAUMETZ and LEBUCQUIERE arriving there at 12 midnight. Battalion H.Q. was at D Brigade H.Q. in Sunken Road in C.20.c. Unable to crowd into some sheds in the village of BEAUMETZ. It was a very wet night.	
	27th.		The 62nd. Division was held in Reserve for an attack by the VI Corps which had as its object the capture of the FLESQUIERES RIDGE and clearing up the HINDENBURG SUPPORT SYSTEM on that Ridge (this to be done by 3rd. Division) and then by exploiting success clear with the object of establishing a bridgehead East of the Canal de ST. QUENTIN in the direction of RUMILLY (this to be done by the 62nd. Division). Zero hour for the attack was at 7.30am. The Battalion moved off by Companies from BEAUMETZ at zero hour plus 10 minutes (5.40am.) and entered by Platoons via P.4.a.2.8. – LONG VALLEY – MATHIESEN R.d., CLAYTON CROSS, PLOWDER VALLEY to a position of assembly south of the RAVRINCOURT – HERMIES Road in K.27.c. Battn.H.Q. was established at the filled in crater about K.26.d.5.1. This move was completed by 10.30am. Each company took its Lewis Gun limber with it and rear Amidst. The journey was made without serious difficulty. The tracks were rather sticky after the rain, which made the going slow. Hostile shelling was not very severe en route although one man was wounded. The weather cleared up.	
			The Battalion remained on its assembly area until 4.30pm. in the afternoon when orders were received to move to area K.10.b. and there await further instructions. The Battalion moved out to the village. At the same time the enemy was heavily shelling HAVRINCOURT and the roads in and out of the village which delayed the move for about 15 minutes. The Battalion moved by Platoons via K.27.c., K.21.b and d., K.15.a and d., along HUGHES TRENCH and STAG ALLEY. Some difficulty was experienced in getting along the trench system after dark and finding locations. The Battalion was eventually settled by 8.0pm. The men lay in the bottom of the trenches and rested as well as they could for a few hours.	
	28th		Orders were received from Brigade at 3.am. that the Battalion was to capture the village of MARCOING and the line of the CANAL de ST. QUENTIN West of it at 5.30am. The 2/4th.Hants Regt. were to pass through the Battalion and rush a bridge head. The 2/4th. Duke of Wellington's Regt. to be in Brigade Reserve and to exploit success by the capture of RUMILLY.	

5th. Batn. of Wellington's (W.R.) Regt.

Army Form C. 2118.

WAR DIARY
or
INTELLIGENCE SUMMARY.
(Erase heading not required.)

Place	Date	Hour	Summary of Events and Information	Remarks and references to Appendices
	1918. Sept.		The battalion moved off from W.T.O.P. at 1.0.a.m. It was an extremely dark night, the men were heavily laden and fired and it was very difficult to keep in touch. Time as very short for the long march, so it was not possible to reach the "starting off" point B. of MASQUIERES until 7.0.a.m. half an hour after zero. The men were all exhausted with the long march carrying Lewis Guns etc. As the battalion had not been able to reach the starting point before zero, O.C. 2/4th. Hants Regt. had not had for to march and he was already formed up, deafned. After reorganising and moving A, B brigade, he send his battalion over behind the barrage in front of this battalion as leap frog through on arrival. The new arrangements had to be explained to company commanders on the spot as the formed up in rear W.19. The battalion moved off from ridge W.19 in artillery formation at V.-Coy. in two waves. A Company was on the right with two platoons. C Company on the right and D Coy (left) and D Coy. (right) in the second wave. No. 1 section of D Company and B.M.G. Corps went forward behind D Company (Infantry) in support of the attack and were absorbed by a reserve platoon of A Company. This left 1 platoon of A Company in battalion reserve at Bn. H.Q. at W.19.a.7.1. The battalion overtook the 2/4th.Hants Regt. in the village of Marcoing. In conjunction with 2/4th. Hants Regt.this was overcome and the line of the Canal de ST. QUENTIN was reached before 9..... In spite of the utmost difficulty B and D companies managed to extricate their companies across the canal before 11..... The bridges had been destroyed by the enemy and the canal bank was very deep, making it a very real obstacle. As our troops crossed the Canal they were subjected to heavy enfilade enemy machine gun fire from W.I.C., and W.I7.D. In addition to the shelling. These companies were only able to keep the enemy fire moderately down by putting Lewis Guns into the attics of houses on the Canal Side and keep the enemy engaged whilst the troops dribbled across. Later on 4 A. a C Companies crossed the Canal. "C" Company left one platoon in Reserve at Company H.Q. on the West side of the Canal. The remaining Companies (except "A") took all platoons on to the East side of the Canal. The 2/4th. Hants Regt. took up a line on the West Bank of the Canal after this battalion had passed through them.	

WAR DIARY
or
INTELLIGENCE SUMMARY.

Army Form C. 2118.

5th Bn. Duke of Wellington's (W.R.) Regt.

(Erase heading not required.)

Instructions regarding War Diaries and Intelligence Summaries are contained in F. S. Regs., Part II. and the Staff Manual respectively. Title pages will be prepared in manuscript.

Place	Date	Hour	Summary of Events and Information	Remarks and references to Appendices
	1918. Sept.		after crossing the Canal companies were a little mixed but all platoons maintained their entirety as all four organised units. All companies on crossing the canal quickly pressed forward and immediately came under heavy M.G. fire from the trench MARCOING SWITCH which was held strongly by the enemy. Heavy enfilade fire was very troublesome, also from the north from the roof but it was not possible. A line was then established along the line of the railway from about L.17.d.8.3. to L.23.d.0.3. All day there was a good deal of sniping by the enemy and ourselves. The enemy by his enfilade M.G. fire from the north prevented the Engineers from repairing the bridges during the hours of day light. The line of the Canal and MARCOING were heavily shelled by the enemy all day. Companies established excellent observation posts in the attics of houses on the eastern side of the Canal Bank. These observers saw numbers of the enemy in marching order enter MARCOING SUPPORT French during the afternoon, at the same time a message was received from Bde. that the enemy were concentrating in RUMILLY being brought there in busses. The Battalion was later ordered to attack the two trench system MARCOING SUPPORT and MARCOING SUPPORT running through L.17., L.23, L.24 the objective being from L.23.a.5.4. to M.19.c.9.1. This was to be done under Artillery barrage at Zero. Barrage commenced at Zero on the line of MARCOING SWITCH and rested there 5 minutes. Then lifted to MARCOING SUPPORT where it rested for 15 minutes. Owing to companies not having had an opportunity to properly organise under cover to the variation of ground had to be gone by all four companies such on one platoon front with one platoon in support and a platoon of each company in Reserve. Our troops advanced with vigour and found a battalion of the enemy in MARCOING SWITCH and MARCOING SUPPORT who greatly outnumbered the attacking troops and were themselves preparing to attack. Our right Company (D) (catching cross about 40 strong) captured their objective and were immediately supported by the remaining 3 platoons (40 strong). They claim 40 prisoners and 9 Machine guns East half Coy objective without serious trouble about L.23.d.0.5. to L.24.c.1.b. The left Coy--- (A) got to about 100 yards of the objective but the supporting Platoons had been in difficulty Reserve Coy the W. bank of the Canal did not reach them to its. The attacking Platoons (C) strong under Capt. .... arrived under the M.J. stops and well under the barrage and cleared an enemy machine gun in MARCOING SWITCH which fired, then rushed, capturing the wounded officer and 3 other ranks in the dugout close by.	

WAR DIARY or INTELLIGENCE SUMMARY

Army Form C. 2118.

(Erase heading not required.)

Place	Date	Hour	Summary of Events and Information	Remarks and references to Appendices
	1918. Sept.		Continuing their advance the Platoon reached MARCOING SUPPORT in which there were many M.G.'s. Not finding anyone on his flanks 2/Lieut. Lloyd sent out to each flank along the trench to get into touch with other troops and meanwhile barricaded the dugouts for the enemy. The men sent to his right had to beat a hasty retreat owing to very M.G. fire and numbers of the enemy seemed to tell men had to be a hasty retreat owing to very M.G. fire and numbers of the enemy appearing to counterattack. They next saw a great number of Huns rolling up the trench in rear (MARCOING SWITCH) who commenced firing on them. Finding he was completely surrounded, 2/Lieut. Lloyd decided to get back and therefore ordered his men to do so. Out of one trench in charge the guns this they did with great élan and shouting vigorously dashed into the enemy and so frightened them that they began hastily, with their equipment on and throwing up their hands. The new was driven back on its own Oasis who desired these men to allow and remained their prisoners took 38 prisoners. All through this action W.Y a Company's Platoon the enemy brought heavy M.G. fire to bear on them from our left flank which really caused as much damage to his own troops as to ours. The spirit of the men in this Platoon was really wonderful and he was only slightly wounded in the leg and arm would not leave until the action was over. The two centre companies B and C between simultaneously with the Companies on right and left, and gained their objectives in MARCOING SUPPORT but finding themselves isolated with the enemy on each side of them rifle and machine gun counter attacks developed on the left flank and they were unable to hold on and had to take up their original line on the railway. Whilst in MARCOING SUPPORT the prisoners they captured in MARCOING SWITCH were, tho' inadequately guarded and tired on their own troops in the rear, large numbers of prisoners were taken - estimated at 450 - and with our troops being disorganised and numerically inferior the greatest confusion arose and the reserve platoons on the line of the railway restored the situation and prisoners were got away. The counter attack battered off and the line established - MARCOING SUPPORT TRENCH from M.23.d.6.5. to L.22.d.1.3. Then back to Railway - M.23.D.4.0. to M.23.b.4.8. In all 25 machine guns were captured and estimated prisoners 500 with 5 officers. In view of the small numbers and exhausted nerves of the attacking force, the immediate capture of large numbers and machine-guns counterattack from the left - the troops showed the greatest resolution and promptitude. During the whole of this operation and throughout the night the enemy very heavily bombarded the bridges over the Canal, the line of the Railway and the village of MARCOING with H.E.'s.	

Army Form C. 2118.

5th. Duke of **WAR DIARY** (W.R.) Regt.

or

INTELLIGENCE SUMMARY.

(Erase heading not required)

Place	Date	Hour	Summary of Events and Information	Remarks and references to Appendices
	1918. Sept.			
	2nd.		During the night the troops recrgamised. Our casualties during the day amounted to 5 officers (1 killed) and 130 other ranks.	
	3rd.	At 7.30a.m.	The 2/4th. Duke of Wellington's Regt. passed through our line under an artillery barrage until the ultimate objective CANAL DU NORD was reached, RUMILLY TRENCH and exploiting this success by capturing the village of RUMILLY. They met with considerable opposition and were heavily counter attacked. Two companies held RUMILLY TRENCH and obtained a footing in RUMILLY SUPPORT. Later on in the evening the 2/4th. Dukes Regt. were sent through to endeavour to clear the situation up and take RUMILLY but they were held up by determined enemy resistance. During the day the battalion became Brigade Support and Labor Brigade Reserve. B Company moved two platoons into MARCOING SUPPORT on the left of "D" Company with A and C Companies still in support on the line of the Railway. A subway lay.	
	4th.		The 145th. Inf. Bde. endeavoured to clear up the situation in RUMILLY SUPPORT TRENCH where there was an obstinate pocket of the enemy who held out very valiantly and prevented our troops getting forward. At night the battalion moved 2 platoons of "D" Company up into the system of trenches astride the Grid line between G.20.a and c to protect any enemy infiltration which the enemy might attempt between RUMILLY and MASNIERES. During the night two companies of 1st. Gordons, 3rd Division, formed up in our area and the battalion was withdrawn from the battle zone at dawn on Oct. 1st. and marched to a bivouac area near Locx 7, K.15. where there was scant accommodation. The casualties sustained by the battalion during the 4 days fighting amounted to - 3 Officers killed, 8 Officers wounded, 1 Officer shell shock.	

Other ranks.
Killed. 14
Died of Wounds. 1
Wounded. (approx.) 250
Wounded at duty. 3
Missing. 82

The captures of the battalion in the same period amounted to 5 Officers and 350 other ranks, and 25 machine guns.

J. Walker ..Lieut.Col.
Commdg. 5th.Duke of Wellington's Regiment

Army Form C. 2118.

5th.Batn. Duke of Wellington's (W.R.) Regt.

WAR DIARY
or
INTELLIGENCE SUMMARY.
(Erase heading not required.)

Place	Date	Hour	Summary of Events and Information	Remarks and references to Appendices
			DRAFTS etc.	
			Lieut. A. Adamson.)	
			2/Lieut. C. Bentley.)	
			" T.S. Davenport) Joined Batn. 5.9.18.	
			" E. Ellis)	
			" G. Monkman)	
			" G.A. Barnett.)	
			" S.E. Briggs)	
			" A. Rossington)	
			2/Lieut. J. Eagan) Joined Batn. 6.9.18.	
			" B. King)	
			2/Lieut. T. Shepherd. Joined Batn. 5.9.18.	
			Lieut. L. Clapham. Joined Batn. 19.9.18.	
			CASUALTIES, TRANSFERS, etc.	
			Capt. J.R. Cockhill DSO,MC. To England. 18.9.18.	Other Ranks.
			" C.H. Isenwood. To Hospital. 28.9.18.	
			" C.B. Foster. Wounded. 2.9.18.	Killed. 5.9.18. 55
			2/Lieut. G.V. Barnett. Killed. 26.9.18.	Died of wounds. 7.9.18. 26
			" G.V. Chriesworth. Killed. 26.9.18.	8.9.18. 7
			" E. Benson. Died of wounds. 16.9.18.	19.9.18. 51
			" S.E. Briggs. Wounded. 26.9.18.	
			" T.R. Morton M.C. Wounded(Gas). 28.9.18.	OTHER RANKS.
			" A. Farrer. Wounded. 15.9.18.	Killed. 34.
			" A. Rossington. Wounded at duty. 13.9.18.	Died of wounds. 11.
			" R. Brook. To Hospital, sick. 10.9.18.	Wounded. 205
				Wounded (gas). 5
			RELINQUISHMENTS etc.	Wounded at duty. 5
			Lieut. (A/Capt.) C.B. McRink relinquished the acting rank of captain on ceasing to command	Missing. 5
			a Company dated 1.9.18.	

Original

5th.Date of WAR DIARY (W.R.) Regt.

or

INTELLIGENCE SUMMARY.

Army Form C. 2118.

Place	Date	Hour	Summary of Events and Information	Remarks and references to Appendices
			APPENDICES (contd.).	
			HONOURS etc. The following have been awarded decorations as stated for gallantry and devotion to duty in the field. 268030 Sergt.Spivey F.M. BAR TO MILITARY MEDAL. 241636 Corpl.Shearsmith L.W. MM. - do - 235653 Pte. Ward T. MILITARY MEDAL. 240663 Pte. Jennings R. do. 14367 Cpl. Roberts G. do. 235629 Cpl. Levy I. do. 268800 L.Cpl.Barker W. do. 34561 Pte. Walker A. do. 347.59 Pte. McClintock W. do. 306513 Pte. Stead H.W. do. 34486 Pte. Key C. do. 306037 L.Cpl. Shaw H. do. 241222 L.Cpl. Rhodes C. do. 200121 L.Cpl. Rushwell S. do. 240139 C.S.M. Rules W. do. 242651 Pte. Watson E. do. 241691 Pte. Cook L.H. do. J.Walker Lieut.Col. Comdg. 5th.Duke of Wellington's Regiment.	

SECRET.　　　　　　　　　　　　　　　　　　　　　　　　　　　　Copy No. 10.

5TH. DUKE OF WELLINGTON'S REGT.

Operation Order No. 154.

Ref. Map. 57.c. 1/40,000. e/c

1. **MOVE.** The Brigade will march to the north west corner of HAVRINCOURT WOOD tomorrow evening 9th inst. The Brigade will probably march in the late afternoon.

2. **RECONNOITRING PARTIES.** (a). Lieut. W.L. Sidders and Sgt. Blakeley M.M. will report to Capt. G.B. Bruce at 62nd. Divisional H.Q. TRIANGLE COPSE at 8.am tomorrow morning. They will proceed by lorry to reconnoitre bivouac areas and roads into the wood and will be prepared to meet the battalion and guide it to its area on arrival during the night.
(b). A reconnoitring party consisting of Major B. Senior and the seconds in command of A, B, C and D Coys. will rendezvous opposite GOMIECOURT CHATEAU 10.am tomorrow where a lorry will be in readiness. The Lorry will then call at Brigade H.Q. where the battalion Reconnoitring Party will receive further instructions from the Commanding Officer. This reconnoitring party will rejoin the battalion on its arrival at HAVRINCOURT WOOD.

3. **CONFERENCE.** There will be a conference of Commanding Officers of Battalions at Bde. H.Q. at 9.30am. tomorrow.

4. **SURPLUS KIT etc.** The battalion has to be prepared to dump all surplus baggage which cannot be carried on the baggage waggons, and packs at the present Waggon Lines. Surplus personnel will also be left here. No lorries are available. Coys. will have packs ready by 10.am. tomorrow. Further orders will be issued as regards transference to Waggon Lines.

8/9/18

............K Sykes............Capt.& Adjt.
5th. Duke of Wellington's Regiment.

Copies to -
A,B,C,D and H.Q. Coys.
2nd. in Command.
Q.M.
Adjutant.
War Diary (2).
Office.

TO - All recipients of O.O. 134.

Ref. para. 1. of O.O.134.   For N.W. read S.W.

..............Capt.& Adjt.
5th.Duke of Wellington's Regiment.

9.9.18.

SECRET.   Copy No. 9

5TH. DUKE OF WELLINGTON'S REGT.

Operation Order No. 135.

Ref. Map. SHEET 57.c. 1/40,000.   9th. Septr. 1918.

1. **MOVE.** The battalion will march from COURCELLES AREA with 186th. Inf. Bde. Group to HAVRINCOURT WOOD tomorrow in accordance with attached March Table.
   The Battalion will parade near Guard Tent at 3.pm. in Mass.
   Transport lines will be West of RUYAULCOURT about P.9.c.

2. **DISTANCES** Distances of 100 yards will be maintained between Companies and between the battalion and the Transport.

3. **BILLETING.** Billeting Officer (Lieut. W.L. Ridders) will meet the Battalion on the BERTINCOURT - HAVRINCOURT Road at P.1.c.4.2.

4. **ADMINISTRA-** Separate administrative instructions have been issued to the
   TIVE.   Q.M.
   Two Storemen will be detailed as under to remain in charge of the Battalion Dump. They will report to Q.M. at 12 noon tomorrow for instructions -
   "B" Coy.   1 other rank.
   "C" Coy.   1 other rank.

5. **STRETCHER** 7 other ranks of the Band will be detailed for duty will
   BEARERS.   2/2nd. W.R. Field Ambulance as stretcher bearers. They will not report until ordered by Bde. Rear H.Q.

6. **GENERAL.** (a). Transport will be hidden as far as possible - any Transport that is left in the open should be split into small groups.
   (b). Care must be taken that no fires or lights are showing after dusk.
   (c). Men must not be allowed to move about by day more than is absolutely necessary.
   (d). Companies and H.Q. will render nominal rolls of all men going into action to the Adjutant by 9.am. 11th. Septr.

7. Acknowledge.

Issued at ..4.30/pm..

..R.Sykes.. Capt. & Adjt.
5th. Duke of Wellington's Regiment.

Copies to -
1 to 5. A, B, C, D and H.Q. Coys.
   6. Senior Major.
   7. Q.M.
8 & 9. War Diary.
  10. Adjutant.
  11. 186th. Inf. Bde.
  12. Office.

MARCH TABLE TO ACCOMPANY Battn.O.O. 13b.

Serial No.	Unit.	Starting Point.	To.	Time to Pass Starting Point.	Route.	Remarks.
1.	185th. Inf.Bde.H.Q.	Junction of road and railway. G.4.c.6.4.	S.W. corner of HAVRINCOURT WOOD.	—	WARLUS – GOUZEAUCOURT – HAVRINCOURT WOOD – road junction W.30.c.5.5. – HAPLINCOURT – RUYAULCOURT.	To join column in front of 5th.D.of W.Regt. at BARASTRE SUGAR FACTORY 5.25pm. Not to enter BERTINCOURT before 6.15pm.
2.	5th. D. of W. Regt.		Brigade H.Q. J.26.d.9.5.	4pm.		
3.	186th. T.M. Battery.			4.15pm.		
4.	2/4th. D.of W.Regt.			4.3pm.		
5.	2/4th. Hants Regt.			4.25pm.		
6.	"D" Coy. 62nd.Bn.M.G.C.			5pm.		To join column at Cross Roads East of HAPLINCOURT C.5.c.c.0. at 9.5pm. in rear of "D" Coy. 62nd. Bn. M.G.C.
7.	9th. D.L.I.			—		

2.9.18.

SHEET: 57c N.E & S.E (Parts of). SCALE:- 1:10,000.

U.T.S. MAP No. 415 / 9.9.18.

MESSAGE FORM.

Map reference, or mark position on back
Alter sentences as necessary.

To ....

1. I am at .... (and am consolidating
2. I am at .... (and have consolidated
   (and am ready to advance to ......

3. I am held up at .... by (Wire.
                                       (M G
                                       (T.M.   at ....
                                       (Enemy

4. I have sent patrols forward to ....

5. I need .... S.A.A.   Very Lights
                         Bombs.   SOS Signals
                         Rifle Grenades   Spare Lewis Gun Drums
                         Water   Stretcher-bearers
                         Wire   Stakes

   Send the above to ....

6. Enemy troops strength estimated at .... (assembling at ....
                                                 (advancing from ....
                                                 (retiring from ....

7. I am in touch with .... on (Right at ....
                                             (Left

8. I am not in touch   on (Right
                             (Left

9. I estimate my present strength at .... rifles.

10. Hostile (M.G.
            (T.M. at .... shooting at ....
            (Bty.

11. I intend to ....

12. Remarks:-

Time .... am   Name .... Platoon ....
                pm
Date ....   Rank .... Coy ....
                                                Battn ....

Copy of letter received from Lieut.Genl. Sir W.P.Braithwaite
K.C.B., C.B. late Commander 62nd. (W.R.) Division.

- -

9th.Sept.1918.

My dear Walker,

So many thanks for the congratulations which you have sent me on behalf of the officers, W.Os, N.C.Os and other ranks of the 5th. Duke of Wellington's Regt. I appreciate them very much indeed. I feel, really, that the K.C.B. belongs to the 62nd. Division for it was the magnificent fighting of the Div. which secured this honour for its late Commander. It is very gratifying to get such a testimony of goodwill as you have forwarded to me from the Battn. you command, a Battn. on which I knew I could always rely not only to do its full share of any fighting but - a bit more.

Thank you again,

Yours sincerely,

(sd). WALTER P.BRAITHWAITE.

185th. Infantry Brigade.	62nd. Bn. M.G. Corps.
186th. Infantry Brigade.	9th. Bn. D.L.I.
187th. Infantry Brigade.	62nd. Div. Signal Coy.
G.O.C. R.A.	A.D.M.S.
C.R.E.	62nd. Divl. Train.

I have great pleasure in publishing for the information of all ranks of the Division, the following extract from a personal letter, dated September 13th, I have received from General Sir Julien Byng, Commanding 3rd. Army -

"I set the 62nd. Division a very hard task yesterday, but the importance of it was so great that I determined to try it.
The Division has done it, and done it splendidly, and so I write to let you know how proud I am of their achievement."

(sd).R.WHIGHAM.
............Major General,
Commanding 62nd. (West Riding) Division.

14.9.18.

The following is a copy of wire received from Maj.Genl.
Sir R. WHIGHAM K.C.B. D.S.O., Commander
62nd. (W.R.) Division.

"Warmest thanks and congratulations to all troops of your Brigade and Batteries that support them."

(sd). R. WHIGHAM. Majr. General.
Commanding 62nd. (W.R.) Division.

12.9.18.

5th Duke of Wellington's Regt.
Operation Orders No. 139.

Ref. Maps. 57c NE and SE 1/20000

1. The Battn. subsector will be readjusted tonight. All movements will take place as soon after dusk as possible.

2. C Coy will remain in their present front line but will not extend further N. than TRIANGLE WOOD which is inclusive to 2/4th Duke of Wellington's Regt. They will establish a liaison post with 34th Div. if possible about K.35.b.2.6. They will also relieve the two posts of A Coy. 9th Durham Light Infantry in K.36.a and d. Liaison will be established with 2/4 Loyal N.L. who are relieving 2/20th London Regt.
   Coy H.Q. will remain in KIN LANE.

   A Coy will establish posts with 1 platoon along the line of the sunk line between K.34.b. and K.35.a. in support of front line. 3 Remaining platoons will establish the return swam of KUT LANE with Platoon HQ. Coy HQ will be with B Coy at K.34a.5.5.

B Coy will relieve A Coy of 9th D.L.I. (less two posts in K.35a and c) in the area K.34a from the FEMY LINE to the TIP. Platoon guides & 1 for Coy HQ will be at present Battn HQ at 7 p.m. to guide B Coy into position. Coy HQ will be in KIN LANE.

D Coy will be in Battn. Resv. Two platoons will be accommodated in dugouts in SWING Trench K.34b. These two platoons will provide liaison posts with 2/4th D. of W (a) at MOAT K.34a.5.6 (b) at junction of STAR Trench and KIN LANE. One platoon and Coy HQ will be in KNUCKLE Trench. Remaining platoon will be at BUTLER Trench.

1 Coy of Durham Light Infantry will withdraw to BUTLER Trench near Battn. HQ. and be under orders of Commanding Officer for immediate counter-attack.

Battn. HQ will remain at its present location.

(2)

3. Rations
Rations for A B C Coys will be delivered if practicable by pack animals to junction of SHROPSHIRE SPUR Road and SWING Trench about K.34.a.9.3. about 10.15 p.m.

D Coys rations will be dumped at Battn HQ.

4. Coys will forward disposition with sketch as soon as possible after relief.

5. Completion of relief will be notified by wiring the figures '1H'

6. On completion of relief these Orders will be destroyed.

7. Acknowledge.

K Sykes
Capt & Adjt
5th D. of Wellingtons Regt.

Copies to:-
A B C D Coys.
O.C. 4th D. of W. Regt (for infm)
HQ 186th I.B. (for infm)
O.C. 9th D.L.I. (   )
War Diary (2)
Office

Secret. War Diary   Copy No. 6
5th Duke of Wellington's Regt.
Operation Order No. 138

Ref. Maps. Sheet 57c NE & 57c SE.
           57c 1/40000.   15.9.18.

1. Boundary.
   After dusk the inter battalion boundary will be readjusted. C Coy will side-slip northwards and take over posts of 2/4th Duke of Wellington's Regt. South of K.29.c.6.0. Similarly 1 Platoon of D Coy (at present in SW'ing Trench) will take over posts of 2/4th D. of W's Regt. in STAR Trench Southwards from K.28.c.8.0. This adjustment will be completed as soon after dusk as possible.

2. Relief.
   The Battn. will be relieved by 1st Herts. Regt. tonight.

3. Guides
   Platoon guides and 1 for Coy HQ (5 per Coy) will report to Lieut. W.L. Sidders at Adv. BHQ at 8.30 p.m. These guides must be sure of their way.

(1)

4. Order of Relief etc.
   D Coy will be relieved by No 2 Coy 1st Herts.
   B "   "   "   "   " 1 "   "   "
   C "   "   "   "   " 4 "   "   "
   A "   "   "   "   " 3 "   "   "

5. Handing over.
   Bombs, S.A.A, S.O.S. Grenades and tools will be handed over and receipt obtained. O.C A Coy will hand over dump of Bombs and SAA at K.34 a.8.3.
   Coy. dispositions will be most carefully handed over.

6. Transport &c.
   Lewis Gun limbers will be at BHQ at 11 pm. Lewis guns will be loaded there and each Coy leave a guard with them.
   Cookers and water carts will be at MILL COTTAGE P.24 b.5.9 at 12 midnight. Troops will stop there for a meal.
   Horses for C.O. Adjt M.O. and Coy Commanders will be at P.24 b.5.9 at 12 midnight.

7. On relief.
   On relief the Battn will march

(2)

"D" Coy independently to BEUGNY
Coy's:— P.24.b.5.9 — RUYAULCOURT —
BERTINCOURT — Cross roads O.5.a.0.0
— BEUGNY.

Guides will meet the Battn. on
arrival at the cross roads south of
BEUGNY 1.28.b.6.2.

The Brigade will march on the
afternoon of the 16th inst. to the
Railway COURCELLES.

8. Completion of Relief
Completion of relief tonight
will be notified to BHQ by wiring
the number "15".
Arrival at BEUGNY will be
notified in usual way.

9. Acknowledge.

Issued at 6.10/pm.

K Sykes Capt & Adj.
5th D. of Wellington's Regt.

Copies to —
A B C(?) D Coys.
Maj. Simon, Rear HQ
War Diary (2)
Office

Copy of letter received from Lieut.Col.C.R.NEWMAN DSO. G.S.O.1.
62nd. (W.R.) Division.

Septr. 16th.

My dear Walker,

I am so sorry not to see you to say good bye before I leave, but there is no time. Your Battalion has once more covered itself in glory. My best congratulations, and I am most sorry to part from you and them. Wishing you all good luck and still further successes.

Yours very sincerely,
(sd). C.R. NEWMAN.

Secret   Copy No 4

5 Duke of Wellington's Regt.
Operation Order.

Ref Map 57 C NW. 1/20,000.

1/ <u>Relief</u> The Battⁿ will be relieved tonight by 1st Batt King's Liverpool Reg^t.

On relief the Batt. proceeds to Railway embankment between GOMIECOURT & COURCELLES.

2/ <u>Order time of Relief</u>
D Coy 1st King's Liverpool R^t. will relieve our A & B. Coys
No 13 + 14 Platoons relieve our A Coy.
" 15 + 16   "   "   " B Coy.
C Coy 1st King's will relieve our C + D. Coy
Nos 9 + 10 Platoons relieve our C Coy
" 11 & 12   "   "   " D Coy
Two reliable guides per Coy will report to Lieut. M. Tod at Batt. HQ at 9.45 pm.

Relief is expected to take place about 10-11 pm.

On relief Coys will proceed independantly to GOMIECOURT

Rear HQ will provide guides to

meet Coys. at Fork Road at A23d 10.35

3. Transport Lewis Gun Limbers will be at Battn HQ H5 d 9.2 at 10.30 pm. 1 Limber will be at Bn. Rear HQ H4c 4.7 at 10.30 pm.
Coys will each provide their own Lewis Gun Guards. Petrol Tins will be brought out of the line.

4) Handing Over All ammunition (in boxes) Very Lights, S.O.S. Signals. Bombs (in boxes) Picks + Shovels will be handed over and receipts obtained
Dispositions will be carefully handed over

5) Report
Coys will report "Relief Complete" by telephone by wiring the word "THANKS" or by runner.
Arrival in new area will be notified to B.H.Q.

6) Rear HQ
Batt. HQ Personnel at H4c 4.7 will move off at 10.30 pm without

... being relieved.
... Acknowledge.

Klyher Capt & Adjt
5 West Rid. Regt.

Issued at 9.15 pm

Copies to:
1 A & B Coys
2 C & D Coys
3 To Sudden
4 Office
5 & 6. War Diary.

S E C R E T.   Copy No. 9

5th. DUKE OF WELLINGTON'S REGT.

Operation Order No.140.

Ref. Map. 57.c. 1/40,000.

1. MOVE.	The battalion will move from GOMIECOURT AREA to-day and will relieve 2/20th. London Regt. in BEHAGNIES AREA about H.5.a.
2. ORDER OF MARCH etc.	The battalion will parade by Companies on the E. side of the Camp at 5.30pm. March off at 100 yards interval in the following order - H.Q., C, B, D, A, Transport. No troops to cross ERVILLERS - BAPAUME Road before 6.30pm.
3. ADVANCE PARTY.	Advance party has proceeded ahead and will meet the battalion on arrival.
4. TRANSPORT.	All Valises, Orderly Room Boxes etc. will be dumped at Q.M. Stores by 4.15pm. this afternoon.
5. REPORTS.	Companies will report themselves "Settled in new area" as usual.
6.	Acknowledge.

Issued at 2.55 pm

K. Lyster... Capt. & Adjt.
5th. Duke of Wellington's Regt.

Copies to -
1 to 5. A, B, C, D and H.Q. Coys.
6. Lieut. Pod.
7. T.O. and Q.M.
8 & 9. War Diary.
10. Office.

SECRET.   Copy No. 9

5TH. DUKE OF WELLINGTON'S REGT.

Operation Order No.140.

26/9/18

Ref. Map. 57.c.N.E. 1/20,000.

1.   The battalion will move from FAVREUIL AREA to position of assembly in the Area BEAUMETZ tonight (Y/Z night).
     Position to be occupied is approximately BEAUMETZ and J.20 with H.Q. in Sunk Road J.20.c.5.9.

2.   Billeting Party proceeds in advance and will meet Battalion on arrival.

3.   Battalion Starting Point will be the FAVREUIL - MORY Road opposite A Coys. H.Q. Order of March - H.Q., D,A,B,C. Time to pass Starting Point will be notified later. It will probably be about 6.45pm.
     Route - FREMICOURT and LEBUCQUIERE.
     The head of Brigade Column will enter FREMICOURT at 8.45pm.

4.   Waggon Lines to-night will be established about I.17.c.

5.   It must be impressed on all ranks that there must be no additional movement in the forward area before dusk on Y/Z night. On Y day there must be no movement of troops during daylight East of a line BEAUMETZ - MORCHIES - LAGNICOURT, and reconnoitring officers and billeting parties approaching this line must do so by routes covered from observation from BOURLON WOOD. No fires must be lit or lights shown in assembly positions.

6.   Acknowledge.

                                          .....K.Sykes.....Capt. & Adjt.
                                          5th. Duke of Wellington's Regiment.

Copies to -
     1 to 5. A,B,C,D and H.Q. Coys.
         6. T.O. & Q.M.
         7. Adjutant.
     8 & 9. War Diary.
        10. Office.

SECRET.   Copy No 1..... 9

ADDENDUM TO OPERATION ORDER No.140.

1. The battalion has to pass Brigade Starting Point (Cross Roads I.19.c.6.1.) behind 2/4th. Duke of Wellington's Regt. at 9.25pm.
   The battalion will pass Battalion Starting Point at 8.10pm. commencing with H.Q. Company and maintaining usual distance of 100 yards between companies. Route will be via cross roads I.28.b.6.2. and LEBUCQUIERE.

2. Guides will meet the battalion at the point where the Railway Crosses the FREMICOURT - LEBUCQUIERE Road I.29.b.6.3.

3. 1 section of "D" Company 62nd. M.G. Battalion will join the battalion at Bde. Starting Point. They will march with H.Q. Coy. O.C. H.Q. Company will arrange their accommodation for to-night.

4. All companies will report arrival at destination.

5. Personnel and vehicles for Waggon Lines proceed direct to new Waggon Lines to-night. They will leave the battalion column in FREMICOURT and proceed by the BAPAUME - CAMBRAI Road direct to I.17.a.6.6. This personnel and vehicles must march in rear of the battalion. There must be no check in FREMICOURT. Cookers, L.G. Limbers, Pack animals, Water Cart and Mess Cart go forward with battalion as already arranged with T.O. They will go behind respective companies.
   It is anticipated that Waggon Lines will be established tomorrow in P.6.

                                        ......Khyber...... Capt.& Adjt.
                                        5th.Duke of Wellington's Regiment.

Copies to -
   1 to 5. A,B,C,D and H.Q. Coys.
        6. Adjutant.
        7. T.O. and Q.M.
    8 & 9. War Diary.
       10. Office.

Extract from British Official Communique dated 29.9.18.

"Later in the day our success was extended to the south, and Gouzeaucourt was captured.   During the morning, also, the 62nd. (Yorkshire) Division captured Marcoing, and made progress to the south east of it.   Before midday the 5TH. BATTALION DUKE OF WELLINGTON'S REGIMENT forced the crossings of the Canal de l'Escaut (Scheldt Canal) at Marcoing, and established itself in the German Defences on the East bank.".

H.Q., 62nd (West Riding) Division
1st October 1918.

The capture of HAVRINCOURT on 12th September was essential to the success of the Operations South of CAMBRAI in which the 62nd Division has been engaged during the last four days.

As a sequel to that brilliant achievement, the Division has now captured MARCOING, MASNIERES, and the high ground North of CREVECOEUR, thus establishing a Bridgehead over the CANAL de ST QUENTIN, which is vital to the further successful prosecution of the campaign.

I have today been visited by the Field Marshal Commanding-in-Chief who has desired me to convey to all ranks of the Division his congratulations and high appreciation of their splendid courage and endurance.

For myself I give you all my warmest thanks for the unfailing cheerfulness with which you have carried out the most arduous tasks, often in conditions of great hardship and discomfort.

It will ever be to me a pride to have commanded so magnificent a Division.

R.W.Whigham

Major-General,
Commanding 62nd (West Riding) Division.

H.Q. 62nd (W.R.) Divn.
1st October 1918.

I have received the following telegram from Lieutenant General Sir W.P. BRAITHWAITE, K.C.B., Commanding IX Corps.

"To: General WHIGHAM,
62nd Division.

Just heard of your great success at RIBECOURT and MARCOING AAA It is all splendid and just like 62 AAA Will you allow me to congratulate you and the Division and to say how very proud I am to have once commanded so splendid a Division."

I have sent him the following reply:-

"To: General BRAITHWAITE,
Cmdg. IX Corps.

62nd Division most grateful for your kind remembrance and congratulations AAA We congratulate you and IX Corps on your splendid successes."

Major General
Commanding 62nd (West Riding) Division.

SECRET.

WD 22

CONFIDENTIAL.

WAR DIARY.

- of -

5th DUNE OF WELLINGTON'S (W.R) REGIMENT.

1st to 31st October, 1918.

(Volume 22)

ORIGINAL.

E. Venour
Major,
Commanding 5th Duke of Wellington's Regt.

ORIGINAL.

5th Duke of Wellington's Regt.

Army Form C. 2118.

WAR DIARY
or
INTELLIGENCE SUMMARY.
(Erase heading not required.)

Instructions regarding War Diaries and Intelligence Summaries are contained in F. S. Regs. Part II. and the Staff Manual respectively. Title pages will be prepared in manuscript.

Place	Date	Hour	Summary of Events and Information	Remarks and references to Appendices
Ref.Maps. 57a 1/40,000 VALENCIENNES 1/100,000	1918 Oct 1st		After being relieved in the Battle Line East of the CANAL de ST. QUENTIN, MARCOING, the battalion marched out via RIBECOURT, FLESQUIERES and HAVRINCOURT to a bivouac area near Lock 7 in K.15. The accommodation was scant, but with the aid of bivouac sheets the men soon made themselves cover from the weather. The Battalion was very tired but was in high spirits.	
	2nd		Battalion rested all day and Officers reorganised their Companies and Platoons.	
	3rd		A little training was done in the morning and the afternoon devoted to recreation. Fine weather.	
	4th		Training was done in the morning. Recreation in the afternoon. The Divisional Commander (Major-General R.D.Whigham, K.C.B. D.S.O.) visited the Battalion during the afternoon and spoke to all the officers and conveyed the Commander in Chief's personal congratulations to the Battalion on its recent fine achievements. Fine.	
	5th		Battalion doing Training.	
	6th		-do- -do- -do-	
	7th		-do- -do- -do-	
	8th		The Battalion was ordered to "Stand By" all day ready to move in conformity with a general advance on the VI Corps front. At 5 p.m. orders were received to move at 7.10 p.m. The Bivouac Camp at Lock 7 K.15.a. was struck and the Battalion moved off by Companies accompanied by Lewis Gun Carts, Cookers, Water Carts and Pack Ponies carrying S.A.A. The Battalion marched via FLESQUIERES, RIBECOURT to trenches in L.21.a. and b. There the Battalion remained for the night.	
57B 1/40,000	9th		The Battalion remained in L.21.a and b during morning and at 2.30 p.m. moved via MARCOING to Area G.14.d. and G.20.b. between RUMILLY and MASNIERES. Most of the Battalion there got some sort of cover from the weather. Battalion H.Q. was in a cellar at the N. end of MASNIERES.	

ORIGINAL.

Army Form C. 2118.

5th Duke of Wellington's Regt.

WAR DIARY
or
INTELLIGENCE SUMMARY.

(Erase heading not required.)

Instructions regarding War Diaries and Intelligence Summaries are contained in F. S. Regs., Part II. and the Staff Manual respectively. Title pages will be prepared in manuscript.

Place	Date	Hour	Summary of Events and Information	Remarks and references to Appendices
	1918 Oct. 10th		Battalion moved at 1430 hours and marched via RUMILLY to SERANVILLERS and was billetted in the N.E. portion of the village. SERANVILLERS showed more recent habitation by civilians than other villages West of it and there were quite a number of good billets not too knocked about by shell fire and air-craft bombing. The Battalion stayed there for the night. Wet and misty early in the morning but turned out very fine and bright in the afternoon. Cold all day.	
	11th		Battalion dumped packs at SERANVILLERS before marching off. The Battalion moved with the Brigade group at 1000 hours and marched via WAMBAIX and ESTOURMEL to CARNIERES. It was a miserable wet day and the march in consequence was an unpleasant one. It was a very great pleasure to the Battalion to pass out of the devastated battle area of four years War and get into country free from trenches, wire, etc. and to land again under cultivation. CARNIERES was a large village with very good houses in it, mostly furnished and must have been evacuated only very recently. The Battalion obtained very good billets in the S.E. portion of the village. There were no civilians left in the village.	
	12th		A little training was done near the Aerodrome on the E. outskirts of the village. Wet and fine at intervals. Very misty.	
	13th		Usual services were held for different denominations during the day. 2/4 Hants. Regt. and 2/4 Duke of Wellington's Regt. moved to BOUSSIERES during the day.	
	14th		Beautiful bright sunny day, but cool. Battalion carried out "Attack Practice" during the morning on ground to the West of the village.	
	15th		Battalion did "Attack Practice" West of the village during the morning.	
	16th		Very wet day. Battalion did training in billets during the morning. Officers reconnoitred forward area East of QUIEVY during the morning with a view to taking over the line from 2nd Coldstream Guards, 1st Guards Division.	

ORIGINAL.

Army Form C. 2118.

5th Duke of Wellington's Regt.
WAR DIARY
or
INTELLIGENCE SUMMARY.
(Erase heading not required.)

Place	Date 1918	Hour	Summary of Events and Information	Remarks and references to Appendices
Ref map 57 B^{NE} 1 S1 A SE 1/20000 Third Mystere map started	Oct 17		Battalion dumped packs at CARNIERES in the morning. At 3.15 p.m. the battalion marched out of CARNIERES via BOUSSIERES, BEVILLERS, to just West of the village of QUIEVY where the men all had tea. The troops moved forward at dusk and relieved two companies and Battalion H.Q. of 2nd Coldstream Guards, First Guards Brigade, in the battle line just west of the village of ST PYTHON. The relief was carried through without hitch or interference from the enemy. On relief dispositions of the battalion were as follows:- A Coy 2 Platoons on railway D.5.b with 2 Platoons and Coy HQ in Support in D.4.d. C Coy 2 Platoons on railway in D.5.d. and 2 Platoons in Support in D.11.a. D Coy were in Battalion Support on the line of "main line of resistance" in the orchard D.10.c. B Coy were in Battalion Reserve and were accommodated in QUIEVY. Battalion HQ was at E. edge of QUIEVY with an advance HQ with D Coy in D.10.c. Transport Lines were located at BEVILLERS. The night passed without special incident except that about 50 civilian refugees from ST PYTHON passed through our front line in D.5.b. and went to ST	

ORIGINAL.

Army Form C. 2118.

5th Duke of Wellington's Regt.

WAR DIARY
or
INTELLIGENCE SUMMARY.
(Erase heading not required.)

Instructions regarding War Diaries and Intelligence Summaries are contained in F.S. Regs., Part II. and the Staff Manual respectively. Title pages will be prepared in manuscript.

Place	Date	Hour	Summary of Events and Information	Remarks and references to Appendices
VAAST.			Rations coming up for the forward companies were caught by hostile shell fire in QUIEVY and one C.Q.M.S. was killed and a C.Q.M.S. wounded and 3 other men wounded. 2 mules and 1 horse were also killed	
	Oct/18		The enemy put down a heavy barrage on our whole front at 4:30 am but no infantry action followed. Very misty morning but visibility later. Quiet day on the whole. At night our A.C.D Coys were relieved by 2 Coys of 2/4 Duke of Wellingtons who side slipped from the right. On relief the battalion withdrew to cellars in QUIEVY and became battalion in Brigade Reserve Support.	
	Oct/19		Men rested all day. At 8 pm the battalion moved off by platoons from QUIEVY to the village of ST PYTHON and assembled amongst the houses west of LA SELLE River at the N end of the village about V.29.d. Assembly was completed in very wet weather by 11 pm. Battalion HQ was established at house V.30.c.05.70.	

ORIGINAL.

5th Duke of Wellington's Regt.

Army Form C. 2118.

WAR DIARY
or
INTELLIGENCE SUMMARY.
(Erase heading not required.)

Instructions regarding War Diaries and Intelligence Summaries are contained in F. S. Regs., Part II. and the Staff Manual respectively. Title pages will be prepared in manuscript.

Place	Date	Hour	Summary of Events and Information	Remarks and references to Appendices
	Oct 20. 1918		The battalion was ordered in conjunction with other units of the Brigade and divisions on either flank to take part in an attack at 2 a.m. The task of the battalion was to cross the LA SELLE RIVER in V.30 c. and to clear the village of ST PYTHON and to capture the defensive positions of LA PIGEON BLANC FARM and the line of the road running between E.1.a.8.9 and W.25.b.2.5. 'C' Coy had to form a defensive flank facing south on the line of the road running through E.1.a.8.9 to D.6.b.6.4. The leading company 'A' had to cross the LA SELLE RIVER first and mop up the village in front of the remaining three attacking companies. B and D Coys were the two companies to attack the final objective at LA PIGEON BLANC FARM. The River LA SELLE was a formidable obstacle, being about 25 ft wide with a still depth of 1 ft. to 6 ft. with thick mud in the bottom. It was well defended by enemy M.G. positions on the E. side of the river which continually fired during the forming up of preparations before Zero hour but caused us no casualties. The river was just fordable	

ORIGINAL.

5th Duke of Wellington's Regt.

WAR DIARY
or
INTELLIGENCE SUMMARY.
(Erase heading not required.)

Army Form C. 2118.

at our front about V.30.c.05.30, where the water was about 4ft deep over the fords. At 1.30 a.m. the 461st Field Coy R.E. commenced putting up light wooden bridges over the river in V.30.c. In all 2 bridges were successfully put up, ready 4 of them were used by the troops of this battalion at 1.30 a.m. "A" Coy crossed the river by the ford at V.30.c.05.30. It was a very moonlight bright night but misty rising to the river. They formed up about 100 yds east of the stream. All this company got across in 15 minutes. The river bank on the Eastern side was muddy and steep, but was easily got up by means of 5' high ladders carried by the men. As "A" Coy had successfully got over the stream without opposition it was decided to push B, C, & D Coys over before zero over the bridge which were then ready and in position. The whole battalion had successfully crossed the river by two minutes before zero hour (2.a.m.) and lay down in the orchards on the eastern side. Each Company carried 5' light ladders which proved indispensable for getting up the river bank. The crossing of the river before zero in face of enemy M.G. fire without casualties and

ORIGINAL.

5th Duke of Wellington's Regt.

WAR DIARY
or
INTELLIGENCE SUMMARY.

(Erase heading not required.)

Army Form C. 2118.

Place	Date	Hour	Summary of Events and Information	Remarks and references to Appendices
			instituted by the enemy was a feat well accomplished by the battalion. The moon throughout the night was most persistent. The attack was made at 3 am under our artillery and M.G. Barrage. The barrage rested on the village of ST PYTHON from 3am until 3am plus 3 minutes. Then lifted to the Eastern outskirts of the village where it rested for 20 minutes. Then advanced to the final objective at the rate of 100 yds in 4 minutes. 'A' Coy went forward and rushed the village close under the barrage and at once met with opposition on the first block of houses and from each flank. After overcoming this opposition the company then proceeded through the village splitting into sections at two points in the main street. The journey was harassed and held by the enemy. After a few minutes of sharp hand to hand fighting this was overcome. Machine guns held them up at a second barricade but these were soon cleared, on proceeding to take up a line of defence on the S.E. outskirts of ST PYTHON another Machine Gun Post was encountered which was	

immediately rushed, the guns and team being captured. This company had quite a formidable task in mopping up the village and in places stiff street fighting took place. A large number of the enemy were bayonetted in the streets in addition to those killed and wounded by our artillery barrage. On the barrage lifting to the eastern edge of the village 'C' Coy immediately moved forward behind 'A' Coy from the position of assembly. In moving to their forming up position at the S.E. corner of ST PYTHON this company met with opposition along the main road through ST PYTHON. This was effectively dealt with and they then pushed on, striking the road at D.6.b.4.4 encountering opposition on the way from an orchard which was rushed and quickly overcome. On coming to the line of the objective the company worked up the road from D.6.b.4.4 in an easterly direction dropping posts on the way until they arrived at road junction E.1.a.8.9 opposition was met with along the road but the enemy were either killed or taken prisoner. Immediate touch was obtained with B Coy at the cross roads E.1.a.8.9. The Company then dug in and formed a defensive

flanks facing SOLESMES in a Southerly direction.
B (right) and D (left) Companies formed up behind A and C Coys and pushed forward behind the barrage to the eastern side of ST PYTHON. Each company attacked on a two platoon front, the leading platoons taking as a first objective about the line Y.30.d.65.70 to D.6.b.99.40 and the rear platoons passing through them and taking the final objective from W.25.b.25 to E.1.a.8.9. The defensive position known as LA PIGEON BLANC FM. was included in left company (D). The line of the first objective was taken by the two Companies without much difficulty but prior to jumping up behind the barrage each company had a little mopping up to do on the eastern outskirts of ST PYTHON. The enemy put up a fight on the final objective especially at LA PIGEON BLANC FARM but after 15' minutes the opposing Machine guns were knocked out of action by Lewis gun fire and the objective gained with many prisoners. Touch was at once obtained with the Cyclists Division on the left and with C Coy on the right. The two Coys then dug in and consolidated each with 2 platoons in front and

ORIGINAL.

5th Duke of Wellington's Regt.

WAR DIARY
or
INTELLIGENCE SUMMARY.
(Erase heading not required.)

Army Form C. 2118.

Place	Date	Hour	Summary of Events and Information	Remarks and references to Appendices
			two platoons about 500 yds in rear.	
		4.10 am	By 4.10 am the whole of the battalion objectives had been taken. The men attacked with a will and dash beyond all praise, tackling each little opposition with great initiative and resource. The battalion positions during the day were very briskly shelled but no counter attack took place.	
		8.5 am	At 8.5 am the 2/20th London Regt passed through the battalion to a further objective. The battalion captured over 300 prisoners, 13 Machine Guns and 4 Trench Mortars in addition to a large amount of rifles,	
	P.S.-		equipment, signalling equipment etc. The casualties of the battalion during the operation amounted to 5 OR killed and 08 wounded.	
			Concluesions: The complete success of the attack is attributed to the following causes 1. To the fact that the men completely understood their task before they started and dealt with every obstacle without hesitation showing the greatest initiative in dealing immediately with any opposition.	
			2. The Barrage was perfect and closely followed, making the surprise complete. 3. The very complete arrangements made by the R.E. and the	

ORIGINAL.

Army Form C. 2118.

5th Duke of Wellington's Regt.
WAR DIARY
or
INTELLIGENCE SUMMARY.

(Erase heading not required.)

Instructions regarding War Diaries and Intelligence Summaries are contained in F. S. Regs., Part II. and the Staff Manual respectively. Title pages will be prepared in manuscript.

Place	Date	Hour	Summary of Events and Information	Remarks and references to Appendices
	Oct 21		Absolute silence maintained during the crossing gave the operation an ideal start. The fact that the attack was made in semi-darkness made the surprise more astounding and disorganised the defence. Throughout the day subsequent to the attack our positions were continually bombarded by enemy artillery and ST PYTHON came in for a great deal of attention. The day was very wet. The battalion was relieved by 2/4 Duke of Wellingtons Regt during the morning, on relief the battalion was withdrawn into Brigade Reserve and accommodated in billets and cellars at the N.W. corner of SOLESMES. Another wet day.	
	Oct 22		During the afternoon the battalion with remainder of 186 Inf Bde was withdrawn and marched to billets at BEVILLERS.	

ORIGINAL.

5th Duke of Wellington's Regt.

Army Form C. 2118.

WAR DIARY
or
INTELLIGENCE SUMMARY.
(Erase heading not required.)

Instructions regarding War Diaries and Intelligence Summaries are contained in F.S. Regs., Part II. and the Staff Manual respectively. Title pages will be prepared in manuscript.

Place	Date	Hour	Summary of Events and Information	Remarks and references to Appendices
	1918 Oct. 23rd		Battalion in billets at BEVILLERS. Men cleaned up and rested.	
	24th		Reorganisation of Battalion continued.	
	25th		Men all had baths at QUIEVY. Fine day with a little rain at night.	
	26th		Battalion did Platoon and Company Training during the morning. Recreation in afternoon. Fine and bright.	
	27th		Usual services in the morning for each denomination.	
	28th		Company and Platoon Training on Aerodrome Ground East of BEVILLERS in the morning. Inter-company Football Matches in afternoon.	
	29th		Half Battalion Attack Practice on Aerodrome Ground in morning. Games in afternoon. Fine.	
	30th		Battalion Attack Practice in the morning on Aerodrome Ground. Inter-company Football Matches in afternoon.	
	31st.		The Battalion marched along with remainder of the 186th Infantry Brigade to billets at SOLESMES via ST. HILAIRE, ST. VAAST and ST. PYTHON. Billets were fairly good, but rather cramped. Dull day with heavy rain at night.	

J. Tevrot Major,
Commanding 5th Duke of Wellington's Regt.

ORIGINAL.

Army Form C. 2118.

5th Duke of Wellington's Regiment.
WAR DIARY
or
INTELLIGENCE SUMMARY.
(Erase heading not required.)

Instructions regarding War Diaries and Intelligence Summaries are contained in F. S. Regs., Part II. and the Staff Manual respectively. Title pages will be prepared in manuscript.

Place	Date	Hour	Summary of Events and Information	Remarks and references to Appendices
			APPENDICES.	
			DRAFTS, etc.	
			Lieut. F.O. Roberts Joined Battn. 2-10-18. 110.	
			Capt. J.B. Cockhill, DSO.MC. do. 6-10-18. 6.	
			Lieut. R.C.M. Broadwood do. 2-10-18. 4.	
			2/Lieut. G.H. Appleby do. 4-10-18. 7.	
			2/Lieut. G. Carruthers do. 5-10-18. 70.	
			2/Lieut. H.L. Martin do. 7-10-18. 12.	
			2/Lieut. G.A. Ward do. 20-10-18. 20.	
			2/Lieut. T. Mudd do. 18-10-18. 33.	
			2/Lieut. G. Hey do. 5-10-18. 3.	
			2/Lieut. F.H. Phillips do. 6-10-18. 13.	
			2/Lieut. M.C. O'Dowd do. 16-10-18. 15.	
			2/Lieut. G.H. Vanstone do. 16-10-18. 1.	
			Capt. G.F. Clay rejoined from 16-10-18. 28.	
			Hospital. 27-10-18. 12.	
			13-10-18. 2.	
			17-10-18. 3.	
			20-10-18. 11.	
			21-10-18. 2.	
			22-10-18. 20.	
			23-10-18. 5.	
			26-10-18. 13.	
			27-10-18. 10.	
			28-10-18. 8.	
			28-10-18. 6.	
			CASUALTIES, etc.	
			Capt. A.V. Broadbent, MC. Trfd. to POW. Coy. 13-9-18.	
			Lieut. S.N. Milnes Trfd. to Employ. Coy.	
			Capt. G.N. Clay, MC. To Hosp. 20-10-18.	
			2/Lieut. W. Briggs Killed. 15-10-18.	
			Lieut. H. Skelsey. To Base MB. 18-10-18.	
			2/Lieut. J. Hogan. To Hosp. 29-10-18.	
			31-10-18.	
			Other Ranks.	
			Killed 7.	
			Died of Wounds 4.	
			Wounded 32.	
			" Gas 1.	
			" at duty. 2.	

ORIGINAL

Army Form C. 2118.

5th Duke of Wellington's Regiment.

WAR DIARY
or
INTELLIGENCE SUMMARY.

(Erase heading not required.)

Instructions regarding War Diaries and Intelligence Summaries are contained in F. S. Regs., Part II. and the Staff Manual respectively. Title pages will be prepared in manuscript.

Place	Date	Hour	Summary of Events and Information	Remarks and references to Appendices
			APPENDICES.	

Appointments, Relinquishments, etc.

Lieut. (a/Capt.) F.D. Roberts relinquished a/Rank of Capt. on joining Battn. 16-10-18.
2/Lieut. G.F. Clay, MC. appointed a/Capt. whilst commanding a Coy. 3-10-18.
Lieut. (a/Capt.) J.B. Cockhill, DSO.MC. relinquished a/Rank of Capt. on ceasing to command a Company 19-9-18.
Lieut. (a/Capt.) J.B. Cockhill, DSO.MC. appointed a/Capt. whilst commanding a company dated 5-11-18.
2/Lieut. W.J. Lloyd, DSO. appointed a/Capt. whilst commanding a company d/ 14.10.18.
Lieut. (a/Capt.) E.G. Watkinson, MC. relinquished a/Rank of Capt. on ceasing to command a company d/ 2-10-18.
2/Lieut. W. Saunders, MM. appointed a/Capt. whilst commanding a company d/ 17-10-18.
    relinquished whilst rank 2/10/18

Honours and Awards.

The following have been awarded decorations, as stated against their names, for bravery and devotion to duty in the field.

Lieut. (a/Capt.) C.G.H. Ellis	DSO.	2/Lieut. (a/Capt.) G.F. Clay MC.
2/Lieut. (a/Capt.) W.J. Lloyd	DSO.	Lieut. E.G. Watkinson MC.
Capt. M. Sykes, MC.	Bar to MC.	2/Lieut. W. Saunders, MM.
Lieut. I.M. Rod	MC.	240358 C.S.M. Fisher, DCM.
25110 L/Cpl. Lee, A. MM.	DCM.	305142 Cpl. Buckley, T. DCM.
34505 Pte. Hardy, H.	DCM.	17016 L/Cpl. Chapman, W. ?.
15664 Cpl. Fairborn, G. MM.	Bar to MM.	240971 L/Cpl. Halliwell, G. MM. Bar to MM.
242034 Pte. Castle, F. MM.	Bar to MM.	242857 L/Cpl. Ibbotson,P. MM. Bar to MM.
268485 L/Cpl. Bell, G.E. MM.	Bar to MM.	235629 Corpl. Levy, I. MM. Bar to MM.
34499 Pte. Peel, H. MM.	Bar to MM.	240157 Sergt. Allen, W.N. MM. Bar to MM.

ORIGINAL.

5th Duke of Wellington's Regiment.

WAR DIARY or **INTELLIGENCE SUMMARY.**

(Erase heading not required.)

Army Form C. 2118.

Instructions regarding War Diaries and Intelligence Summaries are contained in F. S. Regs., Part II. and the Staff Manual respectively. Title pages will be prepared in manuscript.

Place	Date	Hour	Summary of Events and Information	Remarks and references to Appendices
			APPENDICES.	
			Honours and Awards, contd.	
			34506 Pte. Tardy, H. MM.	
			240957 C.S.M. Dennis, W.H. MM.	
			206935 Sergt. Burrows, G. MM.	
			266170 L/Sgt. Southgate, H. MM.	
			268800 L/Cpl. Barker, W. MM.	
			34510 L/Cpl. Wilde, F. MM.	
			235722 Pte. White H.G. MM.	
			201823 Pte. Womersley, E. MM.	
			26204 Pte. Harris, B. MM.	
			34426 Pte. Hill, J. MM.	
			34499 Pte. Peel, H. MM.	
			241659 Pte. Asquith, H.O.K. MM.	
			34464 Pte. Rider, A.J. MM.	
			16100 Pte. Overend, J. MM.	
			34757 Pte. Parkes, A. MM.	
			240623 Pte. Dombavand, E. MM.	
			235736 Pte. Taylor, G. MM.	
			203562 Pte. Armitage, H. MM.	
			235598 Pte. Bashford, E. MM.	
			25908 Pte. Jeffcott, H. MM.	
			240674 Pte. Middleton, W. MM.	
			241857 Pte. Cox, P. MM.	
			334488 Pte. Ball, P. MM.	
			26237 L/Cpl. Ramsay, R.M. MM.	
			26304 Pte. Tippet, G.T. MM.	
			259234 Pte. Leverick, W. MM.	
			34563 Pte. Harrison, E. MM.	
			34410 L/Cpl. Donkin, A.S. MM.	
			241184 Pte. Sevall, S. MM.	
			241855 Pte. Holroyd, G.W. MM.	
			235755 Sergt. Pearson, A. MM.	
			235593 Pte. Bell, M. MM.	
			201575 Pte. Birchenough, J. MM.	
			35158 Pte. Chernock, W. MM.	
			20106 L/Cpl. Hesley, T.A. MM.	
			269091 Pte. Baldwin, R. MM.	
			242979 L/Cpl. Keogh, J.W. MM.	
			267286 Corpl. Simpson, H. MM.	
			34552 Pte. Snowden, J.W. MM.	
			34515 Pte. Anton, R. MM.	
			Awarded French Croix de Guerre avec Palme	
			Capt K Sykes M.C.	

E. Tewart   Major.
Commanding 5th Duke of Wellington's Regt.

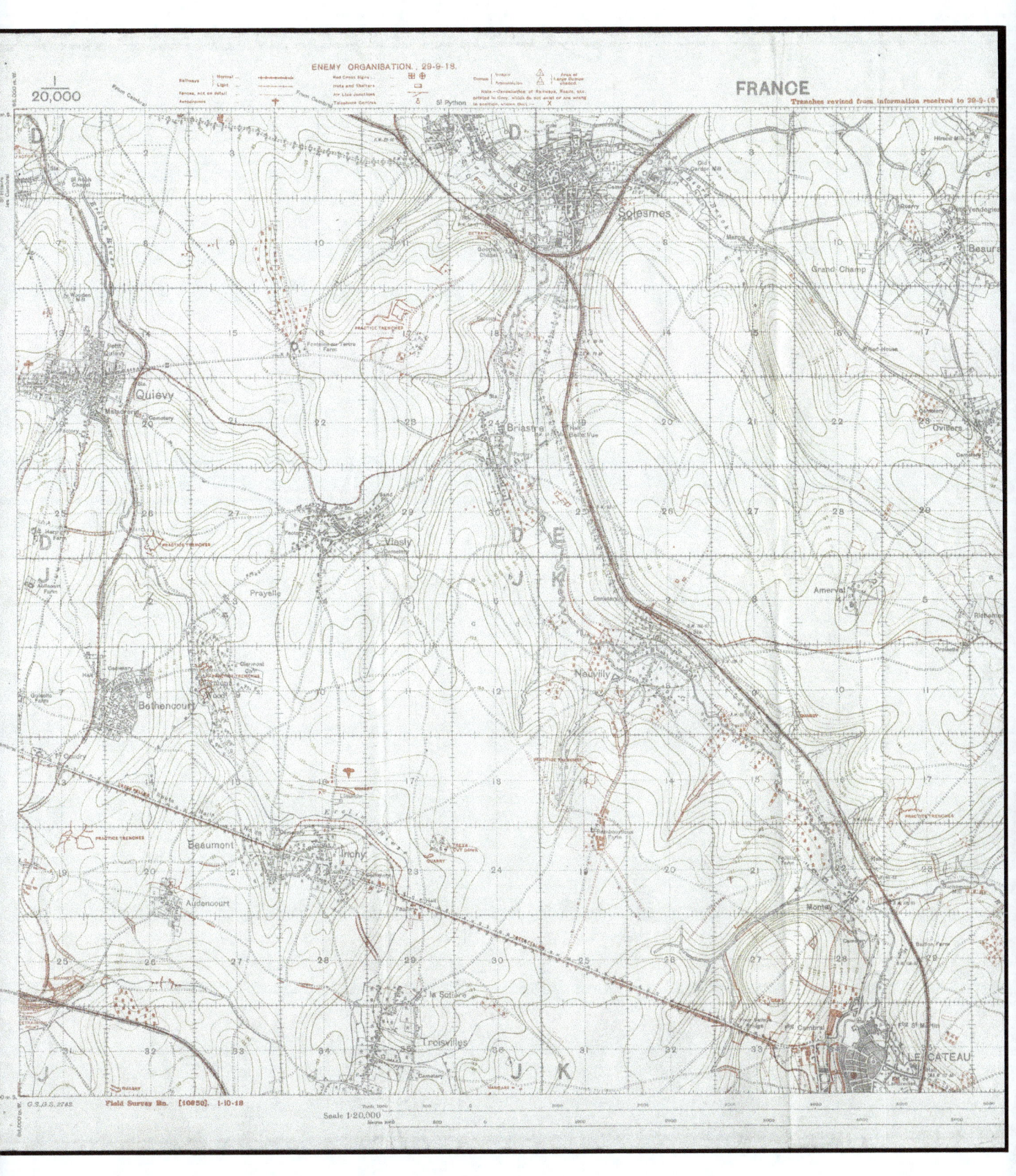

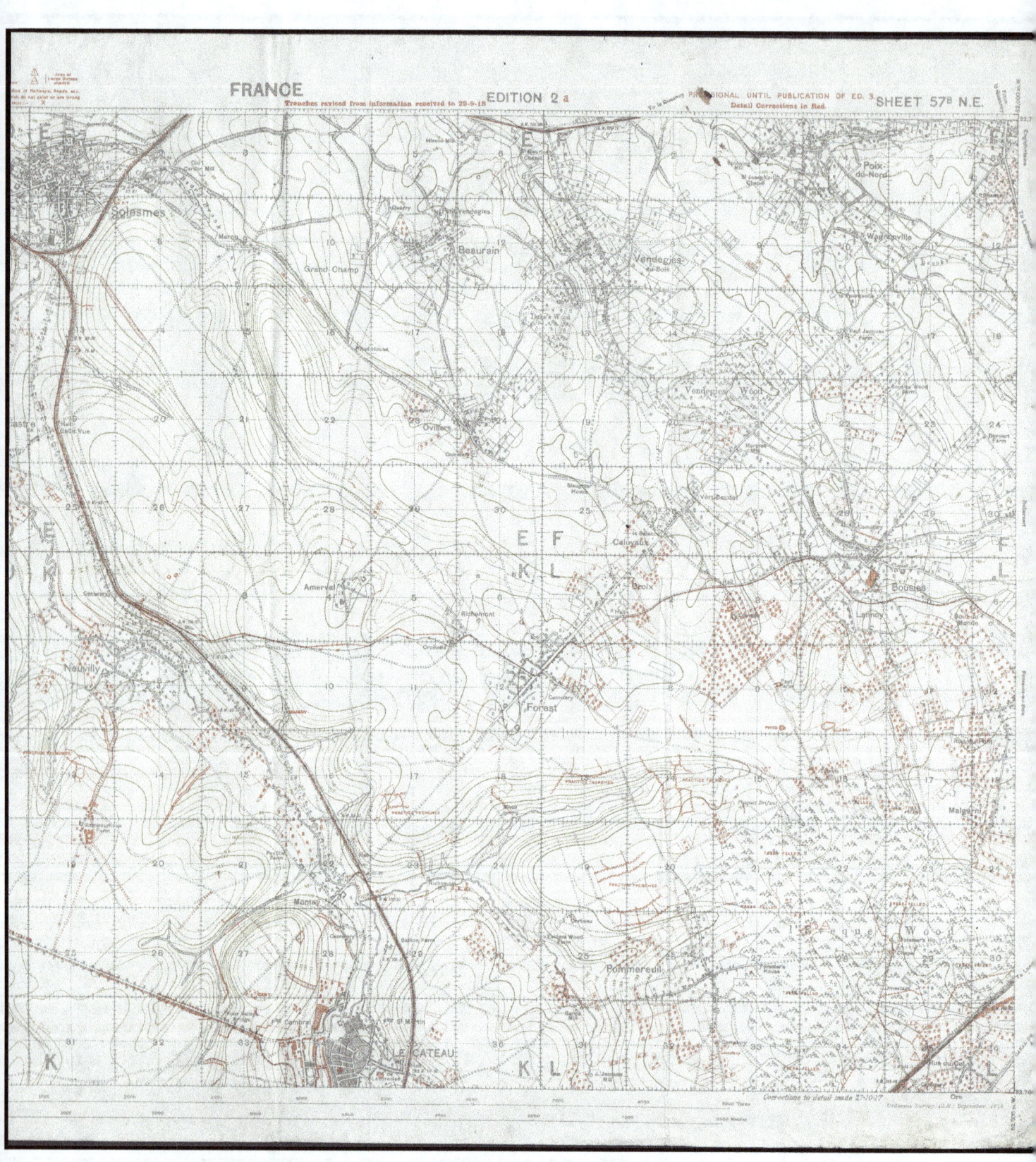

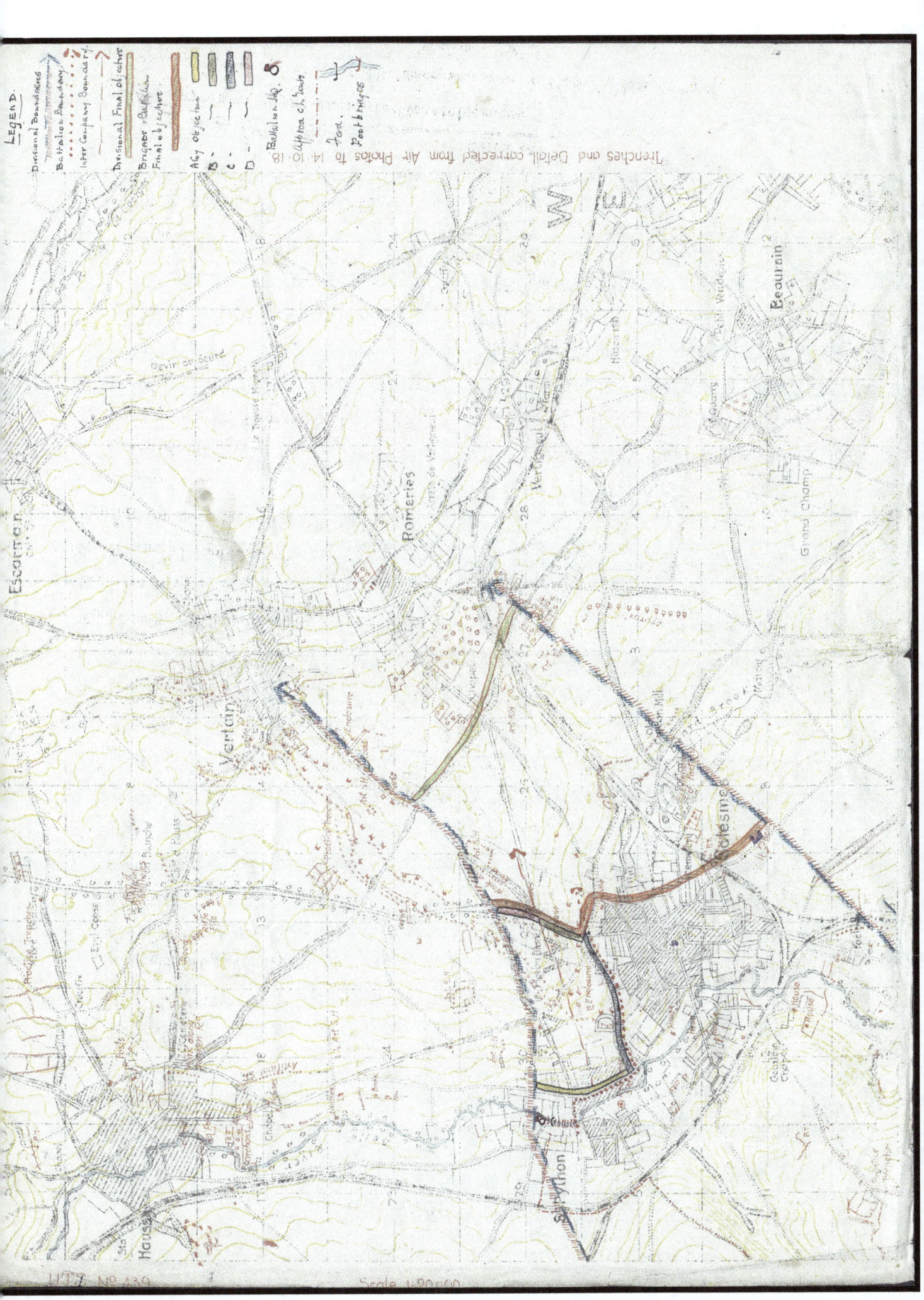

MESSAGE FORM

To _____ No _____

1. I am at _____   {Note:— Either give map reference or mark your position by an "X" on the map on back}
2. My line runs _____
3. My Platoon/Company is at _____ and is consolidating.
4. My Platoon/Company is at _____ and has consolidated
5. Am held up by (a) M.G. (b) Wire at _____ (State where you are.)
6. Enemy holding strong point _____
7. I am in touch with _____ on Right/Left at _____
8. I am not in touch with _____ on Right/Left
9. Am shelled from _____
10. Am in need of :— _____
    _____
11. Counter-attack forming at _____
12. Hostile (a) Battery (b) Machine Gun (c) Trench Mortar active at _____
13. Reinforcements wanted at _____
14. I estimate my present strength at _____ Rifles.
15. Have captured _____
16. Prisoners belong to _____
17. Add any other useful information here :— _____
    _____
    _____
    _____

Time _____ m   Name _____
Date _____ 1918   Platoon _____
                       Company _____
                       Battalion _____

(A). Carry no maps or papers which may be of value to the enemy.

(B). Give no information if captured except the following which you are bound to give :— Name and Rank

(C). Collect all captured maps and papers and send them in at once

141 Copy No. 9

BATTALION OPERATION ORDERS BY LIEUTENANT COLONEL J. WALKER, D.S.O.
COMMANDING 5th WEST RIDING REGT. NO. 142. a/17.10.18.

Ref. Maps – Sheets 57.b. and 51.a. 1/40,000.

1. **RELIEF.**
   The Battalion will relieve Two Companies and Battalion H.Q. of 2nd Coldstream Guards, 1st. Guards Brigade in the Battle Line today.

2. **DISPOSITIONS.**
   Dispositions of Companies will be as follows –
   Two Platoons of A. Coy. 5. D. of W. Regt. will take over from Left Platoon of No. 1. Coy. 2nd Coldstreams on Railway in D.5.b.
   Two Platoons of A. Coy. and Coy. H.Q. 5. D. of W. Regt. will take over from Support Platoon of No. 1. Coy. Coldstreams in D.4.d.
   Two Platoons of C. Coy. 5. D. of W. Regt. will take over from Right Platoon of No. 1. Coy. of Coldstreams on Railway in D.5.d.
   Two Platoons of C. Coy. 5. D. of W. Regt. will take over from Left Platoon No. 2. Coy. Coldstreams in D.11.a.
   C. Coy. H.Q. to take over from No 2. Coy. Coldstreams in D.10. central.
   D. Coy. 5. D. of W. Regt. will take over from present Battalion H.Q. of Coldstreams in Orchard in D.10.c.
   B. Coy. 5. D. of W. Regt. will be in Battalion Reserve and will be accommodated in S.E. portion of QUIEVY.
   Battalion H.Q. 5. D. of W. Regt. will be on E. edge of QUIEVY at Billet marked No. 17. D.14.c.7.2.

3. **GUIDES.**
   Platoon Guides and One for Coy. H.Q. for A. C. D. Coys. will be on Road at D.15.c.5.4. at 18.15. hours.

4. **TIME OF MOVE ETC.**
   The Battalion will parade outside A and B. Coys. Billets on the BOUSSIERES ROAD in the following order at 15.10.hours –
   H.Q. B. D. C. A. Route via BOUSSIERES and BEVILLERS.
   Move off by Coys. at 100 yards interval. Each Coy. will be accompanied by Lewis Gun Carts, Cookers and Ammunition Pack Animal. Tool Cart will go with D. Coy. and each of D. C. A. Coys. will obtain 35 Shovels and 10. Picks from it at the Guide rendezvous. Lewis Guns will be unloaded at the Guide rendezvous. Coys. will have Tea in QUIEVY. Ammunition Pack Animals will accompany Coys. forward.

5. **RATIONS.**
   Rations for A and C. Coys. will be sent by limber to be at Fork Roads, D.10.3.0. at 22.00.hours and carried from there by Coys. Rations for D. Coy. will be sent to D.10.c.2.3. at 22.00.hours. Rations for Battalion H.Q. and B. Coy. will be delivered to respective H.Q. in QUIEVY. Meat for A. C. and D. Coys to be sent up cooked.

6. **TRANSPORT.**
   Transport Lines will be located at BEVILLERS. Officers' Valises will be sent to Q.M. Stores by 14.00.hours today.
   T. O. will collect Orderly Room Boxes today at 14.00.hours. Transport will move independently under T. O's Orders.

7. **GENERAL.**
   Coys. will report "Relief Complete" by wiring the words "10 Required" to Battalion H.Q. and by Runner to Report Centre. A Battalion Report Centre will be established at D. Coy's H.Q. (D.10.c.2.3.) where messages for Battalion H.Q. can be sent. Present Billets in CARNIERES will be left absolutely clean.

O/C. B. Coy. will detail an Officer to obtain a Certificate of cleanliness from Town Major before leaving.   Coys. will very carefully take over and will send sketch of Coy. Dispositions as soon as possible to Battalion H.Q. after relief.

8. ACKNOWLEDGE.

K Sykes Capt & Adjt.
5th West Riding Regt.

Copies to -

1. to 5.	A. B. C. D. H.Q. Coys.
6.	T. O. and Q. M.
7.	186. Inf. Bde. (for inf.)
8.	Adjutant.
9 - 10.	War Diary.
11.	Office.
12.	O/C. 2nd. Coldstream Guards.

Secret.   War Diary   Copy No 5.

5th Duke of Wellington's Regt.
Operation Order No
Ref Map 57A SE & 57 B S.E 1/20000.
d. 19.10.18.

1. The VI Corps has been ordered to capture the high ground East of LA SELLE River in conjunction with Corps on both flanks, at a date to be notified later. The 42nd Div will be on the right of the 62nd Div & the Guards Division on the left.

2. 62nd Div is to capture SOLESMES and the high ground N.E. of it in E 3 W 24 and W 26. 186 Inf Bde. (with 2/4 York and Lancs Regt attached) will capture the town of SOLESMES and the line of the first Objective from E 4. b. 9. 0. to W 25 b. 2. 3.

185 Inf Bde. will pass through 186 Inf Bde. at about zero plus 300 minutes and will capture the final Objective.

3. 5th Duke of Wellingtons Regt will cross LA SELLE River in V.30.c. and will clear St PYTHON and will capture LA PIGEON BLANC FARM and the line of the road running between E.1.a.8.9 and W.25.b.2.3.
One Company (C) will form a defensive flank on the line of the road running through E.1.a.8.9 to D.6.b.4.4
The leading Company (A) will cross LA SELLE River shortly before zero. The two Coys for Battn final objective (B & D) should reach LA PIGEON BLANC FARM at zero plus 75 minutes

3/4. Hants Regt will cross LA SELLE river in V.30.c. as soon as the 5 D of W. Reg are clear and will capture the N portion of SOLESMES

4. The Battalion will assemble in St PYTHON West of LA SELLE River before zero.
A. Coy will cross the ford over LA SELLE River at V.30.c.D.5.60 half an hour before zero. At zero this Company will move forward, turn southwards

and mop up village of ST PYTHON. Lewis Guns from this Coy will be put in houses on W. Side of River to cover the attack at zero. C Coy will cross the river and passing through A Coy. form a defensive flank facing almost due South on the line of the Road running through E.1.a.8.9 and W.25.6.2.3. Platoon posts will be dropped. the leading platoon going furthest.

D Coy and B Coy will follow C Coy over the river each on slip bridges made by R.E. and each on a two platoon front (D Left B. Right) will capture the line of the road running through E.1.a.5.9. to D.6.b.4.4. including the defensive position of LA PIGEON BLANC.

5 Battalion H.Q. will be established in house on ST PYTHON V.30.C.0.7. it will be marked by usual blue flag with 5 on it. All reports will be sent to this H.Q. Coys will report location of their own H.Q. as soon as established.

6. Battalion will leave QUIEVY on Zero night at 8pm. Lewis Gun Limbers will accompany Companies as far as road in D 10 C.

B and D Coys will carry Success Signals these will be sent up from the outside flank of each Company.

Each Coy will carry ground flares & light them when called for by aeroplanes.

Each Coy will carry 5 light ladders all Ranks will wear a white armband on their right arm.

Pass word will be PELICAN

Barrage times will be issued later

R Sykes Capt Adjt

War Diary

62nd (W.R.) Divn. H.Q.
20.10.18

I have great pleasure in publishing the following minute received from Lieut-General Sir Aylmer Haldane, K.C.B., D.S.O., Cmdg. VI. Corps.

"62nd Division.   VI. Corps H.Q.
20th Oct. 1918

My best congratulations on the skilful manner in which the difficult attack of today's date, involving the passage by night of an unfordable stream under the close fire of the enemy, was carried out.

It reflects much credit on Commanders, Staffs and the gallant Officers N.C.Os and men of your Division.

I am particularly pleased with the admirable work of the Royal Engineers and Pioneers in overcoming the difficulty of the river passage, and with the Artillery & Machine Gunners for their able support of the attack.

A. Haldane
Lieut. General

R. Wigham
Major General
Commanding 62nd (West Riding) Division

Secret   War Diary Copy No 6
                5 Duke of Wellington Regt
                Operation Order d 22.10.18

            Ref Maps 57 C NE 57 A SE /20000

1. The 186 Brigade is being replaced
   in SOLESMES by one Battalion of
   each of 8th and 16th Inf Brigade

2. The Battalion will move from
   SOLESMES to-day approximate start
   will be at 15.30 hours. Exact details
   will be notified as an Addendum
   when known move by the road
   through D 6 a 6.9 D 6 d 2.y.
   D 10 d 20 should shelling permit

3. Lewis Gun Limbers have been ordered
   for 14 p.m
   Billeting party will be provided
   by Rear HQ who will place guides
   at the outskirts of BEVILLERS

                            R Sykes Capt Adjt

Copy for War Diary.

Following message from General WHIGHAM begins.

" Hearty congratulations and warmest thanks to you and all ranks under your command for success of today's operations. This fine acheivement is due to most abled and careful arrangements by yourselves and unit commanders and to the magnificent courage of the troops of this splendid division".

SECRET.   Copy No. 9.

5th DUKE OF WELLINGTON'S REGIMENT.
OPERATION ORDER No. 143.

Reference - Sheets 57B and 57A 1/40,000.

1. **Move.**

    The Battalion will march with 186th Infantry Brigade Group to SOLESMES tomorrow.

2. **Order of March, etc.**

    Order of March - H.Q. A. B. C. D. Transport. Battalion (with head facing North) to parade on BEAUVOIS - BEVILLERS Road at 07.10 hours. Band will drop back at each halt.

3. **Distances.**

    A distance of 100 yards will be maintained between the Battalion and the Transport. Halts at 10 minutes to the hour.

4. **Route.**

    Route will be - cross-roads 0.22.d.8.1. - cross-roads 0.10.d. - ST.HILAIRE - ST.VAAST Railway Crossing D.5.b. - ST.PYTHON. The Battalion will not enter SOLESMES before 10.00 hours.

5. **March Discipline.**

    The strictest March Discipline will be maintained. Attention is drawn to B.O. 971 of to-day.

6. **Advance Party.**

    Billeting Party under Lieut. W.D. Ridders will meet the Battalion on the SOLESMES - ST.PYTHON Road D.5.d.2.7.

7. **Acknowledge.**

        Issued at 1645 hrs.   K. Lyles.
                                                Capt. & Adjt.
                                        5th Duke of Wellington's Regt.

Copies to

1. A. COY.   7. Adjutant.
2. B. COY.   8. 186th Inf. Bde.
3. C. COY.   9/10. War Diary.
4. D. COY.   11. Office.
5. H.Q. COY.
6. T.O.&Q.M.

                                                30th October, 1918.

1/20,000 Trenches revised from information received to 12-10-18 FRANCE.

Field Survey Bn. [10569]. 14-10-18. Scale 1 : 20,000

51A. SE.
"B" Coy.

SECRET.

WW 23

C O N F I D E N T I A L.

W A R   D I A R Y

- of -

5th DUKE OF WELLINGTON'S (W.R.) REGIMENT

1st to 30th November, 1918.

(Volume - 9)

Hughes Capt:
Commanding 5th Duke of Wellington's Regt.

O R I G I N A L.

Army Form C. 2118.

5th DUKE OF WELLINGTON'S REGT.
WAR DIARY
or
INTELLIGENCE SUMMARY.
(*Erase heading not required.*)

Instructions regarding War Diaries and Intelligence Summaries are contained in F. S. Regs., Part II. and the Staff Manual respectively. Title pages will be prepared in manuscript.

Place	Date	Hour	Summary of Events and Information	Remarks and references to Appendices
Ref.sheets 57.o. 51.s. 1/40,000.	1918 Novr 1st		Fine day. Battalion trained on ground West of SOLESMES in morning. Recreation in afternoon. News was received that Austria Hungary had concluded an Armistice with the Allies.	
	2nd		Fine day. Battalion moved at dusk from SOLESMES to ESCARMAIN via ROMERIES. Roads were very congested and it was a difficult march.	
	3rd		Fine morning. Wet in afternoon. Battalion rested as much as possible during day.	

ORIGINAL.

Army Form C. 2118.

5th Duke of Wellington's Regt.

WAR DIARY
or
INTELLIGENCE SUMMARY.
(Erase heading not required.)

Instructions regarding War Diaries and Intelligence Summaries are contained in F. S. Regs., Part II and the Staff Manual respectively. Title pages will be prepared in manuscript.

Place	Date	Hour	Summary of Events and Information	Remarks and references to Appendices
Reference sheet 51e. 1/40,000.	1918 Nov 4th		Battalion moved from ESCARMAIN at 00.40 hours and assembled in position behind Bank R.25.a. Lewis Guns were carried on pack animals. **Plan of Attack.** The 186th Infantry Brigade on the Right and the 187th Infantry Brigade on the left were to carry out the attack on the front of the 62nd Division and capture all objectives as far as the RED LINE (a line through M.11.b & d. and M.18.a.a.c.) The 185th Infantry Brigade were in Divisional Reserve in ESCARMAIN. The Guards Division attacked on the left and the New Zealand Division on the right. The attack was part of a big forward advance by the Allies (First, Third and Fourth British armies and First French Army engaged). The attack of the 186th Infantry Brigade was carried out on a one battalion front with a frontage of approximately 1,200 yards. The 2/4 Hampshire Regt. were to capture all the ground as far as the BLUE LINE (from R.12.d. along Road astride grid line between R.17 and 18). The 2/4 Duke of Wellington's Regt. (from R.12.d. along Road astride grid line between R.17 ground as far as the GREEN LINE (from Road just South of FRASNOY N.9.d. along Road in M.15.b. to grid line between M.15 and M.21.) These two attacks of 2/4 Hampshire Regt. and 2/4 Duke of Wellington's Regt. were supported by Artillery barrages. The 5th Duke of Wellington's Regt. were to follow behind these two battalions and leap-frog through them and capture the RED LINE (a line from M.21.c.2.3. through M.18.a.&.c. to grid line between M.18 and M.24.). This attack was to be supported by Artillery, but with no barrage. **Battalion Plans.** The battalion attacked on a two company front D. COY. (left) and B. COY. (right) were to capture and consolidate the first battalion objective - the high ground about grid line between M.16 and M.17. A. COY. (left) and C. COY. (right) were to leapfrog through and take the final battalion objective (RED LINE). Each company attacked on a three platoon front with one platoon in reserve. Two sections of D. COY. 62nd Battn. Machine Gun Corps, on pack, supported the attack of the battalion from positions on the high ground in M.15.d. and M.17.c. respectively. The 186th Trench Mortar Battery with two guns and 100 rounds on pack animals followed the battalion ready to engage any favourable targets.	

ORIGINAL.

Army Form C. 2118.

5th Duke of Wellington's Regt.

WAR DIARY
or
INTELLIGENCE SUMMARY.
(Erase heading not required.)

Instructions regarding War Diaries and Intelligence Summaries are contained in F. S. Regs., Part II. and the Staff Manual respectively. Title pages will be prepared in manuscript.

Place	Date	Hour	Summary of Events and Information	Remarks and references to Appendices
	1918 Novr 4th contd		Companies of 2/4 Duke of Wellington's Regt. held up by Machine Gun fire from an orchard in M.15.c. B. COY. arrived in rear of 2/4 Duke of Wellington's Regt. about 09.30 hours and on coming under machine gun fire extended. The Company Commander in conjunction with O.C. C. COY. 5th Duke of Wellington's Regt. decided to push on although the GREEN LINE had not been taken. He sent one platoon round the left flank and advanced frontally with one platoon, and the enemy retired leaving 30 prisoners in our hands captured in the Sunken Road running East in M.15.c. obtaining touch with D. COY. on the left this Company continued its advance at 11.30 hours. After very little further resistance the objective in M.17.c. was reached. A Liaison Post was at once established with the New Zealand Division at the PONT de l'MOUETTE. Whilst involved with the fighting in front of the GREEN LINE two platoons of this Company somewhat lost direction and reached the objective on the left of D. COY. after some heavy fighting on the Southern outskirts of FRASNOY, where some prisoners were taken. This Company took 30 prisoners, 2 Field Guns and 1 Howitzer, and three machine guns. After capturing the battalion intermediate objective (about grid line between M.16 and M.17). D. and B. Companies reorganized and arranged their line in depth each with two platoons in front and two platoons in support. A. COY. advanced behind D. COY. and leap-frogged through the latter Company on its objective in M.17.c.d. but got too much to its right and rather lost direction and found itself in M.17.d. instead of M.17.b. On finding they were too far to the right the Company reorganized and endeavoured to work round on to its allotted front, but owing to heavy enemy machine gun fire from M.17.b.6.0. and the Company Commander becoming a casualty this was not accomplished. Two attempts were made to take this Railway Bridge and house at M.17.b.6.0. but failed and eventually a line from M.17.d.9.5. to M.17.d.2.8. was taken up and consolidated in touch with C. COY. on the right. This Company captured two Howitzers. C. COY. advanced behind A. COY. and did not encounter any opposition until reaching the Sunken Road at M.15.c.5.9. where they came under heavy enemy machine gun fire from the orchard in M.15.c.s.d. In M.15.c. this Company came across two Companies of 2/4 Duke of Wellington's Regt. who were held up by machine gun fire from the orchard in M.15.c.s.d. After waiting an hour for the 2/4 Duke of Wellington's Regt. to take their objective the officer commanding C. COY. consulted with the Company Commander	

ORIGINAL.

Army Form C. 2118.

Instructions regarding War Diaries and Intelligence Summaries are contained in F. S. Regs., Part II. and the Staff Manual respectively. Title pages will be prepared in manuscript.

5th Duke of Wellington's Regt.

WAR DIARY
or
INTELLIGENCE SUMMARY.
(Erase heading not required.)

Place	Date	Hour	Summary of Events and Information	Remarks and references to Appendices
	1918 Novr. 4th contd		battalion ready to engage any favourable targets. Narrative. The Battalion assembled in R.25.c. about 01.30 hours without any trouble and rested until morning. Zero hour for the attack was at 05.30 hours. At 06.30 hours the battalion moved off by platoons at 30 yards interval from the assembly positions and followed a taped out track through R.25.b., R.20.c.&.d., R.21.a.&.b. to railway about R.16.central. Little difficulty was experienced in reaching the line of the railway about R.16.central. Although the battalion had to go through the enemy barrage comparatively few casualties resulted. It was not necessary to split into smaller formations than platoons. Owing to a very thick morning mist and the fact that the New Zealand Division had to go through our Divisional area at the same time as ourselves in their encirclement of LE QUESNOY, it was rather difficult keeping touch between platoons. On reaching the railway line Companies were able to reorganize in the Sunken Road in R.17.a.&.c. From this point D. COY. (left) and B. COY. (right) went forward in a due Easterly direction in artillery formation of platoons. On reaching the line about grid line between M.14 and M.15 both companies had to extend on coming under Machine Gun fire from Orchards in M.15.b.&.c. It was found that 2/4 Duke of Wellington's Regt. had not quite reached the GREEN LINE and enemy Machine Guns were very troublesome in front of this line. Both companies decided to leapfrog through 2/4 Duke of Wellington's Regt. in M.15.a.&.c. and continue the advance at once. The enemy artillery was particularly active in R.17.c.&.d. and R.18.a.&.c. D. COY. first encountered opposition from Machine Guns in the orchard in M.15.b. which was soon overcome. Later this company was held up for some time from several Machine Gun posts in M.16.a.&.b., which were successfully dealt with by Lewis Gunners and 2 Machine Guns fell into our hands. After overcoming this opposition this Company was able to push on its objective without further trouble and a line was established on the high ground in M.17.c. Touch was at once obtained with 187th Infantry Brigade on the right. This company captured 90 prisoners, 8 4.2" Howitzers, 3 machine guns, and a considerable amount of shells and other stores. B. COY. on the right of D. COY. on reaching the high ground in M.15.a.&.c. found two	

ORIGINAL.

5th Duke of Wellington's Regt.

WAR DIARY
or
INTELLIGENCE SUMMARY.
(Erase heading not required.)

Army Form C. 2118.

Place	Date	Hour	Summary of Events and Information	Remarks and references to Appendices
	1918 Nov. 4th contd		of B. COY. 5th Duke of Wellington's Regt. and decided to push on independently. Lewis Gun fire was brought to bear on the orchard, and on B. COY. advancing the enemy gave himself up. O.C. B. COY. sent one platoon round to the road junction of M.15.c.7.7. to endeavour to outflank the orchard and there be joined up with the left of the New Zealand Division, who had just mopped up M.15.c.3.5. on this platoon approaching. About 100 of the enemy came out of the houses at M.15.c.3.5. on this platoon approaching, but were escorted away by the New Zealand Division. Whilst involved in this fighting O.C. B. COY. completely lost touch with one of his platoons. He, however, collected his remaining 3 platoons and continued the advance behind B. COY., leap-frogging through them in M.16.d. An enemy machine gun in CUMBERLAND CHURCH and another one firing from the house at M.17.d.7.0. caused a good deal of trouble and were not overcome. The Railway in M.17.d. was eventually crossed in spite of very heavy machine gun fire, and the advance pressed on. On crossing the railway New Zealand troops were seen well on the right and the right platoon of ends got into touch with them with the result that the Company worked 200 yards too much to the right, but which did not materially matter seeing that A. COY. were in close touch on the left of the Company front. A house in M.13.c.7.0. was held by the enemy and an attempt with one platoon was made to take it. The house, however, proved to be held in strength and had machine guns on either flank and also in the upper rooms of the house. The platoon, after losing its platoon Commander and several men, had to fall back. The enemy waved a white flag from the skylight of the house but made no effort to give himself up. The O.C. Company then decided to take up a line in M.17.d. and M.13.c. West of the Sunken Road. The New Zealand Division attempted to take the house at M.13.c.7.0. with three platoons but failed. C. COY's. line was established at 13.30 hours after much fighting. This company took about 100 prisoners and 6 machine guns. At dusk the battalion line was reorganized with D. COY. on the left from M.11.c.0.3. to M.17.b.3.0. C. COY. on the Right in M.17.d. and M.13.c. with a line of posts from left of C. COY. along grid line between M.17.b. and C. connecting up to right of D. COY. held by A. COY. B. COY. was in Battalion Reserve in M.17.c. Battalion H.Q. was at M.16.d.3.4. The day's fighting had been hard, after 4 very long march up to the point where resistance was met. Direction was very difficult to keep owing to the numerous hedges which	

ORIGINAL.

Instructions regarding War Diaries and Intelligence Summaries are contained in F. S. Regs., Part II. and the Staff Manual respectively. Title pages will be prepared in manuscript.

Army Form C. 2118.

5th Duke of Wellington's Regt.

WAR DIARY
or
INTELLIGENCE SUMMARY.
(Erase heading not required.)

Place	Date	Hour	Summary of Events and Information	Remarks and references to Appendices
	1918 Nov. 4th contd		were very strong, and enclosed country, and in many cases Platoons had to work round. Immediately after dusk the enemy once nearer and commenced digging in opposite our whole front, but on the New Zealand Division reaching LA CARCY at 21.30 hours opposition ceased and no further machine gun fire was heard after 23.00 hours. The casualties of the Battalion during the day amounted to 5 officers and 80 other ranks. 13 guns were captured, 230 men were captured and 15 machine guns, besides large quantities of munitions, etc.	
	5th		At 06.00 hours 185th Infantry Brigade attacked through the battalion front and encountering no opposition made a rapid advance. It was a miserable wet day. The battalion became Brigade Reserve and was moved during the morning in-to the Sunken Road in N.17.b. At 15.00 hours the battalion marched in pouring rain to billets at LA CAVEE (N.7.c.) Men were all drenched and very tired.	
	6th		Another very wet day. At 08.00 hours the battalion marched on to a point just West of FOREST de MORNAL about N.10.c.8.8. Still in Brigade Reserve. A halt was made in pouring rain in an orchard until 12.30 hours when the battalion moved on to OBIES (N.12.d.) and went into billets.	
	7th		The Battalion along with 1/5 Devon Regt. in centre and 5th West Yorks Regt. were ordered to continue the advance at 06.00 hours from the line of the Main Road in O.9.a.2.d., O.15.b.5.d. In order to get to meet up in time it was necessary to leave OBIES at 02.00 hours as the path was a difficult one. Thanks to the Intelligence Officer and Scouts of 2/4 Duke of Wellington's Regt. the battalion successfully reached the forming up ground in O.15.d. well before zero hour. The battalion plans were as follows - A. Coy. to capture the first objective, the line of the Road in COUTANT from Cross Roads O.16.b.5. to O.17.c.5.0. C. Coy. to take the second objective from O.17.a.8.3.to Southern Divisional boundary at O.17.a.2.0. And B. Coy. to take the third objective on the line of the Road from O.18.a.3.2. to O.18.c.0.0. D. Coy. was in Battalion	

ORIGINAL.

Army Form C. 2118.

Instructions regarding War Diaries and Intelligence
Summaries are contained in F. S. Regs., Part II.
and the Staff Manual respectively. Title pages
will be prepared in manuscript.

5th Duke of Wellington's Regt.

WAR DIARY
or
INTELLIGENCE SUMMARY.
(Erase heading not required.)

Place	Date	Hour	Summary of Events and Information	Remarks and references to Appendices
	1918 Novr 7th contd		Reserve. The attack was supported by artillery, but with no regular barrage. Each company formed up behind each other attacked on a three platoon front with one platoon in support. Companies leap-frogged through one another. No opposition of any kind was met with and each company took its objective without trouble. Touch was left with the 1/5 Devon Regt. the whole time, but liaison was not kept with the 42nd Division on the right, as their attack did not start until all our objectives had been gained. By 10.00 hours all objectives had been taken and arranged in depth. Some little difficulty in direction was experienced owing to a think early morning fog. Some casualties were caused amongst our advancing troops from the artillery covering the Division on our right. 3 prisoners and 3 machine guns were captured during the advance. At 12 noon D. COY. was ordered forward to leap-frog through B. COY. in 0.18.c. and take a line approximating to the grid line between 0.18.d. and P.13.c. D. COY. successfully carried out this operation encountering enemy machine gun fire from Ferm PRI MOUTON P.13.c. on the line of the objective. At 15.00 hours orders were received to continue the advance in conjunction with 42nd Division on the right and the 1/5 Devon Regt. on the left. C. COY. was therefore detailed to leap-frog through D. COY. and capture the line from the Southern Point of BOIS MOYAUX in P.13.b.5.5. - along road to P.13.c.3.8.- then a line due South to a grid line at P.13.d.3.0. on North side of the stream, but orders were given that it much opposition was met with the attack had not to be pressed and they must consolidate on position won. They were ordered also to conform absolutely with the action and progress of 1/5 Devon Regt. This Company formed up and moved forward after dark with 3 platoons in line and 1 platoon in support. It was not possible to get into touch with units on the flank before the attack commenced. The Company therefore leap-frogged through D. COY. and the right platoon under 2/Lieut. Monkman actually reached its objective. Meanwhile the O.C. COY. got into touch with the 1/5 Devon Regt. and found that their attack had been cancelled. Finding that his flanks were in the air and units on either flank had not advanced it was decided to withdraw the line to its original place and this was done without any casualties.	

ORIGINAL.

5th Duke of Wellington's Regt.

Army Form C. 2118.

WAR DIARY
or
INTELLIGENCE SUMMARY.
(Erase heading not required.)

Instructions regarding War Diaries and Intelligence Summaries are contained in F. S. Regs., Part II. and the Staff Manual respectively. Title pages will be prepared in manuscript.

Place	Date	Hour	Summary of Events and Information	Remarks and references to Appendices
	1918 Nov 8th		The advance through our line was continued by the 187th Infantry Brigade at dawn. The battalion then withdrew into billets A. and B. COYS. to GOUSAUX C. COY. to BELECOURT FARM (0.17.d.) D. COY. to l'ERMITAGE (0.11.c). The day was very wet and the men were all very tired, but morale high.	
	9th		A fine day. Battalion marched from GOUSAUX Area at 08.00 hours via MARNES and VIEUX MESNIL, NEUF MESNIL, MON PLAISIR, BOUS le BOIS to LOUVROIL and became Support battalion to 187th Infantry Brigade who were holding a line of outposts East of LOUVROIL. All bridges over the river SAMBRE had been blown up by the retreating enemy and a single plank bridge temporarily erected by the R.E. at Q.14.c.3.9. Men were comfortably housed in billets.	
	10th		Another fine day. Battalion moved to Pdg. ST. LAZARE in the morning and became Support Battalion to 186th Infantry Brigade who took over the outpost line from 187th Infantry Brigade. Men were comfortably housed in billets. During the operations & hostilities on this day the battalion advanced over 25 kilometres of new ground, captured 11 Howitzer guns, 2 Field Guns, 18 Machine Guns, 2 33 prisoners and vast quantities of munitions, materiel, Q ogn, etc. The Casualties of the battalion in the same period amounted to:- 7 Officers wounded 1 Officer wounded (at duty) 11 O.R. killed. 2 O.R. died of wounds. 77 O.R. wounded 2 O.R. wounded at Duty. 3 O.R. missing.	

ORIGINAL.

5th DUKE OF WELLINGTON'S REGT.

WAR DIARY
or
INTELLIGENCE SUMMARY.

(Erase heading not required.)

Army Form C. 2118.

Instructions regarding War Diaries and Intelligence Summaries are contained in F. S. Regs., Part II. and the Staff Manual respectively. Title pages will be prepared in manuscript.

Place	Date	Hour	Summary of Events and Information	Remarks and references to Appendices
	1918 Novr 11th		Fine day. Battalion rested. News received at 8.30 a.m. that hostilities were to cease at 11 a.m. that day.	
	12th		Fine. Battalion did Physical Training and Close Order Drill in morning. Recreation in afternoon.	
	13th		-do-	
	14th		-do-	
	15th		-do-	
	16th		-do-	
	17th		Preparations completed for the commencement of the Advance next day. Very cold.	
Ref. Map. NAMUR.8. 1/100,000.	18th		The battalion moved with 186th Infantry Brigade Group from MAUBEUGE AREA to billets at COLLERET. A very cold day with some snow.	
	19th		Foggy day and damp. Roads very dirty. Battalion marched from billets at COLLERET to LEERS ET FOSTEAU, a distance of 11 miles via BOUSIGNIES - Road Junction S.S.E. of SARTIAU. It was an unpleasant march, the only interest being in crossing the Belgian Frontier. Billets at LEERS were moderate.	
	20th		Battalion moved very early from LEERS et FOSTEAU with remainder of 186th Infantry Brigade Group. The Battalion marched via RAGNIES, MARBAIX and HAM-sur-HEURE to billets at NALINNES - a distance of 12½ miles. Billets were very good and the Belgian population very well disposed towards the troops. The little town was decorated with Belgian National colours.	
	21st		A very foggy, damp day. Battalion rested at NALINNES.	
	22nd		-do-	
	23rd		The major portion of the battalion marched (in light order) to CHARLEROI accompanied by Band, and cookers. They greatly enjoyed it.	

ORIGINAL.

Army Form C. 2118.

5th DUKE OF WELLINGTON'S REGT &

WAR DIARY

or

INTELLIGENCE SUMMARY.

(Erase heading not required.)

Instructions regarding War Diaries and Intelligence Summaries are contained in F. S. Regs., Part II. and the Staff Manual respectively. Title pages will be prepared in manuscript.

Place	Date	Hour	Summary of Events and Information	Remarks and references to Appendices
Ref. Map NAMUR.8. 1/100,000.	1918 Novr 24th		Battalion marched from NALINNES via GERPINNES and FROMIEE to billets at BIESME in very fine frosty weather.	
	25th		Battalion marched from BIESME via GRAUX to DENEE in heavy rain. En route the Battalion marched past the Fourth Army Commander General Sir H.S. Rawlinson. Billets at DENEE were quite good.	
	26th		Battalion marched from DENEE via BIOUL, WARNANT, YVOIR, EVREHAILLES, PURNODE to a very small village named DORINNE, where billets were not very commodious. The march was a very long one over heavy roads and the long hill from YVOIR to EVREHAILLES was very trying to transport and troops.	
	27th		Battalion marched in heavy rain from DORINNE to CONNEUX via SOVET CHATEAU and ACHENE. CONNEUX was a very tiny village and billeting the Battalion was difficult. The civilian inhabitants numbered 200.	
	28th		Battalion remained at CONNEUX and cleaned up generally. The 62nd Division became part of the IX Corps commanded by our old Divisional Commander Lieut-General Sir W.P. Braithwaite KCB.	
	29th		Battalion remained at CONNEUX. Companies did some training in the morning and held inspections. The weather was dull and very damp.	
	30th		Battalion rested at CONNEUX. Baths under company arrangements were provided. It was a clear sharp day. Games were played in the afternoon.	

Capt.
Commanding 5th Duke of Wellington's Regt.

ORIGINAL.

Army Form C. 2118.

5th DUKE OF WELLINGTON'S REGT.

WAR DIARY
or
INTELLIGENCE SUMMARY.
(Erase heading not required.)

Instructions regarding War Diaries and Intelligence Summaries are contained in F. S. Regs., Part II. and the Staff Manual respectively. Title pages will be prepared in manuscript.

Place	Date	Hour	Summary of Events and Information	Remarks and references to Appendices
			APPENDICES.	
			DRAFTS, etc.	
			Capt. H.S. Jackson, DSO. joined Battn. 17.11.18. 5 o.r. ... 30.10.18.	
			" C.S. Floyd. " " 13.11.18 22 o.r. ... 13.11.18.	
			" G.V. Bernays, MC. " " 23.11.18 3 o.r. ... 13.11.18.	
			3 o.r. ... 15.11.18.	
			4 o.r. ... 16.11.18.	
			5 o.r. ... 17.11.18.	
			3 o.r. ... 23.11.18.	
			5 o.r.) ... 24.11.18.	
			5 o.r.)	
			3 o.r.) ... 25.11.18.	
			6 o.r.)	
			CASUALTIES, etc.	
			Capt. C.W. Lockwood to 186th Infantry Brigade as T.O. 12.11.18.	
			" C.H. Lockwood Class. Bii. 18.11.18.	
			Lieut. E. Clapham Wdd. and Died of Wds. 5.11.18.	
			" F.D. Roberts to 186th T.M.B. 31.10.18.	
			2/Lieut. E. Ellis to England wounded 13.11.18.	
			" G. Caruthers Wounded 7.11.18.	
			" H.H. Martin to England wounded 11.11.18.	
			" J.H. Vanstone wounded 5.11.18.	
			" J.A. Ward to England wounded 9.11.18.	
			" W. Saunders, MC.MM. do. 8.11.18.	
			" B. King Transferred to 62nd Bn. M.G.C. 3.11.18.	
			Other Ranks. Killed 12.	
			Died of wounds 3.	
			Wounded 82.	
			Wounded at duty 2.	
			missing 3.	

ORIGINAL.

Army Form C. 2118.

5th DUKE OF WELLINGTON'S REGT.

WAR DIARY
or
INTELLIGENCE SUMMARY.
(Erase heading not required.)

Place	Date	Hour	Summary of Events and Information	Remarks and references to Appendices
			APPENDICES.	
			Appointments, Promotions, etc.	
			Lieut. (a/Capt) G.V. Bernays, MC. appointed a/Capt. whilst in command of a company d/24.11.18.	
			" " H.S. Jackson, DSO. appointed a/Capt. whilst in command of a company d/25.11.18.	
			Lieut. (addtl.a/Capt) C.S. Floyd appointed a/Capt. (addtl) d/25.11.18.	
			" (a/Capt) W.J. Lloyd, DSO.MC. appointed a/Capt. (addtl) d/10.11.18.	
			" " relinquished a/rank of Captain on ceasing to command a company d/10.11.18.	
			2/Lieut. (a/Capt) G.F. Clay, MC. relinquished a/rank of Captain on ceasing to command a company d/17.11.18.	
			Honours and Awards, etc.	
			Major E. Senior DSO.	
			Capt. W.J. Lloyd, DSO. MC. Lieut. W.L. Sidders MC.	
			2/Lieut. G.G. Hoyle MC. 2/Lieut. T. Briggs. MC.	
			266035 Sgt. Burrows, G. MM. DCM. 25262 L/Cpl. Linsey, B. MM. DCM.	
			202042 L/Cpl. Booth, E. MM. DCM.	
			240847 Sgt. Garside, MM. Bar to MM. 24726 L/Cpl. Ackroyd, J.A. MM. Bar to MM.	
			22602 Pte. Frank, T.S. MM. Bar to MM.	

ORIGINAL.

5th DUKE OF WELLINGTON'S REGT.

Army Form C. 2118.

WAR DIARY
or
INTELLIGENCE SUMMARY.
(Erase heading not required.)

Instructions regarding War Diaries and Intelligence Summaries are contained in F.S. Regs. Part II and the Staff Manual respectively. Title pages will be prepared in manuscript.

Place	Date	Hour	Summary of Events and Information	Remarks and references to Appendices
			APPENDICES.	

Honours and Awards, etc. (contd).

203657	Pte.	Darlington, H.	MM.	245075	L/Cpl. Buckley, J.	MM.
247.26	Pte.	Ackroyd, J.A.	MM.	26653	Pte. Cartledge, E.A.	MM.
30850	Corpl.	Hinchaliffe, J.	MM.	35639	Pte. Johnson, T.	MM.
241956	Sergt.	Draper, F.H.	MM.	266957	Pte. Fletcher, G.H.	MM.
307334	Pte.	Talbot, N.	MM.	240204	L/Cpl. Shaw, L.	MM.
266352	Corpl.	Tillotson, S.	MM.	345557	Pte. Bell	MM.
242106	Corpl.	Whitteron, W.	MM.	266072	L/Cpl. Rowley, G.	MM.
34408	Pte.	Dewhirst, I.	MM.	202065	Pte. Ellis, E.D.	MM.
33500	Pte.	Gracie, D.	MM.	33754	Pte. Pallet, A.	MM.
497707	L/Cpl.	Hall, R.	MM.	305187	Pte. Hollingworth, H.	MM.
203297	Pte.	Daft, C.	MM.	263016	Pte. Fox, A.	MM.
17112	Pte.	Wilson, G.	MM.	238190	Corpl. Almond, D.	MM.
205420	Pte.	Drake, B.	MM.	241352	Pte. Heywood, H.	MM.
238188	L/Cpl.	Straker, R.	MM.	240858	L/Cpl. Ball, E.	MM.
241707	L/Cpl.	Garbutt, J.	MM.	266451	Pte. Parrington, T.	MM.
12275	CSM.	Handley, K.	FRENCH CROIX de GUERRE.			
241700	L/Cpl.	Glossop, J.W.	MEDAILE MILITAIRE.			

Capt.
Commanding 5th Duke of Wellington's Regt.

SECRET.   Copy No. 7

5th Battn. DUKE OF WELLINGTON'S REGT.

INSTRUCTIONS No. 1.

Ref. Sheet 51a. 1/40,000.   2nd November, 1918.

1. General.

   a. The Allies are continuing the advance to the line AVESNES - MAUBEUGE - MONS on the 4th November.

   b. The attack is to be pressed right through without delay to the BROWN LINE (i.e. the AVESNES - BAVAI - MONTIGNIES SUR ROC Road).

   c. Maps showing proposed objectives and dividing lines have being issued to Companies. These are liable to modification.

2. Action of Flank Divisions.

   a. The New Zealand Division propose to capture LE QUESNOY by moving troops round both flanks of this town.
   On reaching the DOTTED BLUE line, there will be a halt of 20 minutes to enable two battalions, N.Z. Division, to be passed through to capture VILLEREAU and POTELLE in conjunction with the advance of the 62nd Division from the DOTTED BLUE line.

   b. The Guards Division will go straight through to the BLUE line by Zero plus 100 minutes, will leave the BLUE line at Zero plus 135 minutes and go straight through to the GREEN line which they will reach at Zero plus 245 minutes.
   During the advance to the GREEN line the right of the Guards Division will keep in touch with the left of the 62nd Division.

3. Plan of Attack.

   a. The 186th Infantry Brigade on the Right and the 187th Infantry Brigade on the Left will carry out the attack on the front of the 62nd Division, and will capture all objectives as far as the RED line inclusive.

   b. The 185th Infantry Brigade will be in Divisional Reserve in ESCARMAIN and will pass through the leading Brigades on the RED line and continue the advance.

   c. When the 185th Infantry Brigade has passed through them, the 186th and 187th Infantry Brigades will re-organize and be prepared to take up the advance later from the 185th Infantry Brigade.

4. Artillery.

   a. The attack will be covered by the following artillery -

              62nd Divisional Artillery
               3rd Divisional Artillery
              76th Army Brigade R.F.A.
              84th Brigade R.G.A.

4. <u>Artillery</u>, contd.

    b.   No definite artillery barrage will be practicable East of the GREEN line. The C.R.E. will arrange for crossing places over the RHONELLE River to be constructed as soon as possible to enable batteries to be pushed forward in close support of the Infantry for offensive action as guns of opportunity. With this object, Brigades R.F.A. will move up and cross the RHONELLE River as soon as they drop out of effective range.

5.   <u>Time Table</u>.

    The following is the proposed Time Table -

    Zero plus 135 minutes -- Infantry commences moving forward from BLUE line. Barrage lifts at rate of 100 yards in 3 minutes.

    Zero plus 185 minutes -- Infantry reach BLUE DOTTED line and halt for 20 minutes.

    Zero plus 205 minutes -- Infantry Advances from BLUE DOTTED line. Barrage lifts at 100 yards in 3 minutes.

    Zero plus 235 minutes -- Infantry reaches GREEN line and halts for 15 minutes.

    Zero plus 250 minutes -- Infantry advances from GREEN line. Artillery barrage ceases.

6.   <u>Contact Aeroplanes</u>.

    Contact aeroplanes will fly over the objectives at Zero plus 2, 4 and 6 hours and thereafter as may be required.

    Average distance from GREEN to RED line 2.100 yards.

                                                   Capt. & Adjt.
                                      5th Duke of Wellington's Regt.

Copies to -

    1. A. Coy.
    2. B. Coy.
    3. C. Coy.
    4. D. Coy.
    5. HQ. Coy.
    6. Signal Officer.
  7/8. War Diary.
    9. Office.

SECRET.   Copy No. 4

5th DUKE OF WELLINGTON'S REGT.

INSTRUCTIONS No. 2.

Reference Sheet 51a. 1/40,000.   3rd November, 1918.

1. The attack of 186th Infantry Brigade will be carried out on a one Battalion front.
    2/4 Hants. Regt. will capture all ground as far as the BLUE line.
    2/4 D. of W. Regt. will leapfrog through 2/4 Hants. Regt. and will capture all ground as far as the GREEN line.
    5th D. of W. Regt. will leapfrog through 2/4 D. of W. Regt. and will capture all ground as far as the RED line.

2. The Battalion will establish Laison Posts with units on either flank at points shown on tracings to be issued separately.

3. When Battalions have captured their objectives, they will consolidate in depth, and will be prepared to reorganize, when ordered, with a view to continuing the advance.

4. 'D' Company, 62nd Battn. M.G.C. is attached to the Brigade to assist in the capture and consolidation of the Brigade objectives.
    Two sections, on pack, will support the attack of 5th D. of W. Regt. from positions on the high ground in M.15.d. and M.17.c. respectively. These guns will engage any favourable targets which present themselves.
    One section, on limbers, will move forward to positions in the vicinity of the RED LINE to cover consolidation.
    One section will be in Brigade Reserve.

5. 186th T.M. Battery will carry 2 Mortars and 100 rounds on pack animals. They will follow the attack of 5th D. of W. Regt. as closely as possible and will be prepared to engage any favourable targets which present themselves. O.C. 186th T.M. Battery will act in close liaison with O.C. 5th D. of W. Regt.

6. Battalions will assemble in the following positions --

    2/4 Hants. Regt. on the line of the Railway from R.16.d.9.5. to R.16.central, and on West edge of track from R.16.b.1.0. to R.10.c.5.1. To be in position by zero minus 2 hours. On arrival of this Battalion in its assembly position, the troops of 187th Infantry Brigade holding front line posts will be withdrawn.

    2/4 D. of W. Regt. in Sunk Road in R.21.d. To be in position by zero minus 1 hour. Moves forward at approximately zero.

    5th D. of W. Regt. under bank in R.25.c. To be in position by zero minus 30 minutes. Moves forward at approximately zero plus 1 hour.

    Further instructions regarding the approach march to positions of assembly will be issued later.
    All units will carefully reconnoitre the track from R.31.a. which is being staked out by 460th Field Coy. R.E. 2/4 Hants. will tape out a track from the East end of the R.E. track about B.21.b.3.4. to the Railway about R.16.central.
    Each company will detail a reconnoitring party of one officer and one NCO. to meet the Intelligence Officer at Battn. H.Q. at 16.30 hours to-day.

7. Zero hour will be 05.30 hours, 4th November.

8. **Battalion Objectives.**

   The Battalion will attack on a two Company front. D. COY. (Left) and B. COY. (Right) will take the first Battalion objective - the high ground about grid line between M.16. and M.17. A. COY. (Left) and C. COY. (Right) will leapfrog through and take the final objective (the RED line). Each Company will attack on a three platoon frontage with one platoon in Reserve.

9.   Probable Battalion H.Q. will be firstly in trenches M.14.b.2.3. and secondly at FME. L'EVEQUE (M.16.c.1.6.)

Capt. & Adjt.
5th Duke of Wellington's Regt.

Copies to -

1. A. Coy.
2. B. Coy.
3. C. Coy.
4. D. Coy.
5. HQ. Coy.
6. Signal Officer.
7/8. War Diary.
9. Office.

SECRET   Copy No. 7

5th DUKE OF WELLINGTON's REGIMENT.

INSTRUCTION No. 1.

3rd November, 1918.

1. 2/Lieut. M.G. O'Dowd will act as Liaison Officer with 2/4 D. of W. Regt., and will report there at 23.30 hours on Novr. 3rd.

2. During operations three daily situation reports will be rendered to Battn. HQ. in addition to others of more than ordinary importance such as progress of attack, etc. Times 02.30 hours 08.00 hours and 14.30 hours.

3. The Battalion will rendezvous at Cross Roads about W.24.b.7.4. at 00.40 hours on November 4th in order HQ. D.B.A.C. with head of column facing North.

    Move from there to Assembly Area by platoons at 40 yards interval.

4. The Battalion will move from Assembly Position R.25.c. about 06.15 hours on November 4th.

5. Two sections 186th T.M. Battery will move with the Battalion. They will move with Reserve platoon of D. COY. and will be available to assist any part of the front.

6. One Anti-Tank Rifle and 10 rounds ammunition will be issued to D. COY. who will hand it over to A. COY. when they have passed through.

7. The attack of 187th Infantry Brigade is to be carried out as under -

    To capture the BLUE objective - 5th K.O.Y.L.I. with one Coy. 2/4 K.O.Y.L.I. attached.
    to capture the GREEN do. - 2/4 K.O.Y.L.I.
    to capture the RED do. - 2/4 York & Lancs. Regt.

8. Success signals will be sent up on both flanks of Battalions on reaching the following objectives -
    a. the BLUE Line.   b. the DOTTED BLUE line.
    c. the GREEN Line.   d. the RED Line.
    D. and B. COYs. will each fire a white Very light as a signal for A. and C. COYs. to move forward.

9. An officer from each Coy. will be sent to the Adjt. at 19.30 hours today to synchronise watches.

10. No S.O.S. Signal will be responded to by Artillery between Zero minus 7 hours and Zero.

11. During the attack O.C's Companies will ensure that the closest touch is kept along the Brigade boundaries lines with the Units on their flanks.

Copies to -
1. A. COY.   5. Hq. COY.
2. B. COY.   6. Signal Offr.   Capt. & Adjt.
3. C. COY.   7. War Diary.   5th Duke of Wellington's Regt.
4. D. COY.   8.   do.
               9. Office.

SECRET.   Copy No. 7

5th Batt'n. DUKE OF WELLINGTON'S REGT.

INSTRUCTIONS No. 4.

Administrative.   3rd November, 1918.

1. Three Pack Animals per company will be provided for carrying Lewis Guns and a proportion of panniers.
   The five Pack Animals carrying S.A.A. will be packed and taken with Batt'n. H.Q.

2. Companies will send Prisoners down via Battalion H.Q. and obtain receipts. Battalion H.Q. will be marked by a blue flag with large white 5 painted on it.

3. The Q.M. will issue hot Cocoa to companies before moving off from ENGARMAIN. Rum will be taken on Pack Pony to Assembly Position at R.25.c. and there issued to companies.

4. Should there by any civilians found in a captured village the companies concerned will picquet the exits in order to prevent their leaving. If approximate number of civilians can be ascertained this will be sent to Batt'n. H.Q.

                                              K. Sykes.
                                              Capt. & Adjt.
                                         5th Duke of Wellington's Regt.

Copies to --

   1. A. COY.
   2. B. COY.
   3. C. COY.
   4. D. COY.
   5. HQ. COY.
   6. Signal Officer.
 7/8. War Diary.
   9. Office.

S E C R E T.   Copy No. 8

AMENDMENT TO INSTRUCTION NO. 1. 5th DUKE OF WELLINGTON'S REGT.

1. Cancel para. 2 (a) and substitute

   The New Zealand Division, on the right of the 62nd Division propose to capture LE QUESNOY by moving troops round both flanks of the town. In order to facilitate this, the tactical boundary between the New Zealand and 62nd Divisions for the attack on the 1st objective (BLUE LINE) will run from the Level Crossing at R.16.d.9.5. due East to R.18.c.3.5., and, on the capture of the BLUE LINE, one Battalion N.Z. Division will take over the front as far North as R.18.a.0.0. and will advance in conjunction with the troops of the 62nd Division on its left to the DOTTED BLUE LINE in M.19. and 20. with its left at M.14.d.2.0. The dividing line between this Battalion and the 62nd Division will be the line R.18.a.0.0. – M.14.d.2.0.

   After a halt of 20 minutes on the DOTTED BLUE LINE, troops of the N.Z. Division are continuing the advance in conjunction with the right of the 62nd Division and will capture the villages of VILLEREAU and POTELLE.

2. Cancel para. 5 and substitute

   The following is a Time-Table of the attack –

   Zero plus (141 minutes (on Right Bde.   ) Infantry
            (front.)   ) advances from
            (135 minutes (on Left Bn.   ) BLUE LINE.
                 of Left Bde. front)   )

   Zero plus 206 minutes   ...   Infantry advances from
                                   DOTTED BLUE LINE.

   Zero plus 251 minutes   ...   Barrage ceases and Infantry
                                   advances from GREEN LINE.

   Zero plus 350 minutes   ...   Infantry reaches RED LINE.
                                   185th Infantry Bde. passes
                                   through to continue advance.

                                       K Sykes.
                                              Capt. & Adjt.
                                       5th Duke of Wellington's Regt.

Issued to all recipients of Instructions No.1.

SPECIAL ORDER OF THE DAY.

The 62nd (West Riding) Division has in three days advanced 9½ miles capturing eight villages, over 800 prisoners, several guns including two 8" Howitzers, and a large number of machine guns.

During this advance, troops of 8 enemy Divisions, comprising elements of no less than 17 Regiments, have been encountered and defeated. This splendid achievement, inspite of the miserable weather conditions of the last two days, could not have been attained but for the constant care and forethought of Brigade and Unit Commanders and, above all, the indomitable resolution and endurance of the men under their Command.

The enemy is retreating everywhere in front of us and the Division has been called on to maintain this same relentless pressure for a little while longer to hasten his ultimate defeat.

In thanking all ranks for the steadfastness and loyalty by which I have always been supported and for their wonderful indifference to hardship, I know I can rely on them once more to respond to the call and to add yet again fresh lustre to the glorious records they have already won.

signed   R. WHIGHAM,

Major-General,
Commanding 62nd (West Riding) Division.

6th November, 1918.

62nd Division.

A.C.311.

The Commander in Chief visited the Corps Commander to-day and expressed his high satisfaction at the manner in which the Guards and 62nd Divisions carried out the attack yesterday and the good progress which they had since made.

To be communicated to all ranks.

signed   G. W. STRATFORD,
Captain,
Brigade Major,
186th Infantry Brigade.

6th November, 1918.

62nd (WEST RIDING) DIVISION.

SPECIAL ORDER OF THE DAY
by
Major General Sir. R.D.WHIGHAM, K.C.B., D.S.O.

10th November 1918.

The Major General Commanding has great pleasure in publishing for the information of all ranks of the Division the following letter which he has received from the Corps Commander :-

"G.O.C., 62nd Division.

My best congratulations to you and all ranks of the 62nd Division on the highly successful advance made last night and this morning which has carried the head of the Corps well East of the fortified City of MAUBEUGE.
The advance of the Division since the 4th November has been carried out through an intricate country and in bad weather and has been constantly opposed. The result obtained is most satisfactory and redounds to the credit of your gallant Division.

9/11/1918.

(Sd) A. HALDANE. Lieut. General
Commanding VI Corps."

                                             Lieut. Colonel,
A.A.& Q.M.G., 62nd (West Riding) Division.

.. copy ..

5th Duke of Wellington's Regt.

...

G.S.347.   7th.

Following from General WHIGHAM aaa Warmest congratulations and thanks to you and all ranks including artillery on splendid day's work.

...

62nd (WEST RIDING) DIVISION.
SPECIAL ORDER OF THE DAY.

11th November 1918.

Hostilities are suspended, and in the glorious part which the British Army has played in bringing this to pass the 62nd (West Riding) Division has borne its full share.

In the changed conditions which await us there is no less need for the soldierly qualities which have brought us this success than in the past.

These qualities will now be apparent by the smartness in dress and appearance of every individual officer and man, in precision in drill and the handling of arms, in perfect march discipline, particularly on the part of working parties and transport, in order and cleanliness in billets, wagon and transport lines, and above all in the strictest observance of the principles of security on the part of all troops on guard or outpost duty.

Let us prove that in these all important matters we are still second to none.

signed   R. WHIGHAM
                       Major-General.

S E C R E T.   Copy No. 10

5th DUKE OF WELLINGTON'S REGIMENT.

OPERATION ORDER No. 144.

Reference
   sheets   1/100,000   VALENCIENNES.
            1/100,000   NAMUR.   16th November, 1918.

1. **Advance.**

    The first stage of the Advance of the Fourth Army to the Rhine will commence tomorrow 17th November, 1918.

2. **Advance Guards.**

    The 185th Infantry Brigade Group are to form the Advance Guard of the 62nd Division.

3. **March.**

    The Battalion follows in rear of 2/4 Duke of Wellington's Regt. and 2/4 Hants. Regt. and passes Brigade Starting Point (Road Junction just S.W. of L in LA MACHINE) at 09.14 hours and proceeds to Area COUSOLRE – COLLERET.

4. **Order of Companies, etc.**

    The Battalion will rendezvous on RUE de LOUVROIL outside Orderly Room with head of Column facing East at 08.40 hours. Order of March -- Band - Signallers - A. B. C. D. - Transport & Battn. H.Q. Nuclei will march in immediate rear of leading company each day. The transport will form up in RUE de ROUSIES and follow the column.

5. **March Discipline.**

    The strictest March Discipline will be maintained on all marches.
    Distance of 10 yards between Companies and 50 yards between Battalions will be maintained on all marches.
    All Companies will report arrival in billets and location of Company H.Q. as soon as they arrive. Notice Boards will be displayed. Halts at 10 minutes to the hour. Commanders will blow whistle. Company closes up and falls out on right of the road on second Whistle.
    The Battalion Quarter Guard marches in rear of the Battalion to pick up stragglers. No one will be allowed to fall out without a chit.
    The Battalion will march into its billeting area always at attention.
    The Band will march in threes.

    / two minutes before a halt and the Company will march to attention.

6. **Picquet.**

    The Brigade Group is responsible for its own protection and will picquet all roads leading into its area. Detailed instructions will be issued on arrival in each area.

Transport.

Officers Valises, Company Mess Boxes, Orderly Room Boxes will be sent to present Q.M. Stores by 07.30 hours.

On the troops reaching their billets, all vehicles (including civilian carts, etc.) will be turned off the lorry route into side Roads and fields so as to leave the lorry Route absolutely clear.

The baggage lorries attached to the battalion will be sent off to pass the Brigade Starting point not less than half an hour before the leading unit, and should they overtake other troops, will follow them until these troops halt and clear the road, when lorries can pass. Lieut. and Q.M. P.R. Hammond will go in charge of the baggage lorries.

Baggage Waggons will move with 527th Company ASC. They will accompany the battalion to Brigade Starting Point where they will be parked <u>clear</u> of the road, and will join 527th Company ASC. as it passes. Baggage Waggons will be returned to the Battalion with the supply Waggons on arrival in new area.

8. Synchronisation.

Companies etc. will send a representative to the Adjutant at ~~19.00~~ 2/00 hours to-day at H.Q. Mess to synchronize watches.

9. Dress.

Full Marching Order. Waterproof sheet folded underneath pack flap. Steel Helmet carried on back of pack. S.B.R's to be carried on top of pack. Soft Caps to be worn. Company Commanders will wear Sam Brownes and no packs. Subaltern Officers will be dressed exactly like the rank and file.

10. ACKNOWLEDGE.

K Sykes.
Capt. & Adjt.
5th Duke of Wellington's Rgt.

Issued at 1800 hours.

Copies to -

1 - 4. A. B. C. D. Companies.
5. Adjutant.
6. R.S.M.
7. T.O.
8. Q.M.
9. H.Q. Mess.
10/11. War Diary.
12. 186th Infantry Brigade (for information)
13. Office.

SECRET.

WR 24

ORIGINAL.

CONFIDENTIAL WAR DIARY

-of-

5th DUKE OF WELLINGTON'S (W.R.) REGIMENT

1st to 31st December, 1918.

Volume 10.

11-U.
11 sheets +
2 maps

[signature]
Lieut-Colonel.
Commanding 5th Duke of Wellington's Regt.

ORIGINAL

Army Form C. 2118.

5th Duke of Wellington's Regt.

WAR DIARY
or
INTELLIGENCE SUMMARY.
(Erase heading not required.)

Instructions regarding War Diaries and Intelligence Summaries are contained in F. S. Regs., Part II. and the Staff Manual respectively. Title pages will be prepared in manuscript.

Place	Date	Hour	Summary of Events and Information	Remarks and references to Appendices
Ref.Map MARCHE 1/100,000	1918 Dear 1st		Battalion in billets at COMBEUX.	
	2nd		Brigade practice ceremonial parade in morning. Games in afternoon.	
	3rd		Brigade Ceremonial Parade on ground off the GURBION - CORJOUX ROAD about midway between the two villages. Major-General Sir H.S. Whigham, KCB, commanding 62nd Division shook hands and congratulated recent recipients of immediate honours, on this parade.	
	4th		A very wet day. It was only possible to give lectures to the men indoors. Recreation in afternoon.	
	5th		A fine day. Usual close order parades and physical drill in the morning. Recreation in afternoon.	
	6th		The battalion moved from COMBEUX to BEIGNON and took over billets from 1/5th Devon Regt. A beautiful day.	
	7th		Sultry day. Training in the morning. Recreation in afternoon.	
	8th		Brigade should have moved forward again to-day, but it was cancelled. Battalion did Training in morning. Recreation in afternoon.	
	9th		Very wet day. Lectures to men within billets.	
	10th		Sultry day with some rain. Battalion marched with 186th Infantry Brigade Group from Leignon at 0900 via PESSOUX to BARVAUX-CONDROZ.	
	11th		Wet day. Battalion marched from BARVAUX-CONDROZ to OCQUIER (2 companies and Bn.) and VERNOX (1 company) via MAFFE and BONSIN. En route the battalion marched past the LK Corps Commander (Lieut-General Sir Walter Braithwaite, KCB).	
	12th		A very wet day. Battalion marched from OCQUIER to FARRIERES - 15 miles.	
	13th		Another pouring wet day. Battalion marched on to CHEVRON, BOUVILLE and FORGES through very beautiful scenery.	
	14th		Battalion marched to GRAND HALLEUX. Weather at first very wet but cleared later.	
	15th		Battalion rested and cleaned up at GRAND HALLEUX. Voluntary Church of England service in the morning.	
Ref.Map Germany I.M. 1/100,000	16th		The battalion marched with remainder of the 186th Infantry Brigade Group from GRAND HALLEUX area in very wet weather. The battalion was billeted at PETIT THIER and BLANCHE FONTAINE.	

ORIGINAL

5th Duke of Wellington's Regt.

Army Form C. 2118.

WAR DIARY
or
INTELLIGENCE SUMMARY.
(Erase heading not required.)

Instructions regarding War Diaries and Intelligence Summaries are contained in F.S. Regs., Part II. and the Staff Manual respectively. Title pages will be prepared in manuscript.

Place	Date	Hour	Summary of Events and Information	Remarks and references to Appendices
Ref.Map Germany I.M. 1/100,000.	1918 Decr 17th		Another very wet cold day with some sleet and snow. The battalion marched from PETIT THIER area to AMEL crossing the German frontier at PONTAU. The battalion marched over the frontier at "attention", the band playing the Regimental March. Examining Posts were placed at each exit to the village of AMEL and the inhabitants were confined to their houses between 7 p.m. and 5 a.m. except those provided with proper passes issued by the British Military Authorities. Battalion remained at AMEL. Wet.	
	18th		-do-	
	19th		-do-	
	20th		Wet. With a good fall of snow.	
	21st		Battalion at AMEL. Fine but very cold.	
	22nd		Very cold with more snow in the afternoon. Battalion marched from AMEL to LORRINGEN where the inhabitants were not well inclined or helpful. Billets indifferent.	
	23rd		A very wet boisterous day. Very gusty and a great deal of rain, hail and sleet. The battalion marched to BLUMENTHAL, a distance of 27½ kilometres. The men marched very well in spite of the awful weather and long distance.	
Ref.Map Germany I.L. 1/100,000.	24th		A fine, sharp frosty day. Battalion marched to WAHLENTHAL (A. Company only) and SCHEVEN. Billets on the whole good, but scattered [25th] much snow during the day and more again during the day.	
	25th		The battalion marched to MECHERNICH, where billets were very crowded, the 2/4 Hants. Regt. and Brigade H.Q. being in the same village.	
	26th		A bright cold day. A Christmas day. Service was held in one of the Cinemas MECHERNICH for the battalion during the morning. After dinners the battalion, (less B. Company,) was ordered to move to OBERG-RUZEM and PIRMANICH. The battalion arrived there after dark and found billets crowded.	
	27th		A draft of details etc. joined battalion, 250 strong.	
	28th		Battalion changed billets again and was disposed as follows :- A. Coy. Transport and H.V. details at OBERGARZEM. B. Company at HOSTEL. C. Company at PIRMANICH and D. Company at EIZEN. Battalion Orderly Room was at OBERGARZEM and the Mess at EUZEN. The battalion area from end to end stretched over 13 kilometres. The men were all comfortably housed.	
	29th		Battalion cleaned up and settled itself. Wet.	
	30th		-do-	
	31st		Sultry day and mild.	

J. Wall Lieut-Colonel.
Commanding 5th Bn. of Wellington's Regt.

Army Form C. 2118.

5th Duke of Wellington's Regt.

WAR DIARY
or
INTELLIGENCE SUMMARY.
(Erase heading not required.)

Instructions regarding War Diaries and Intelligence Summaries are contained in F. S. Regs., Part II. and the Staff Manual respectively. Title pages will be prepared in manuscript.

Place	Date	Hour	Summary of Events and Information	Remarks and references to Appendices

APPENDICES.

Drafts, etc.

Lieut.	W. Wallace.	Joined Battalion from England	3.12.18.
"	W. Yates.	" " " "	18.12.18.
2/Lieut.	B. Brierley.	" " " "	26.12.18.
"	H. Greenwood.	" " " "	26.12.18.
"	W. Nield.	" " " "	26.12.18.
"	W. Rawson.	" " " "	26.12.18.
"	J. Shannon.	" " " "	26.12.18.
"	J. Hogan.	" " " Hospital	26.12.18.

246 O.r.   " " "   26.12.18.

Casualties, etc.

Lieut. H. Johnson   To Hospital sick   31.12.18.

(signature)
Lieut-Colonel.
Commanding 5th Duke of Wellington's Regt.

SPECIAL ORDER

by

Major-General Sir R.D. WHIGHAM, K.C.B., D.S.O.

Commanding 62nd (West Riding) Division.

The following Christmas Greeting from the Corps Commander is forwarded for communication to all ranks of the Division at the first opportunity.

                signed   Harold F. Lea.
                                            Lieut-Colonel.
26th Decr. 1918.   A.A.&Q.M.G., 62nd (West Riding) Division.

TO ALL OFFICERS, WARRANT OFFICERS AND MEN OF THE IX CORPS.

After a difficult and troublesome march, you have reached your final destination in Germany, at a time when it is most difficult to arrange the cheery Christmas to which you are accustomed.

You have borne the discomforts of the march with the same cheerful discipline as you did the hard fighting which brought us the resounding victories of the last two months of the war.

During the march, you have taught the civil inhabitants of Germany, by your discipline, soldierly bearing, smart turnout and forbearance towards a beaten people, as great a lesson as you did the German Army by the defeats you inflicted on it during the final phases of the war.

I am proud to be in command of Troops specially selected to occupy German territory on this historic Christmas, and I wish you all as merry a Christmas as possible under the circumstances, and a Happy and Prosperous New Year.

                signed ...   WALTER BRAITHWAITE.

SPECIAL ORDER OF THE DAY

To all ranks of the 62nd (West Riding) Division.

The last hours of 1918 are passing and tomorrow will see the opening of a new year ushered in with high hopes of an era of peace and the prosperity that peace should bring in its train.

The verdict of history will decide whether 1918 has been the greatest of all the years of the war, but for the 62nd Division it has been one long period of unbroken success in battle from BUCQUOY to MAUBEUGE.

In no Division has the spirit of comradeship and mutual understanding between all units and all ranks been more highly developed than in the 62nd, and without it the successes won in battle could never have been attained.

In the new era of peace now dawning, that spirit will be the keystone of the fabric of prosperity which has its foundations in peace.

It will fall to the lot of some to return to their homes and their callings in civil life earlier than others, but whether we go sooner or later let all of us to whom it has been granted to survive the dangers and stress of war, retain that bond of comradeship throughout the remainder of our lives.

In this spirit I now wish each one of you a very happy New Year and peace and prosperity in the future.

        signed   ...   R. WHIGHAM,

                                Major-General,
        Commanding 62nd (West Riding) Division.

31st December 1918.

Copy No. 10

5th Battn. DUKE of WELLINGTON'S REGT.

OPERATION ORDER No.146

Reference Maps   MARCHE 1/100,000.
                 Germany I.M. 1/100,000.   15.12.18.

1. The IX Corps will continue the Advance in two columns until the heads of columns reach the neighbourhood of the RHINE, East of COLOGNE.
The left column (probably 6th and 62nd Divisions) by BOHLEIDEN on ZULPICH, using the LOSHEIMMERGRABEN - HOLLERATH - HELLENTHAL Road.

2. The 62nd Division will continue the advance on the 16th and 17th December in two columns.
The Right Column (185th and 186th Brigade Groups) by POTEAU, RECHT and AMEL.

3. The 5th Battalion Duke of Wellington's Regiment will march on the 16th instant in accordance with the attached table.

4. 1 Billeting Party NCO. per company will proceed on foot tomorrow, and 1 representative per company by first lorry, reporting to Capt. C.S. Floyd and Lieut. W.L. Sidders, MC. at PETIT THIER at 09.00 hours. Those marching will go together under Senior NCO.

5. Rear Party and Orderly Officer will report to Captain of the Week at Orderly Room at 10.30 hours.

6. Watches will be synchronised at Orderly Room at 07.30 hours tomorrow.

7. First lorry load will leave Q.M. Stores at 08.00 hours.

8. Refilling Point tomorrow - RECHT. Brigade H.Q. will be at RECHT.

K. Sykes
Capt. & Adjt.
5th Duke of Wellington's Regt.

Issued at 2040 hours.
Copies to ..

1/4. A.B.C.D. Coys.
   5. HQ. details.
   6. R.S.M.
   7. Q.M.
   8. T.O.
   9. Adjutant.
10/11. War Diary.
  12. O.C. 2/4 Dukes Regt. (for information)
  13. Office.

Reference Maps :- MARCHE 1/100,000.
Germany I.M. 1/100,000.

MARCH TABLE TO ACCOMPANY BATTN. OPERATION ORDER NO. 145.

Serial No.	Battn. Starting Point	Time to be at Battn. Starting Point	Order of Coys	Brigade Starting Point.	Time to be at Brigade Starting Point	ROUTE FROM	TO
4.	Cemetery South of GRAND HALLEUX	09.20 hours	B. C. Band D. A.	Road Junction 300 yards West-North-West of the H in HOURS.	09.35 hours	GRAND HALLEUX	PETIT THIER & BLANCHE FONTAINE	VIELSALM

Remarks.

5th Battn. Duke of Wellington's Regt. follows 2/4 Hants. Regt. Care will be taken not to block the road with troops and transport prior to 2/4 Hants. Regt. passing through.

15th Decr 1918

Kyles
Capt. O Adjt.
5th Duke of Wellington's Regt.

WAR DIARY.

62nd (WEST RIDING) DIVISION.

SPECIAL ORDER OF THE DAY
BY
Major-General Sir R.D. Whigham, K.C.B. D.S.O.

3rd December 1918

The Divisional Commander publishes for the information of all ranks a letter received from the Corps Commander VI Corps ...

                                            H.Q. VI Corps.
                                                    B.E.F.
                                       27th November 1918.

My dear Whigham,

    Will you kindly express to all ranks of the 62nd Division my regret at losing them from the Corps. I have had occasion several times to convey to you my warm appreciation of the splendid work they did these last three months, so I will not now refer in detail to their achievements.

    The Division has built up a proud record and each time that it has gone into action with the VI Corps it has gained fresh laurels.

    I had hoped that the four Divisions of the Corps who had taken part together in so many hard fights would together march into the enemy's country. I much regret that this is not to be.

    Will you please convey to your staff, C.R.A. C.R.E. A.D.M.S. and Infantry Brigadiers and their Staffs how highly I appreciate their unstinted efforts which have helped so much towards the very successful operations of the 62nd Division.

                      Yours sincerely
        signed.   C. HALDANE.

        signed   HAROLD P. LEA
                                  Lieut- Colonel.
        A.A. & Q.M.G. 62nd (West Riding) Division.

O.C. A. Coy.
    B. Coy.
    C. Coy.
    D. Coy.
  HQ. details.
  R.S.M.
  T.O.
  Q.M.
  War Diary.

B.549.

The following telegram was received by the Commanding Officer on November 30th.

Col. Walker
Commanding Officer
5th Battn. West Riding Regiment.

The inhabitants of Huddersfield at a Town Meeting held this evening Friday November 22nd 1918 in support of the Huddersfield Thanksgiving Week desire to offer to Colonel Walker their most sincere and hearty congratulations on the signing of the armistice with the enemy powers and on the prospect of an early and victorious peace. The home town and county trust that Colonel Walker and his officers and men will accept their affectionate greetings and congratulations in the termination of hostilities in which the old fighting qualities of the havercake lads have been shown as bravely as ever.

                        CARMI SMITH. MAYOR.

The following reply was sent ..

The Mayor of Huddersfield.

Dear Mr. Mayor,

On behalf of the officers, warrant officers, non-commissioned officers and men of the 5th Duke of Wellington's Regt. I beg to thank you most sincerely for your very kind telegram of congratulations and greeting on the cessation of hostilities. Your message is greatly appreciated by us all. As a battalion we are proud to be associated with the town of Huddersfield and it gives us great satisfaction to know that our fighting services have been so much appreciated and valued by our fellow-townsmen at home.

                Yours faithfully

        signed ..   K. SYKES.   Capt.
        Comdg. 5th Duke of Wellington's Regt.

2nd
Decr.
1918.

SECRET

CONFIDENTIAL WAR DIARY

-of-

5TH DUKE OF WELLINGTON'S (W.R) REGT.

1st to 31st January 1919.

......

Volume 11.

E. Vernon. Major.
Commanding 5th Duke of Wellington's Regt.

ORIGINAL

ORIGINAL

5TH DUKE OF WELLINGTON'S REGT.

Army Form C. 2118.

WAR DIARY
or
INTELLIGENCE SUMMARY.
(Erase heading not required.)

Instructions regarding War Diaries and Intelligence Summaries are contained in F. S. Regs., Part II. and the Staff Manual respectively. Title pages will be prepared in manuscript.

Place	Date	Hour	Summary of Events and Information	Remarks and references to Appendices
Ref. Map Germany I.I. 1/100,000	1919 Jany 1st.	(m)	Battalion disposed as follows:- A. Coy, Battalion Headquarters & Transport at OBERGARTZEM, B. Coy, at HOSTEL, C. Coy. at FIRMANICH, D. Coy. at ENZEN. Each Company held its Christmas Dinner in each village Hall and it was greatly enjoyed. The Halls were very well decorated and the Banquets were made possible by generous friends of the battalion in Huddersfield.	
	2nd.		Much cooler with rain at intervals.	
	3rd.		Fine day. Troops did a little training in morning. Recreation in afternoon.	
	4th.		A. & C. Coys had baths under their own arrangements in respective villages.	
	5th.		Church Parade for A, C, D, Coys. was held in A. Coys. Dining Hall, OBERGARTZEM. Very boisterous day.	
	6th.		Fine windy day. A little training during the morning and games in the afternoon.	
	7th.		Very nice day. A little training in morning. Recreation in afternoon.	
	8th.		Very nice day. A little training in morning. Recreation in afternoon. Lieut. Col. J. Walker DSO. went to Brigade (H.Qs. (186th Infantry Brigade) to command the Brigade Group in the absence on leave of Brigadier General J.G. Burnett C.M.G. D.S.O.	
	9th.		Nice day. Usual training parades in morning. Platoon Association Competitions etc in afternoon.	
	10th.		Nice day. Usual training parades in morning. Platoon Association Competitions etc., in afternoon.	
	11th.		Fine day. battalion all had Baths.	
	12th.		voluntary Church Services for different denominations.	
	13th.		Dull day. Usual training in morning and for making Miniature Ranges for each Company.	
	14th.		Dull Day. Usual training in morning and for making Miniature Ranges for each company. Battalion Education Scheme commenced. As only one set of books were available it was only possible to start with one Company. A start was made in C. Coy. with 48 students and 3 Teachers, in Elementry Subjects. Classes for Carpentry, Tailoring, Bootmaking, Haircutting, and Shoeing were also started.	
	15th.		Usual training and recreation.	
	16th.		Usual training and recreation.	
	17th.		Dull wet day. Usual Training and recreation.	
	18th.		Wet cold day. Troops had baths and Inspections under Company arrangements.	

ORIGINAL.

Army Form C. 2118.

5TH DUKE OF WELLINGTON'S REGT.

WAR DIARY
or
INTELLIGENCE SUMMARY.
(Erase heading not required.)

Instructions regarding War Diaries and Intelligence Summaries are contained in F. S. Regs., Part II. and the Staff Manual respectively. Title pages will be prepared in manuscript.

Place	Date	Hour	Summary of Events and Information	Remarks and references to Appendices
Re.Map Germany I.L. 1/100,000	1919. Jany. 19th.		Dull Day. Voluntary Divine Service for battalion in A. Coys. Dining Hall in OBERGARTZEM. The battalion played an Association Match against 2/2nd. West Riding Field Ambulance in the first round of the Brigade Group Competition for the Divisional Cup. The match ended in a draw - 2 goals each.	
	20th.		A. bright day. The usual training and recreation was carried out. B. Coy vacated HOSTEL and moved to ULPENICH.	
	21st.		A Bright frosty day. The battalion/played the replay of the 1st Round of the Divisional Cup, against the 2/2nd West Riding Field Ambulance at HOHHEIM and lost after a hard game by 2 goals to nil.	
	22nd.		Still frosty but, dull. Training and recreation continued as usual. A short route march was done during the morning.	
	23rd.		Frosty and a fall of snow during the morning. Lectures and indoor training occupied the training hours, outdoor recreational was cancelled on account of the hard state of the ground. News was received that Capt C.G.H. Ellis D.S.O. and 2/Lieut Hogan had been awarded the Military Cross. The Divisional Concert party - The PELICANS - gave a variety concert at ENZEN.	
	24th.		Bright and frosty. Training and recreational as usual. News was received that 3 Warrant Officers and 1 N.S.O. of the battalion had been awarded the meritorious Service Medal in the New Years Honours Gazette.	
	25th.		Kit inspections carried out and bathing.	
	26th.		Services were held at OBERGARTZEM and ENZEN for the battalion. The weather continued to be frosty.	
	27th.		Usual training carried out. Little outdoor recreational on account of the hard ground.	
	28th.		Training done under company arrangements.	
	29th.		The battalion went for a short route march during the morning. The day was dull and very cold.	
	30th.		Training continued by companies - Slight fall of snow at intervals during the day.	
	31st.		Dull day and frosty. Training was carried out during the morning. Little outdoor recreation could be done as the ground was very hard.	

E. Secuer. Major.
Commanding 5th Duke of Wellington's Regt.

ORIGINAL.

Army Form C. 2118.

Instructions regarding War Diaries and Intelligence Summaries are contained in F. S. Regs., Part II. and the Staff Manual respectively. Title pages will be prepared in manuscript.

5TH DUKE OF WELLINGTON'S REGT.

WAR DIARY
or
INTELLIGENCE SUMMARY.
(Erase heading not required.)

Place	Date	Hour	Summary of Events and Information	Remarks and references to Appendices
			APPENDICES.	
			Drafts, Etc.,	
			Other Ranks.	
			12 Other ranks 3.1.19.	
			4 do 8.1.19.	
			17 do 14.1.19.	
			3 do 29.1.19.	
			Casualties etc. Transfers etc.	
			Lieut. W. Yates. Left battalion for Demobilization 10.1.19.	
			2/Lieut. J. Bentley. do 20.1.19.	
			Honours and Awards.	
			The following Officers, N.C.Os. and Men have been awarded decorations as stated against their names for gallantry and devotion to duty in the field.	
			Capt. C.G.H. Ellis D.S.O. M.C.	
			" C.W. Lockwood. M.C.	
			Lieut. F.H. Waite M.C.	
			2/Lieut. J. Hogan. M.C.	
			" G. Monkman. M.C.	
			240076 Sgt. Lee S.H. D.C.M. Bar to D.C.M.	
			240088 " Merriman H.S. M.M. D.C.M.	
			240742 Pte. Tomlinson R. M.M. French C. de G. with Palm.	
			240623 " Donbavand E. M.M. French C. de G. with Silver Star.	
			25902 " Jefcoates A. French C. de G. with Bronze Star.	
			240320 Sgt. Micklethwaite F. M.S.M.	
			240829 C.Q.M.S. Airey W. M.S.M.	
			240451 " Pedley J. M.S.M.	
			240001 S/Sgt. Sykes G. M.S.M.	

5TH DUKE OF WELLINGTON'S REGT.

WAR DIARY
or
INTELLIGENCE SUMMARY.
(Erase heading not required.)

Army Form C. 2118.

ORIGINAL

Instructions regarding War Diaries and Intelligence Summaries are contained in F. S. Regs., Part II. and the Staff Manual respectively. Title pages will be prepared in manuscript.

Place	Date	Hour	Summary of Events and Information	Remarks and references to Appendices
			APPENDICES.	
			Honours and Awards (cont^d)	
			Lieut-Colonel G.P. Norton D.S.O. Mentioned in Despatches.	
			do J. Walker D.S.O. do	
			Capt. H.C. Golding M.C. do	
			" J.B. Cockhill D.S.O. M.C. do	
			" C.G.H. Ellis D.S.O. M.C. do	
			" G.B. Bruce M.C. do	
			Lieut. F.H. Waite M.C. do	
			2/Lieut. F.R.W.I. Thorpe do	
			242148 Sergt. Denny P.	
			E. Tenson Major.	
			Commanding 5th Duke of Wellington's Regt.	

SPECIAL ORDER.

by

Major-General Sir R.D. WHIGHAM, K.C.B., D.S.O.

Commanding 62nd (West Riding) Division.

December 31st 1918.

The Divisional Commander has the honour to announce that His Majesty The King has conferred the VICTORIA CROSS on No. 34506 Private HENRY TANDY, D.C.M., M.M., 5th Duke of Wellington's (W.R.) Regt.(T.F.) for the following action of gallantry.

"For desperate bravery and great initiative during the capture of the Village and the Crossings at MARCOING, and the later counter-attack on September 28th 1918.
During the advance on MARCOING this soldier's platoon was held up by machine gun fire, and stopped: He at once crawled forward under heavy fire, located the machine gun position, led a Lewis Gun Team into a neighbouring house from which they were able to knock out the gun, and his platoon continue the advance. On arrival at the Crossings the plank bridge was broken, and under heavy fire, and seemingly impassable, he crawled forward, putting planks into position, and making the bridge passable under a hail of bullets, thus enabling the first crossing to be made at this vital spot. He must have seen that the chance of losing his life amounted to almost a certainty.
Later in the evening during an attack by his Company to enlarge the bridge-head and capture MARCOING Support Trench, he, with 8 comrades were surrounded by an overwhelming number of Germans, and though the position was apparently hopeless, he led a bayonet charge through them, fighting so fiercely that 37 of the enemy were driven into the hands of the remainder of his Company in rear, and taken prisoners, the party winning clear, though he was twice wounded. Even then he refused to leave, leading parties into dug-outs and capturing over 20 of the enemy, and though faint from loss of blood, stayed till the fight was won."

Lieut-Colonel,
A.A.&.Q.M.G., 62nd (West Riding) Division.

ORIGINAL. SECRET.

CONFIDENTIAL WAR DIARY

-of-

5TH DUKE OF WELLINGTON'S (W.R.) REGT.

1st to 28th February 1919.

Volume ... ... 12.

.... Lieut. Colonel.
Commanding 5th Duke of Wellington's Regiment.

ORIGINAL.

Army Form C. 2118.

5th Duke of Wellington's (W.R.) Regt.

WAR DIARY
or
INTELLIGENCE SUMMARY.
(Erase heading not required.)

Instructions regarding War Diaries and Intelligence Summaries are contained in F.S. Regs., Part II and the Staff Manual respectively. Title pages will be prepared in manuscript.

Place	Date	Hour	Summary of Events and Information	Remarks and references to Appendices
Ref. Map. Germany I.I. 1/100,000	1919 Feb. 1st.		Bathing and Inspections occupied the morning. The frost continued making outdoor recreation difficult.	
	2nd.		Church parade was held at ENZEN and a United Evening Service at OBERGARTZEM.	
	3rd.		Usual training under company arrangements was carried out. A & C Coys competed in a 3 mile cross country run, every man in the company having to turn out. C. Coy provided the winners.	
	4th.		The weather continued to be frosty. Usual training and recreation were carried out.	
	5th.		Frosty weather. Usual training and Education in morning. Games in afternoon.	
	6th.		Frosty weather. Usual training and Education in morning. Games in afternoon.	
	7th.		Frosty weather. Usual training and Education in morning. Games in afternoon.	
	8th.		Frosty weather. Usual training and Education in morning. Games in afternoon.	
	9th.		Church parades for in morning for B. & D. Coys at ENZEN and A & C. Coys at OBERGARTZEM.	
	10th.		Frosty weather with bright sunshine. Usual training and Education in morning. Games in afternoon.	
	11th.		Frosty weather with bright sunshine. Usual training and Education in morning. Games in afternoon.	
	12th.		The battalion marched to MECHERNICH in the morning taking Field Kitchens. The weather was beautifully fine and frosty. After dinners in 2/4th Hants Regt., Dining Halls the battalion attended Cinema performance at Brigade Cinema Hall and then marched back to billets.	
	13th.		Usual training in morning. Recreation in afternoon.	

Army Form C. 2118.

5th Duke of Wellington's Regt

WAR DIARY
or
INTELLIGENCE SUMMARY.
(Erase heading not required.)

Place	Date	Hour	Summary of Events and Information	Remarks and references to Appendices
Ref. Map. Germany I.L. 1/100,000	1919. Feb. 14th		Battalion parade in the morning on D. Coys Parade Ground at ENZEN. Recreation in afternoon. Thaw set in.	
	15th.		Men all had baths and cleaned up generally.	
	16th.		Usual services for all denominations.	
	17th.		Military and Educational Training in morning. Recreation in afternoon.	
	18th.		Military and Education Training in morning. Recreation in afternoon.	
	19th.		Battalion went a Route March in morning. Inter League Football Matches in afternoon. Heard that the battalion was likely to be reduced to a Cadre establishment.	
	20th.		Usual training in morning. Recreation in afternoon. News was received that the Infantry Battalions of the 62nd Division were all to be relieved by Scotch Battalions and the Division called Highland Division. The battalions of the 62nd Division to be reduced to Cadres or transferred to other divisions.	
	21st.		Usual Military training and work on Range in morning. Recreation in afternoon. Very mild weather.	
	22nd.		Men had baths in the morning. At night a Fancy Dress Ball was arranged for the battalion in D. Coys Dining Hall at ENZEN and was thoroughly enjoyed.	
	23rd.		Usual Church Services.	
	24th.		Usual Military training in morning. Football in afternoon.	
	25th.		The final of the Inter Company Cup Tie Association Football Competition was held at ENZEN in the morning. A. Coy. versus D. Coy. The latter won easily by 7 goals to 1.	

'ORIGINAL.'

5th Duke of Wellington's (W.R) Regt

Army Form C. 2118.

Instructions regarding War Diaries and Intelligence
Summaries are contained in F. S. Regs., Part II.
and the Staff Manual respectively. Title pages
will be prepared in manuscript.

WAR DIARY
or
INTELLIGENCE SUMMARY.
(Erase heading not required.)

Place	Date	Hour	Summary of Events and Information	Remarks and references to Appendices
Map. Ref 1919 Germany 1/100,000	Feb. 26th.		Battalion went on Route March via KOMMERN, EICKS, and SCHWERFEN during the morning.	
	27th.		Usual Military and Educational training during the morning. Recreation in the afternoon.	
	28th.		A wet day with some snow. Usual training in morning. Games in the afternoon.	

................J. Walker............Lieut-Colonel.

Commanding 5th Duke of Wellington's Regiment.

ORIGINAL.

Army Form C. 2118.

5TH DUKE OF WELLINGTON'S REGT.,
WAR DIARY
or
INTELLIGENCE SUMMARY.
(Erase heading not required.)

Instructions regarding War Diaries and Intelligence Summaries are contained in F. S. Regs., Part II. and the Staff Manual respectively. Title pages will be prepared in manuscript.

Place	Date	Hour	Summary of Events and Information	Remarks and references to Appendices
			APPENDICES.	
			Drafts, etc.,	
			Lieut. H. Johnson. Rejoined from Hospital 20.2.19.	
			2 Other Ranks 4.2.19.	
			2 do 1.2.19.	
			6 do 16.2.19.	
			4 do 22.2.19.	
			Casualties, etc., Transfers etc.,	
			Lieut. W.I. Sidders MC. Demobilized whilst on leave 28.1.19.	
			Lieut. E.G. Watkinson MC Demobilized (Long Service) 14.2.19.	
			Lieut. H.D. Wraith Demobilized (Pivotal) 2.2.19.	
			Lieut. C.A.W. Williams do do 20.2.19.	
			2/Lieut T. Mudd do do 27.2.19.	
			Capt. C.S. Floyd Hospital Sick. 8.2.19.	
			2/Lieut. J. Shannon do 2.2.19.	
			Capt. G.B. Bruce MC To 2nd Inf. Bde. Staff Capt. 31.1.19.	
			TOTAL Demobilized since 11th November 1918. 7 Officers, 265 Other Ranks.	
			Promotions, Relinquishments etc.,	
			2/Lieut(a/Capt) W.J. Lloyd DSO, MC relinquished Acting Rank of Captain 6.1.19.	
			Lieut W. Wallace appointed Additional a/Capt. 21.1.19. and relinquished 20.2.19.	

........Walker........ Lieut. Colonel.
Commanding 5th Duke of Wellington's Regiment.

CONFIDENTIAL.

WAR DIARY
- of -

5th. DUKE OF WELLINGTON'S REGT.

1st to 31st. March. 1919.

(Volume - 13).

[signature] ...Lieut.Col.
Commdg. 5th. Duke of Wellington's Regt.

ORIGINAL.

5th. DUKE OF WELLINGTON'S REGT. N.A.

Army Form C. 2118.

WAR DIARY
or
INTELLIGENCE SUMMARY.
(Erase heading not required.)

Instructions regarding War Diaries and Intelligence Summaries are contained in F.S. Regs., Part II. and the Staff Manual respectively. Title pages will be prepared in manuscript.

Place	Date	Hour	Summary of Events and Information	Remarks and references to Appendices
Ref. Map. GERMANY. I.L. 1/100,000.	1919 Mon. 1st.		A fine day. Cleaning up generally. Battalion sent a Rugby Football Team to EGGENDORF in the afternoon to play 5th. Battn. Gordon Highlanders. The Battalion was beaten by 24 points to 3.	
	2nd.		Church of England Parade Service for the battalion in 'A' Coy's Dining Hall conducted by Senior Divisional Chaplain.	
	3rd.		The Battalion sent off a detachment of 5 officers and 220 other ranks under Capt. G.V. Bernays MC to HERBERSTAHL on the German Frontier as railhead Guard relieving a similar detachment of the 2nd. Battn. Royal Scots. The detachment entrained at ZURICH at 07.01 hours. When this detachment had left the battalion only numbered 18 officers and 187 other ranks.	
	4th.		Mild wet weather.	
	5th.		A battalion Soccer team played against the 18th. Auxiliary Horse Transport (IX. Corps) at BURNHEIM in the afternoon. The match ended in a draw.	
	6th.		Mild weather. Games.	
	7th.		- do -	
	8th.		The battalion less HERBERSTAHL Detachment was relieved in the villages of FINLANICH, OBERHARTEN, EM-ZEN, and HELFENICH by the 1/5th. Argyle and Sutherland Highlanders who joined the 186th Inf. Brigade to replace this battalion on its being ordered to reduce to a Cadre Establishment. The battalion marched to billets at MECHERNICH	

ORIGINAL.

Army Form C. 2118.

5th. DUKE OF WELLINGTON'S REGT.

WAR DIARY
or
INTELLIGENCE SUMMARY.
(Erase heading not required.)

Instructions regarding War Diaries and Intelligence Summaries are contained in F.S. Regs., Part II. and the Staff Manual respectively. Title pages will be prepared in manuscript.

Place	Date	Hour	Summary of Events and Information	Remarks and references to Appendices
	1919 Mch. 9th.		The Detachment at HERBESTHAL returned. Of this detachment 4 officers and 122 other ranks were transferred to 2/4th. Duke of Wellington's Regt. and detrained at ZULPICH. Remainder of the detachment consisting of personnel able to be demobilized returned to the battalion at MECHERNICH.	
	10th.		The retainable men of the battalion (those joining the colours subsequent to 1st. Jany. 1916) were transferred to 2/4th. Duke of Wellington's Regt. and marched to ZULPICH. In all yesterday and to-day 12 officers and 228 other ranks were transferred. In the afternoon there was a German disturbance at NEDHUTTE in the neighbourhood of VUSSEM. The battalion was ordered to keep 2 officers and 50 men "standing by". The Military Mounted Police with assistance of 186th. Trench Mortar Battery quelled the disturbance and the ringleaders were arrested. No troops of this battalion were used.	
	11th.		A fine day. 186th. Inf. Bde Headquarters moved out of MECHERNICH and this battalion ceased to be under their command and came under orders of 62nd. Divisional H.Q. direct.	
	12th.		Battalion sent 30 other ranks away for demobilization including T/R.S.M. B. Earle MC who has been Regtl. Sergt. Major of the battalion since the amalgamation in January 1918 and with the 2/5th. Duke of Wellington's Regt. since March 1916. He was Sergeant Instructor for "H" (Holmfirth) Company on mobilization of the Territorial Force in August 1914. The battalion all had baths at the Divisional Baths MECHERNICH during the day.	
	13th.		A dull cool day. The Commanding Officer presented the French Croix de Guerre Medal (with Silver Star) to No. 240623 Pte. A. Donbavand MM on parade at 10.00 hours. Ribbon Brooches were presented to the following at the same time :- Territorial Force Efficiency Medal. Meritorious Service Medal. Military Cross. No. 240042 Pte. Dewhurst H. No. 240329 C.Q.M.S. Ellis W. Capt. C.F.H. Ellis, DSO, MC. 2/Lieut. C. Henkmar, MC. 2/Lieut. C.G. Bowle MC. The battalion went for a Route march in the morning.	

ORIGINAL.

5th. DUKE OF WELLINGTON'S REGT.

Army Form C. 2118.

WAR DIARY
or
INTELLIGENCE SUMMARY.

(Erase heading not required.)

Instructions regarding War Diaries and Intelligence Summaries are contained in F. S. Regs., Part II. and the Staff Manual respectively. Title pages will be prepared in manuscript.

Place	Date	Hour	Summary of Events and Information	Remarks and references to Appendices
	1919. Mch. 14th.		Fine cold day.	
	15th.		Battalion went for a Route March in morning. Draft of 30 men sent away for demobilization. Soccer Match in the afternoon against 18th. Auxiliary Army Horse Transport. Game was easily won by us.	
	16th.		Church parade in Coliseum Theatre in the morning conducted by Rev. A.W. Wheeler C.F.	
	17th.		Very nasty wet day which later turned to snow. Working parties were supplied for Railhead Supply Officer at Mechernich Station	
	18th.		Quite a good fall of snow making it very nasty underfoot. Supplied further working parties for R.S.O. at the Station.	
	19th.		Very bright sunny day. Snow remains.	
	20th.		Bright frosty day. Snow all disappeared.	
	21st.		Fine day. Men went a Route March in the morning.	
	22nd.		Fine. 58 men of the battalion went to Baths at BUSHFELDEN.	
	23rd.		Fine and Bright. No Chaplain available for divine services.	
	24th.		Heavy fall of snow.	
	25th.		More snow and very nasty.	
	26th.		Rapid thaw. Sent 30 men away for demobilization.	

ORIGINAL.

5th. Duke of Wellington's Regt. Inf..

Army Form C. 2118.

WAR DIARY
or
INTELLIGENCE SUMMARY.
(Erase heading not required.)

Instructions regarding War Diaries and Intelligence Summaries are contained in F. S. Regs., Part II. and the Staff Manual respectively. Title pages will be prepared in manuscript.

Place	Date	Hour	Summary of Events and Information	Remarks and references to Appendices
	1919 Mar. 27th 28th		More snow again which did not stay.	
			Snowed again. Very cold. Sent 5 Officers and 44 men away for demobilization. Major B. Senior D.S. left the battalion for demobilization.	
	29th		Sent the remainder of the demobilisable men away. 2 officers and 40 men.	
	30th		A fine day. Preparations made for Cadre to move the following day.	
	31st		Battalion reduced to Cadre Establishment (4 officers and 49 other ranks) ordered to move to Fourth Army Area. Lorries which should have arrived to convey Cadre and Stores to DURAN arrived two hours late and the train was missed in consequence. The Cadre was billetted for the day in DURAN by Highland Division Reception Camp.	

Walker
Commdg. 5th/Duke of Wellington's Regiment. Lieut. Col.

(10540) Wt W5300/1715 750,000 3/18 E 2688 Forms/C2118/16.

ORIGINAL.

5th. DUKE OF WELLINGTON'S REGT., D.L.

Army Form C. 2118.

WAR DIARY
or
INTELLIGENCE SUMMARY.
(Erase heading not required.)

Instructions regarding War Diaries and Intelligence Summaries are contained in F.S. Regs., Part II. and the Staff Manual respectively. Title pages will be prepared in manuscript.

Place	Date	Hour	Summary of Events and Information	Remarks and references to Appendices
			APPENDICES.	
			CASUALTIES, TRANSFERS etc.	
			Lieut. E. Johnson. Left unit for demobilization - 29.3.19.	
			2/Lieut. C. Hoy. do - 29.3.19.	
			Major E. Senior DSO. do - 28.3.19.	
			Lieut. A.S. Thorpen. DSO. do - 19.3.19.	
			Lieut. I.L. Dod. MC. do - 19.3.19.	
			2/Lieut. C.E. Clay. MC. do - 19.3.19.	
			2/Lieut. O.G. Hoyle MC. do - 26.3.19.	
			2/Lieut. G. Monkman. MC. do - 19.3.19.	
			2/Lieut. H.C. O'Dowd. do - 28.3.19.	
			2/Lieut. W. Field. do - 28.3.19.	
			Lieut. W.J. Lloyd. DSO.MC. do - 21.3.19.	
			Lieut. G.V. Berrays. MC.	
			Lieut. J.B. Goodhill DSO.MC. Demob. in U.K. - 6.2.19.	
			Lieut. W. Wallace.	
			2/Lieut. G.H. Appleby.	
			2/Lieut. B. Brierley.	
			2/Lieut. E.H. Phillips. Transferred to 2/4th. Duke of Wellington's Regt. 19.3.19.	
			2/Lieut. W. Barber.	
			2/Lieut. W. Rowson.	
			2/Lieut. J. Hogan MC.	
			2/Lieut. H. Greenwood.	
			2/Lieut. H. Shepherd.	
			Lieut. F.S. Devenport.	
			2/Lieut. H. Shepherd. To Hospital - Accdtly injured - 4.3.19.	

ORIGINAL.

5th Duke of Wellington's Regt. T.F.

Army Form C. 2118.

Instructions regarding War Diaries and Intelligence Summaries are contained in F. S. Regs. Part II. and the Staff Manual respectively. Title pages will be prepared in manuscript.

WAR DIARY
or
INTELLIGENCE SUMMARY.
(Erase heading not required.)

Place	Date	Hour	Summary of Events and Information	Remarks and references to Appendices
			MEDICIS. (continued).	
			18 Officers and 452 other ranks in the battalion have been demobilized since the Armistice - 11th November 1918.	
			The following Officers and other ranks comprised the Cadre of the 5th. Duke of Wellington's (W.R.) Regt. T.F.:-	
			Lieut.Col. J. WALKER. DSO.	
			Capt. & Adjt. K. SYKES. MC.	
			Capt. & Q.M. P.E. HAMMOND.	
			Lieut. S.G.H. ELLIS. DSO., MC.	
			241096 C.S.M. S. Kemp V.C. 34416 Pte. Coy C.	
			305907 Sergt. Blakeley J.H. MM. 242169 Pte. Hargreaves H.	
			242148 Sergt. Denny R. 34496 Pte. Hill J.H.	
			240128 Sergt. Downs A. 240480 Pte. Harding H.	
			240950 Sergt. Mitchell R. MM. 266656 Pte. Jowett A.	
			241418 Sergt. White J. 240571 Pte. Lee C.	
			242452 Corpl. Bird A.E. 268002 Pte. Lees W.	
			242392 Corpl. Brook H. MM. 242684 Pte. Middleton H.	
			241056 Corpl. Carrol T. 29318 Pte. Oldham C.	
			240607 Corpl. Lees J.A. 263028 Pte. Overend J.	
			235757 L.Cpl. Bickle G.A. 240704 Pte. Pollard J.	
			240971 L.Cpl. Holliwell J.E. MM. 266451 Pte. Parrington S. MM.	
			35157 L.Cpl. McDowell M. 240542 Pte. Rowley A.	
			242184 Pte. Blackburn W. 307387 Pte. Rushworth J.	
			240243 Dmr. Beevers H. 240413 Pte. Smith S.	
			14593 Pte. Barber E. 240366 Pte. Sykes S.	
			242130 Pte. Barker F. 242915 Pte. Silverwood W.M.	
			52967 Pte. Barber H. 34554 Pte. Shaw J.	
			236592 Pte. Bone G. 266361 Pte. Sykes A.	
			36327 Pte. Bale F.H. MM. 240510 Pte. Taylor G.H. MM.	
			200440 Pte. Crothers R. 305520 Pte. Thackeray N.	
			230867 Pte. Guest H. 307301 Pte. Foulcher O.	

ORIGINAL.

Army Form C. 2118.

5th Duke of Wellington's Regt. T.F.

WAR DIARY
or
INTELLIGENCE SUMMARY.
(Erase heading not required.)

Instructions regarding War Diaries and Intelligence Summaries are contained in F.S. Regs. Part II. and the Staff Manual respectively. Title pages will be prepared in manuscript.

Place	Date	Hour	Summary of Events and Information	Remarks and references to Appendices
			APPENDICES. (continued).	
			17112 Pte. Wilson G. MM.	
			241399 Pte. Ward F. "	
			18045 Pte. Wood M. "	
			240908 Pte. Moorhouse W. "	
			305187 L.Cpl. Hollingworth H. MM.	
			Lieut. H.S.H. BROADWOOD (attd - awaiting Repatriation to Canada).	
			PROMOTIONS, RELINQUISHMENTS etc.	
			Lieut. (a/Capt.) A. Johnson relinquishes the acting addtl. rank of Captain on leaving the unit for demobilization - 29.3.19.	
			Lieut. (a/Capt.) H.S. Jackson DSO. relinquishes the acting rank of Captain on leaving the unit for demobilization - 19.3.19.	
			Lieut. (a/Capt.) G.V. Bernays MC. relinquishes the acting rank of Captain on ceasing to command a Company (transferred to 2/4th.Duke of Wellington's Regt.) 10.3.19.	
			Lieut. (a/Capt.) J.B. Cockhill DSO., MC relinquishes the acting rank of Captain on ceasing to command a Company (transferred to 2/4th.Duke of Wellington's Regt.) 10.3.19.	
			Lieut. (a/Capt.) C.S. Floyd relinquishes the acting additional rank of Captain on leave to U.K. being extended - 10.3.19.	
			2/Lieut. (a/Capt.) W.J. Lloyd DSO, MC relinquishes the acting rank of Captain on leave to U.K. being extended - pending demobilization - 7.1.19.	
			Lieut. (a/Capt.) G.G.H. Ellis relinquishes the acting rank of Captain on ceasing to command a Company dated 31.3.19.	
			HONOURS & AWARDS.	
			Lieut.Col. J. WALKER. DSO. Awarded French Legion D'Honneur (Croix de Chevalier) - L.G.d/11.3.19. 26035 Sergt. Burrows G. DCM, MM, awarded French Medaille Militaire - L.G.d/11.3.19.	

...................Lieut.Col.
Commdg. 5th. Duke of Wellington's Regt.

SECRET.   Copy No...7....

5th Duke of Wellington's Regt.

Order No. 149.

Ref. Map. Germany 1A. 1/100,000.   7th March 1919.

1. **RELIEF.**   The battalion will be relieved in the villages of
   FIRMENICH, OBERGARTZEM, ENZEN and ULPENICH on 8th March
   by 1/5th Argyle and Sutherland Highlanders. On relief the
   battalion will be billeted at WACHENDORF and ANTWEILER.

2. **GUIDES.**   Capt. E. Johnson, 1 H.Q. Runner and 1 Runner from A. Coy.
   will meet the incoming battalion at MECHERNICH and guide them
   to this area. They will report to Brigade H.Q. MECHERNICH
   by 6 p.m. today (7th March). The Other Ranks will be in
   possession of rations for the 8th. The officer will report
   to the Adjutant before leaving the battalion.

3. **HANDING OVER.**
   All billets, stores etc., will be most carefully handed
   over under the Ass.-Adjutants arrangements. Each Company
   will leave the following officers and 1 O.R. behind to hand
   over in respective villages.-
   FIRMENICH 2/Lieut. Monkman MC., OBERGARTZEM 2/Lieut Nield.,
   ENZEN 2/Lieut. Rawson., ULPENICH 2/Lieut Barber.,

4. **MOVE TO NEW AREA.**
   The battalion will parade in full marching Order at 10.30
   hours tomorrow on SATZVEY Road, just West of O of
   OBERGARTZEM. All Coys. will parade together under Capt.
   G.C.H. Ellis D.S.O. M.C. All details with Band will
   parade under R.S.M.

5. **TRANSPORT**
   Regimental Transport will accompany the battalion.

6. **BILLETS.**
   A.B.C.D. Coys. as one composite Coy. will be billeted in
   ANTWEILER under the command of Capt. G.C.H. Ellis D.S.O. M.C.
   H.Q. Transport and Q.M. Stores at WACHENDORF.
   Billeting Party of 1 N.C.O. per Company will meet Capt.
   H.S. Jackson D.S.O. at ANTWEILER Church at 16.00 hours today
   to be allotted billets. 1. N.C.O. from each of H.Q.
   Transport and Q.M. Stores, will meet Lieut. I.M. Tod MC
   at WACHENDORF SCHLOSS at 16.00 hours today.

7. **ACKNOWLEDGE.**

   Issued at ..10.30 hrs..

                                    ....K Sykes.......Capt. & Adjt.
                                         5th Duke of Wellington's Regiment.
Copies to-
1. "A" Coy.
2. "D" Coy.
3. "H.Q" Details.
4. "Q.M. & T.O."
5. O.C. HERZERSTAHL Detachment (for information)
6. "186th Infantry Brigade" (for in-formation)
7. & 8. War Diary.
9. "Office".

All recipients of Order 148.

    Order No. 148 is cancelled.

7.3.19.

                                ......K Sykes......Capt. & Adjt.
                                5th Duke of Wellington's Regiment.

SECRET.   Copy No. 7

5TH DUKE OF WELLINGTON'S REGT.

Order No. 149.

Re. Map. Germany 1 : 1/100,000.   7th March 1919.

----

1. **RELIEF.**   The battalion will be relieved in the villages of
                   FIRMENICH, OBERGARTZEM, ENZEN, and ULPENICH on 8th
                   March by 1/5th Argyll and Sutherland Highlanders, on
                   relief the battalion will be billeted at MECHERNICH.

2. **GUIDES.**   Capt. H. Johnson, 1 H.Q. Runner and 1 runner from A. Coy.
                   will meet the incoming battalion at SATZVEY and guide
                   them to this area.

3. **HANDING OVER.** All billets, stores etc., will be most carefully handed
                   over under the Asst. Adjutants arrangements. Each Coy.
                   will leave the following officers and 1 O.R. behind to
                   hand over in respective villages.—
                   FIRMENICH, 2/Lieut. Monkman MC., OBERGARTZEM 2/Lieut
                   Mold., ENZEN 2/Lieut Rawson., ULPENICH, 2/Lt. Barber.,

4. **MOVE TO NEW AREA.**
                   The battalion will parade in full Marching Order at 10.30
                   hours tomorrow on road opposite OBERGARTZEM Church.
                   All Coys will parade together under Capt. G.G.H. Ellis DSO,
                   All Details with Band will parade under R.S.M.

5. **TRANSPORT.** Regimental Transport will proceed independently.

6. **BILLETS.**   Billeting Party consisting of Major E. Senior D.S.O.
                   Lieut. I.M. Tod MC., 1 N.C.O from A.B.C.D. Coys H.Q.
                   Transport & Q.M. Stores, will meet outside Burgermasters
                   Office MECHERNICH at 1000 hours tomorrow.

Issued at..19 30 hrs

                                                    ...K.Sykes..... Capt. & Adjt.
Copies to.—   5th Duke of Wellington's Regiment.
1. "A" Coy.
2. "D" Coy.
3. "H.Q." Details.
4. "Q.M. & T.O."
5. O.C. HERBERTSAM Detachment (for information)
6. "186th Infantry Brigade (for information)
7. & 8. War Diary.
9. Office.
10. Major E. Senior D.S.O.

Copy No. 4......

5th. DUKE OF WELLINGTON'S REGT.

ORDER No. 150 dated 30.3.19.

Ref. Map. GERMANY. I.L. 1/100,000.

1. **CADRE.** The Battalion will be reduced to Cadre on 31st.March. 1919 and will move from MECHERNICH (Germany) to CHARLEROI (Belgium)

2. **TRANSFER.** The Cadre will be transferred from Highland Division, Second Army to 5th. Division, Fourth Army.

3. **EMBUSSING.** Lorries are to be provided for conveyance of Stores and Cadre from MECHERNICH to DUREN. The Cadre will parade at Ration Store, in the Square, MECHERNICH at 0745 hours tomorrow.

4. **ENTRAINMENT.** Entraining will take place at DUREN at 10.00 hours. 4 Trucks on the Demobilization Train will be available for the Cadre. Lieut. H.C.H. Broadwood will proceed in advance to-night to DUREN and meet the Cadre on arrival at the Station tomorrow.

5. **RATIONS.** The Q.M. will arrange for 1 full days rations to be available on completion of journey to CHARLEROI. Rations will be provided on the train by Demobilization Staff.

6. **STORES.** The Q.M. will arrange for Orderly Room Boxes and Stores at the Mining College to be conveyed to the Ration Store to-night. Blankets rolled in bundles of 10 to be at Ration Store at 0730 hours tomorrow.

7. **COLOUR PARTY.** Capt. C.G.H. Ellis and Capt. & Q.M. P.E. Hammond, Sergt. Blakeley, MM, L.Corpl.Hollingworth MM, and Pte. Overend MM, will be responsible for the safeguarding of the Colours on the journey.

........K. Sykes........Capt.& Adjt.
5th.Duke of Wellington's Regt.

Copies to -

    1. Highland Division (for information).
    2. Quartermaster.
    3. Capt. C.G.H. Ellis. DSO, MC.
4 & 5. War Diary.
    6. Office.

ORIGINAL.

CONFIDENTIAL.

W A R   D I A R Y.

-of-

5th. DUKE OF WELLINGTON'S REGT.

1st to 30th April 1919.

(Volume 14.)

J. Waller
Comdg. 5th. Duke of Wellington's Regt. ...... Lt. Col.

Original.

Army Form C. 2118.

5th.Duke of Wellington's Regt.

WAR DIARY
or
INTELLIGENCE SUMMARY.
(Erase heading not required.)

Instructions regarding War Diaries and Intelligence Summaries are contained in F. S. Regs., Part II. and the Staff Manual respectively. Title pages will be prepared in manuscript.

Place	Date	Hour	Summary of Events and Information	Remarks and references to Appendices
Ref.Map.	1919. April 1st.		The Battalion Cadre left DUREN on the Base Details Train at 11.30am. Stoves and fuel were provided in the trucks and the journey was a comfortable one. The train stopped at VERVIERS on route for 40 minutes to allow of a hot meal. The Cadre detrained at CHARLEROI at 11.pm. None met the train as the Cadre was not expected until next day. The men and stores were accommodated in a civilian waiting room on the Station for the night.	
GERMANY. I.I. 1/100000				
NAMUR. 1/100000	2nd.		The Battalion Cadre was transferred from 186th Inf. Bde. Highland Division (62nd) to 95th Infantry Brigade 5th. Division. The Cadre remained in Charleroi for the day and was accommodated at 5th. Division Reception Camp.	
	3rd.		The Cadre was moved by lorry in the afternoon from CHARLEROI to MAURUS and there joined the 95th. Infantry Brigade in readiness to take over equipment and vehicles of the 1st. Battn. East Surry Regt.	
	4th.		A very bright sunny day. Beyond usual inspections nothing else was done.	
	5th.		Another fine day.	
	6th.		Church Parade (c.of E.) was held in the Hotel de Ville, MAURUS in the morning	
	7th.		The Battalion Cadre took over Transport Vehicles and equipment of 1st. Battalion East Surrey Regt. at CHARLEROI.	
	8th.		Very fine day. Continued the taking over of equipment of 1st. East Surrey Regt.	
	9th.		Completed taking over equipment etc. of 1st. East Surry Regt.	
	10th.		Dull and cooler.	
	11th.		Some rain. Battn. Cadre took over equipment and guns of 95th. Inf. Bde. Trench Mortar Battery at CHARLEROI.	

ORIGINAL.

5th Duke of Wellington's Regt.

WAR DIARY
or
INTELLIGENCE SUMMARY.
(Erase heading not required.)

Army Form C. 2118.

Instructions regarding War Diaries and Intelligence Summaries are contained in F.S. Regs., Part II. and the Staff Manual respectively. Title pages will be prepared in manuscript.

Place	Date	Hour	Summary of Events and Information	Remarks and references to Appendices
	1919 April 12th			
	13th		A very wet day. The Cadre all had baths at one of the nine baths near FLEURUS.	
	13th		A wet day. Church of England Church Parade was held in the Hotel de Ville, FLEURUS during the morning.	
	14th		A very wet gusty day.	
	15th		A very wet gusty day.	
	16th		Another wet day.	
	17th		Weather changed for better. Bright and fine.	
	18th		Fine.	
	19th		Fine.	
	20th		Divine Service in Hotel de Ville, FLEURUS for Nonconformists only. No Church of England Chaplain available.	
	21st		Very fine and bright.	
	22nd		do	
	23rd		do	
	24th		Nine cool day. The men of the Cadre went to Charleroi for baths and clean change of underclothes	
	25th		Fine day.	

5th Duke of Wellingtons Regt.

Army Form C. 2118.

WAR DIARY
or
INTELLIGENCE SUMMARY.
(Erase heading not required.)

Instructions regarding War Diaries and Intelligence Summaries are contained in F.S. Regs., Part II. and the Staff Manual respectively. Title pages will be prepared in manuscript.

Place	Date	Hour	Summary of Events and Information	Remarks and references to Appendices
	April 26th	8.45pm	Wet day with fair intervals	
	27th	9.30am	The Battn. Entre entrained with baggage, vehicles and interned at HAUTEVILLE Station CHARLEROI at 3.4am for ANTWERP en route for PREES HEATH Camp.	
	28th	8am	The Battn. Bodies arrived at ANTWERP Dock before at 6.30am. Sun was lovely morning to unload the baggage into barges, to deliver the remainder of the baggage to the Transport Buffalo Regt. At noon to proceed was satisfactorily accomplished.	
	29th to 30th		Wet day with fine intervals. Very wet day.	
	May 1st		Very wet day.	
	2nd		The battalion Cadre with Colours, Vehicles and stores embarked on S.S. PRETORIAN at Antwerp Docks en route for ENGLAND. Very wet day.	

J Walker LT. COL.
COMMDG. 5th WEST RIDING REGIMENT.

5th. DUKE OF WELLINGTON'S REGT.

Order No. 181.

1. **MOVE.** Cadre 'A' of 5th. Duke of Wellington's Regt. will entrain for transfer to the United Kingdom via Antwerp tomorrow. Destination in United Kingdom is PRESS HEATH.

2. **LOADING etc.** Vehicles are being loaded to-day with stores. The R.M. with 1 N.C.O. and 10 men will proceed to CHARLEROI by first train tomorrow and complete loading.
The painting of destination station on vehicles and stores will be carried out forthwith.

3. **ENTRAINING.** Loading on train at CHARLEROI - HAUTEVILLE station will commence at 09.00 hours tomorrow. Train departs at 18.00 hours. Lieut. C.G.H. Ellis will be Entraining Officer for 5th. Div. Cadres tomorrow and will report to R.T.O. at the Station at 09.00 hours.

4. **BAGGAGE.** A lorry has been demanded to report to the Battalion at 09.00 hours tomorrow. Lieut H.C.H. Broadwood will ensure that all Baggage, Officers Kit etc. is loaded and taken to HAUTEVILLE station.

5. **COLOURS.** Lieut. H.C.H. Broadwood, Lieut. C.G.H. Ellis, DSO.,MC, Sergt. Blakeley MM, L.Cpl. McDowell, and L.Cpl. Bickell will be responsible for safeguarding the Colours throughout the journey to England.

6. **IMPREST a/c.** The Adjutant will proceed to WIMEREUX tomorrow and close the Battalion Imprest a/c. and obtain Clearance Certificate from the Chief Paymaster. He will rejoin the Cadre in England.

...K. Sykes... Capt. & Adjt.
5th. Duke of Wellington's Regiment.

Copies to -

1. Q.M.
2. Lieut. Ellis, DSO.,MC.
3. Lieut. H.C.H. Broadwood.
4. Adjutant.
5 - 6. War Diary.
7. Office.

BELGIUM AND PART OF FRANCE

1:40,000

ALL HEIGHTS IN METRES.   CONTOUR INTERVAL 10 METRES.

BELGIUM AND PART OF FRANCE

EDITION 2.

SHEET 51.

NAMUR

FOR OFFICIAL USE ONLY

NAMUR. 8.

BELGIUM

Scale $\frac{1}{100,000}$.

1 OSTEND	2 GHENT	3 ANTWERP	4 MAESEYCK
5A HAZEBROUCK	5 TOURNAI	6 BRUSSELS	7 LIÈGE
11 LENS	12 VALENCIENNES	8 NAMUR	9 MARCHE
			10 ARLON

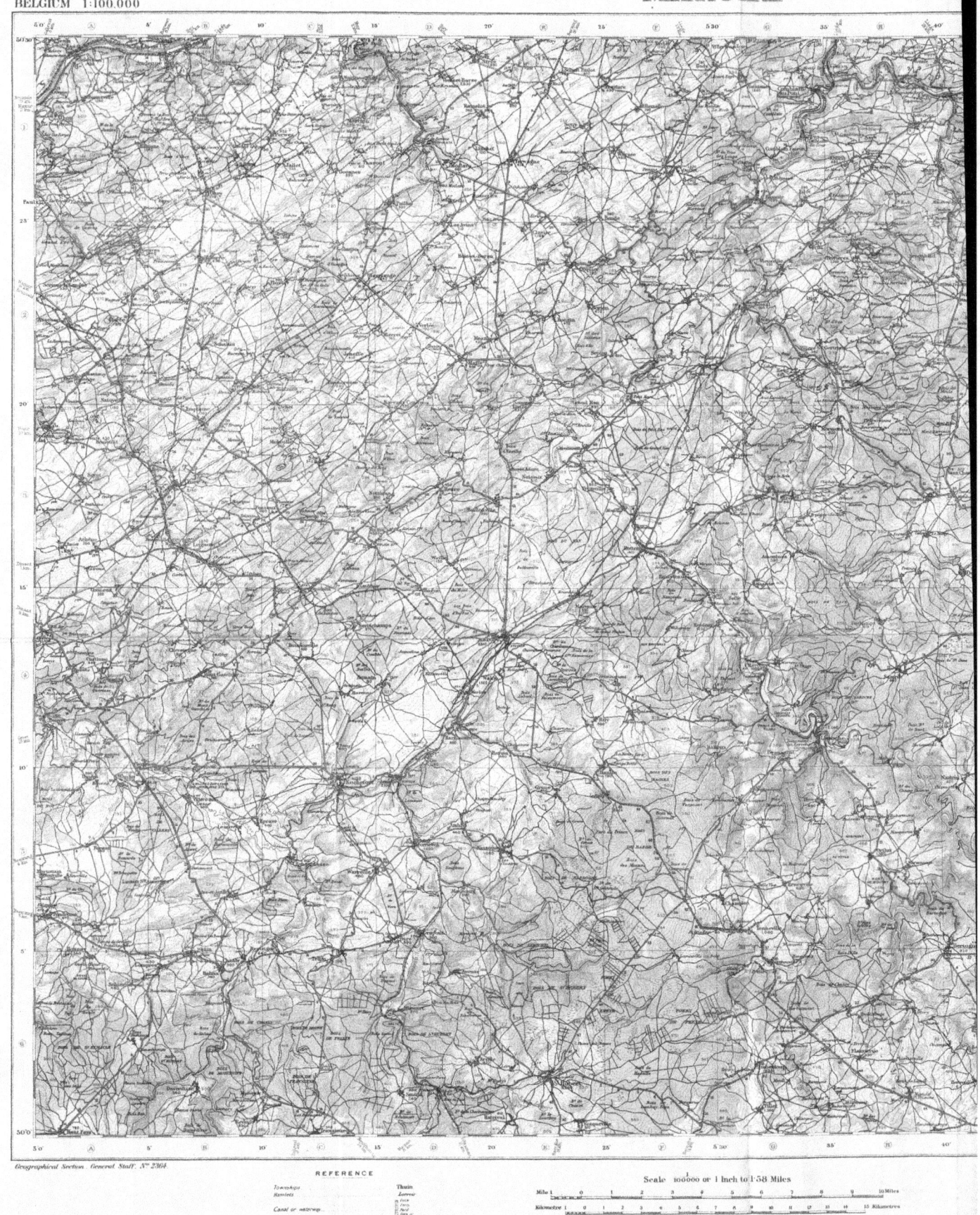

MARCHE 9

BELGIUM

Scale $\frac{1}{100,000}$.

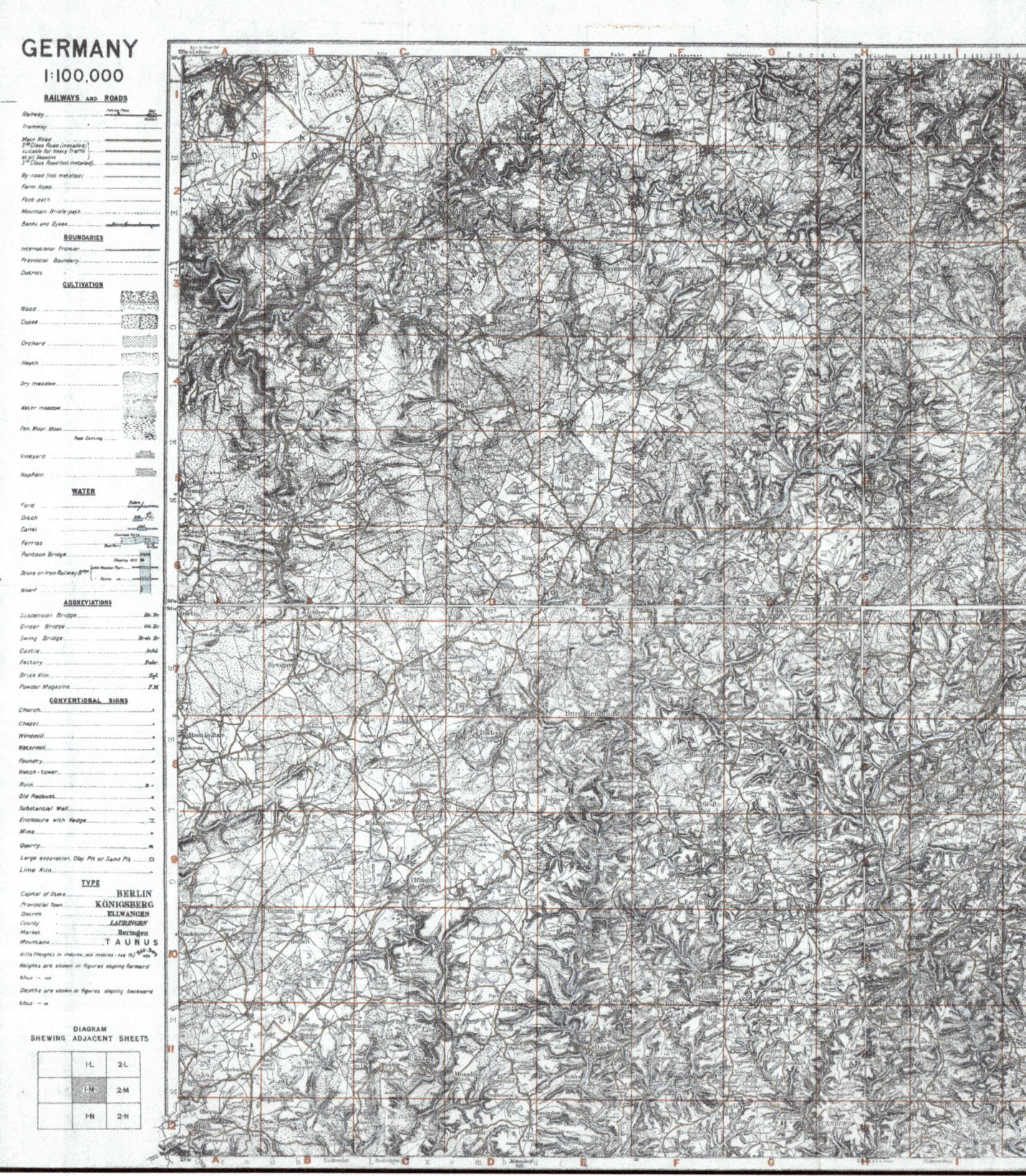

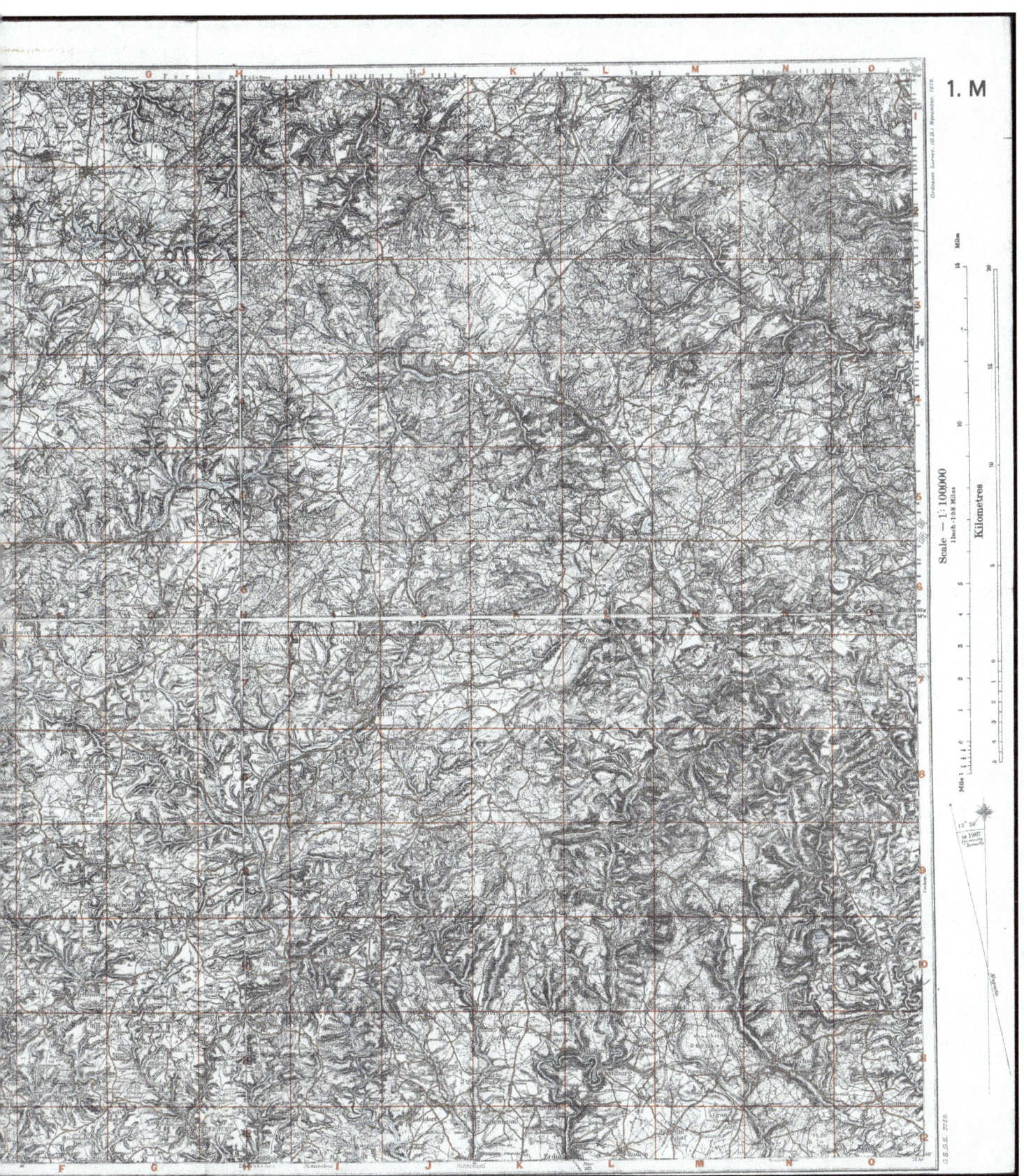

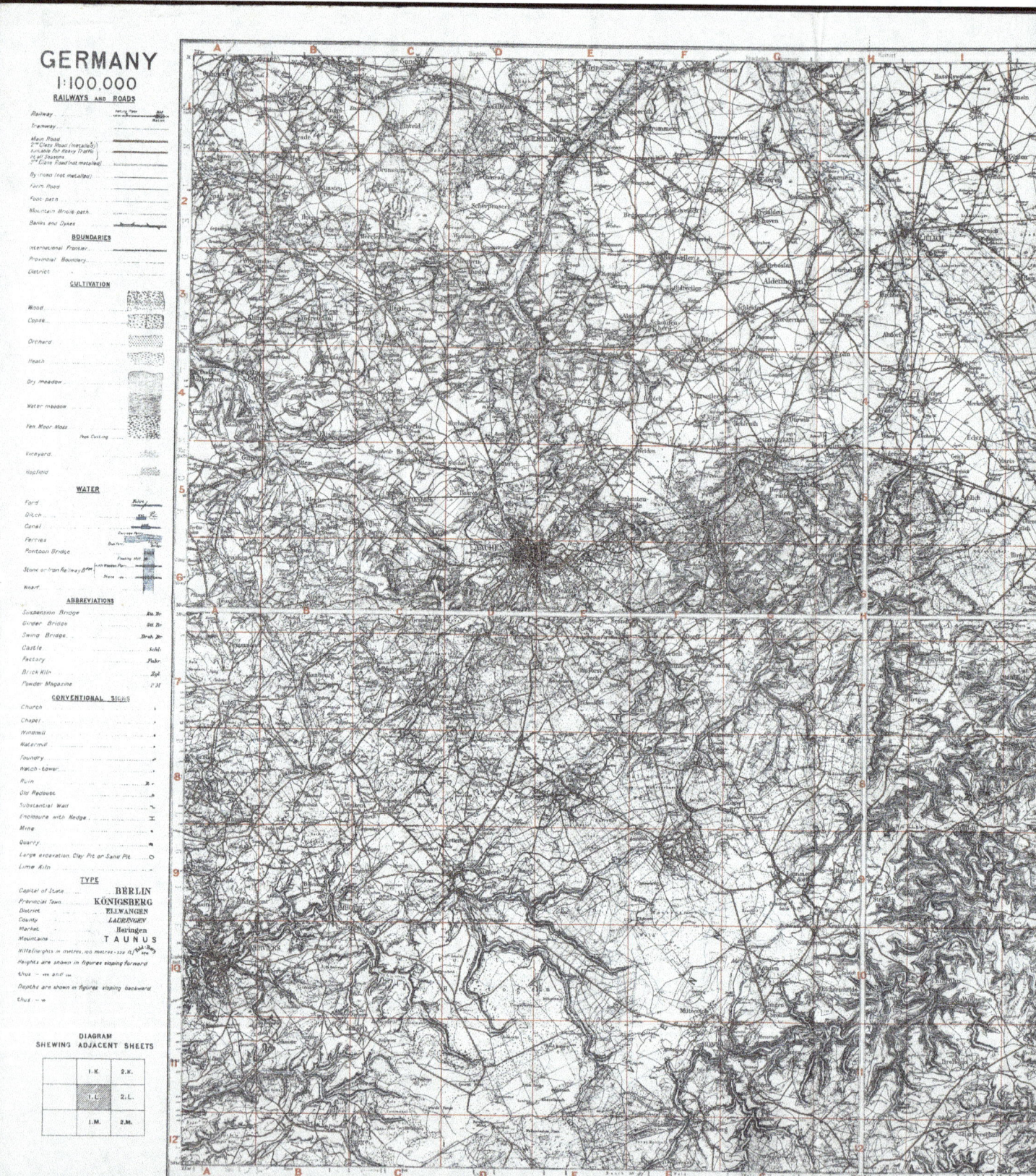

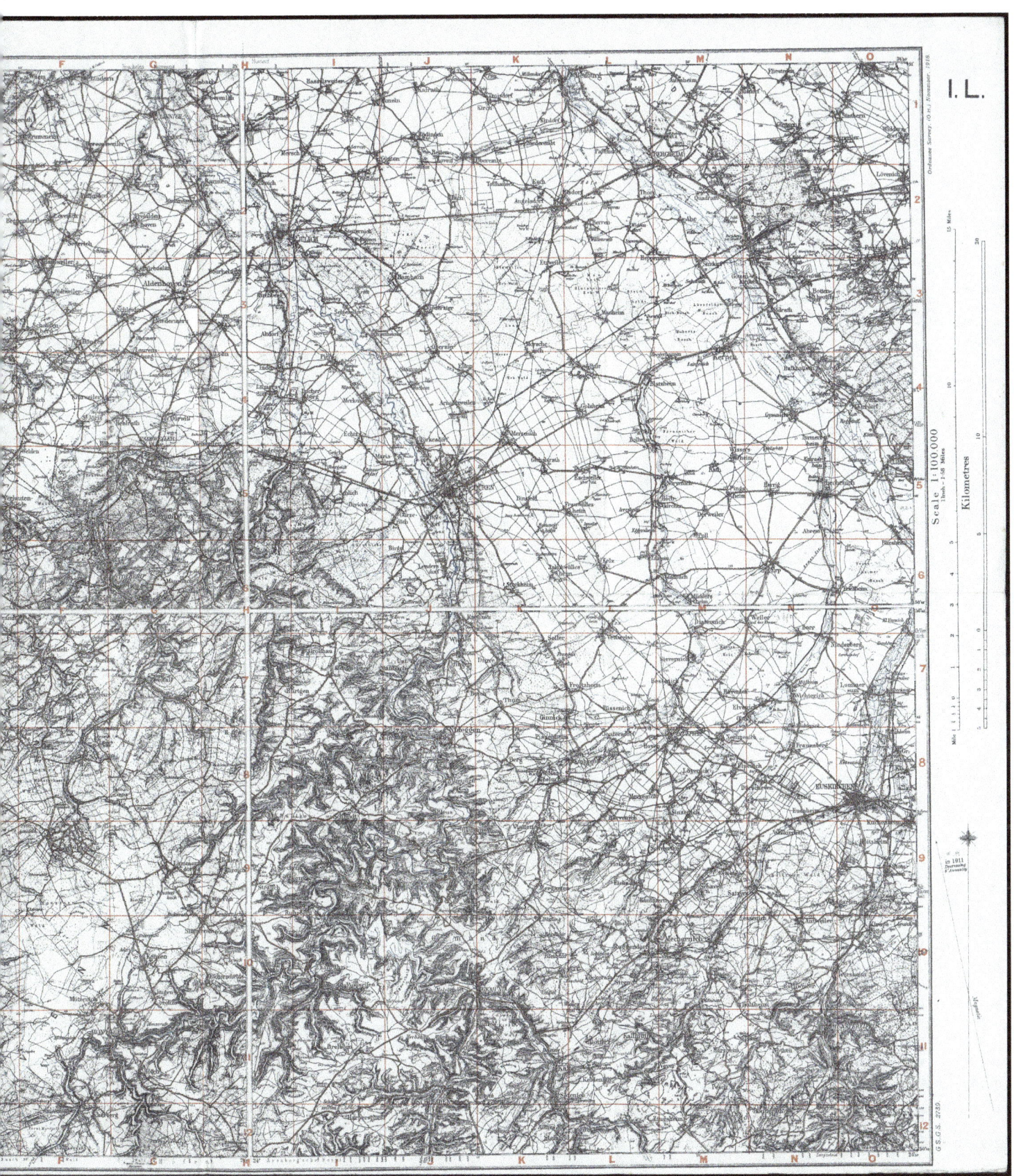

www.ingramcontent.com/pod-product-compliance
Lightning Source LLC
Chambersburg PA
CBHW080917230426
43668CB00014B/2143